6SD

MW00465615

THE SEVENTH SHADOW

THE SEVENTH SHADOW

By RCMP Staff Sergeant (ret)
Michael Eastham
with Ian McLeod

Warwick Publishing
Toronto Los Angeles
www.warwickgp.com

© 1999 Michael Eastham and Ian McLeod

All rights reserved. No part of this publication may be reproduced,
stored in a retrieval system or data base, or transmitted in any form
or by any means, electronic, mechanical, photocopying, recording,
or otherwise, without prior permission of the publisher.

ISBN: 1-894020-47-2

Published by Warwick Publishing
162 John Street, Toronto, Ontario M5V 2E5

Design: Kimberley Young
Maps: Heidi Gemmill
Editor: Melinda Tate

Printed and bound in Canada

To the many peace officers out there
who, in spite of the odds that seem to be against
them, stick with their determination to bring a
perpetrator to justice. It's people like them who
do make a difference, and make our communities
safer places to live.

TABLE OF CONTENTS

ACKNOWLEDGEMENTS

To the surviving members of the Johnson and Bentley families — thank you for your support and cooperation. I know it still hurts greatly, but now the message is clear: "None of us will ever forget."

My thanks to BCTV and CKNW Radio — the unknown crime fighters in this province who allowed our investigative team to abuse them, who criticized us when necessary and kept us on our toes, and who supported us when the chips were down. You kept this horrible crime in the public's mind, and greatly helped us in solving one of Canada's worst mass murders.

Thank you also to Ken, Gerry, Dwight, Len, Frank, Ann, and countless other members of our "Team" — our success was only because of your determination; to my literary consultant, Johanna Bates, whose passion for the story quickly convinced me to co-write this book; to John and Carol McLeod, for their endless support throughout the past year, and of course for letting me borrow their oldest son for a year to help me write this book.

And finally, to my wonderful wife Corinne, who kept her promise not to read the book until it was published: Thanks for your encouragement, support, and most of all, patience.

INTRODUCTION

INTRODUCTION

This book is about one of the most infamous crimes in North American history. The whole story has never been told until now. One of the reasons is that cops don't generally write books. It's against all the rules. But as you will see, I've always had trouble following rules anyway.

As a cop, I was often described as a "maverick" or "on the edge" for my sometimes unorthodox methods of achieving results. That may be true. But that's why they call it that "thin blue line." Perhaps this is just another way for me to continue displaying my "screw 'em" attitude.

I retired in 1996 after a career of 35 years in the RCMP. Thirty of those years were spent as a detective. Not long after, I was approached to tell the Wells Gray Park murder story the way it happened, the way only people inside the RCMP know it happened. I wrestled with myself over whether I could tell the story, and if so, how much blood and guts I should leave out to protect the reader and the victims' family from the reality of the events. I debated how much I should talk about the inner feelings and thoughts that RCMP investigators have when they are consumed with an investigation as we were over a long period of time.

This story contains very graphic details that some people may find disturbing, but this is the way it happened. Although I have changed some names of peripheral individuals, this book is an entirely accurate account of how fate sent us on one of the most extensive manhunts in history and of how we eventually solved this horrendous crime.

It is a story about a family summer vacation that turned into a nightmare in the Canadian wilderness. It is one that fiction writers of murder mysteries could never dream up. It actually happened. It's not a pretty story. It's a horror story.

I lived the nightmare of this investigation for almost two years, and while I knew I had some of my old police notes and photographs for accuracy, most of what appears in the following pages has been impregnated in my memory, beginning with the phone call I got on September 13,

1982. It was on that day that I learned three generations of a single family had been brutally executed. A monster, an evil person, had come out of the night to destroy six innocent lives. That was one of the reasons I decided to write this book: so we don't forget.

There's another reason this story needs to be told. I recently received a copy of a composition that reveals the inner thoughts and feelings of a young relative of the victims.

This young lady lost her grandparents, her aunt and uncle, and her cousins in this tragedy. The following is part of her composition:

I was little, still young and naive enough to think the world was a happy place. My parents told me that my grandparents had died both at the same time. I never asked any questions, but thought it was odd that they had died together. I remember picturing a glass filled with blue liquid, poison, which I believed was to blame for their deaths.

As I grew older, I learned more and more about their deaths. Slowly, bits and pieces of the story were uncovered of why these two people were missing from my life. Then came quite a surprise. Not only did my grandma and grandpa die at the same time, but also my aunt, uncle, and two cousins. No longer was the poison to blame, instead now, a name.

I learned that my family had all been murdered on a family camping trip, an event that changed my parents' lives forever, and although I was not born yet, mine also. I cannot think of any way to describe this event other than "horrible". I don't think there will ever be a word that quite describes the person responsible for such a cruel act.

They asked my mom and dad and my other auntie and uncle to come but they couldn't. If my parents had gone, I would not exist at all. Although I am thankful for the family I am lucky to have, I miss the people I never knew. I miss the memories I would have made.

I wish my grandma were here to teach me how to bake a pie. I wish my grandpa were here to tell me stories of war and how he fell in love with my grandma. I want my aunt and uncle to tease me, and my cousins to talk with me about the stuff that cousins talk about. I'm sure I would have been a flower girl in their weddings and helped with their baby showers. So much they missed out on, so much I missed out on not knowing them.

It really scares me to think this person may soon be walking the same streets as me, shop in the same stores, and lead a normal life. My family, six people who were in the wrong place at the wrong time, will never get a second chance at life, but whoever took their lives away will.

That, folks, is a good reason for writing this book.

This book is dedicated to the memory of George and Edith, Jackie and Bob, and Karen and Janet, and to their surviving families who miss them so much. It is also dedicated to every cop out there who can relate to the frustrations of trying to bring murderers to justice. I know what you are going through, because it's one hell of a lot tougher now than it was in the early '80s.

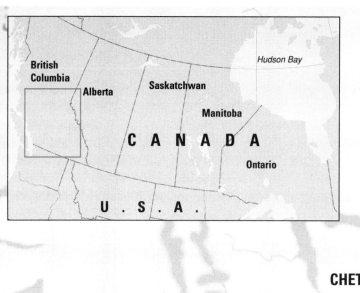

British Columbia
Alberta
Saskatchwan
Manitoba
Hudson Bay
C A N A D A
Ontario
U . S . A .

CHETWYND
DAWSON CREEK
TUMBLER RIDGE

WELLS GRAY PARK
Clearwater

POWELL RIVER
KAMLOOPS

NANAIMO
VANCOUVER
KELOWNA

Sometime during the first week of August 1982, the Johnson and Bentley families got together in Wells Gray Park for a family reunion. For the next few days, George and Edith Bentley, their daughter Jackie Johnson, her husband Bob and daughters Janet and Karen explored the provincial park for berries, wildlife, and the perfect campsite.

George and Edith Bentley, both in their late sixties, enjoyed the luxury of their new truck and camper. Although the two of them were used to setting up their own campsite, they couldn't deny the camper was a convenience that was becoming more necessary with age. They'd been carrying around their camping gear for over 50 years; now their camping gear could carry them. George had room for his fishing rods and some tools he thought he'd need to keep himself busy, and Edith could bake pies for the family if the berries around their campsite were ripe.

The camper helped them enjoy their vacations, no matter what the season. The Bentleys had been retired for three years, and spent a lot of that time touring the province. They had recently rented out their house in Coquitlam, BC, and when they weren't living out of their camper in a quiet campsite, they were staying with their son Brian or with one of their two daughters, Jackie and Sharon.

Jackie (Bentley) Johnson and her husband Bob had been married for 21 years, and they also enjoyed camping with Jackie's parents. Bob Johnson, in his early forties, worked as a sawyer for Gorman Mills in Westbank near Kelowna. He was a family man and dedicated employee. His hard work around the mill was an inspiration to his co-workers, and his practical jokes always kept his friends on their toes. While Bob had an aptitude for hard work, when the whistle blew at the end of the day he was also very good at having fun. Depending on the season, you could find him either roaring around on a motorcycle, or mounted on a snowmobile cutting tracks in snow that would intimidate a caribou. When all the tracks had been worn, like the pure-bred Canadian he was, Bob enjoyed sitting back with a frosty bottle of Extra Old Stock to watch hockey on TV.

Jackie was as devoted to her family as Bob was to his work. She was never far from a camera and spent a lot of her free time taking pictures. It was a new hobby, so the rest of the family was getting really good at posing for the camera. She enjoyed camping with the family, and when they left their house on the second of August, 1982, she made sure they had enough film to last until the 16th, which was the day Bob had to be back to work.

Jackie and Bob's daughters Janet, 13, and Karen, 11, were involved in Girl Guides. The two girls were both very cheerful, and spent most of their young lives being driven between school, piano lessons, and their Girl Guide meetings. Karen looked up to her older sister, and while there was the odd conflict, they mostly enjoyed each other's company. They were an honest reflection of a tightly knit Canadian family, living the Canadian dream.

Although exactly what the Johnson and Bentley families did throughout their vacation is for the most part unknown, Sharon (Bentley) Sarchet later reported that on August 6, 1982, her mother Edith contacted her from the Chamber of Commerce telephone in Clearwater, BC. Edith told her they were having a great time camping, and that they were going to be meeting the Johnsons in Wells Gray Provincial Park. After a few loving words between mother and daughter, Edith hung up the phone and headed back to the camper where George was waiting.

Nobody from either family was ever heard from again.

At midday on August 23, 1982, Al Bonar of Gorman Mills filed a missing persons complaint to a member at the Kelowna RCMP detachment. In this complaint, he insisted that Bob Johnson and his family were supposed to have been back from their vacation in Wells Gray Park on the 16th of August, and that Bob still hadn't shown up for work. Mr. Bonar explained that the sawyer hadn't missed a day's work in 20 years, and by this time had missed almost a week.

The report was passed on to Sergeant Baruta of Clearwater detachment, who made several local inquiries but came away empty handed. The Johnson and Bentley families were promptly put on the system as missing persons. While police made further inquiries around Clearwater, including Wells Gray Park, whose southernmost entrance was 20 miles to the north, Brian Bentley and his wife Linda set out to circulate their families' photographs in the area between Clearwater and Valemount.

It wasn't long before they received an encouraging lead. A service station attendant named Reg Bedard at the Avola Petro Can, about 40 miles east of Clearwater, recalled seeing George and Jackie and the two grandchildren. While the car was being refueled, George had asked her if she knew some good areas for berry picking. It was a promising lead that was eventually brought to the attention of police and ultimately led to a massive search of south central BC.

This search, led jointly by Frank Baruta and Staff Sergeant Norm Schafer of Kamloops, focused on Wells Gray Park and involved police, parks personnel, private citizens' clubs, and local pilots. It included the use of every sort of all-terrain and 4x4 vehicle imaginable. The searchers scoured the park tirelessly for any sign of the missing families, but none was to be found.

It wasn't until September 13, 1982, that information was received from a source in Abbotsford, BC. A gentleman by the name of Kurt Krack believed he had seen the Johnson vehicle while he was picking mushrooms in Wells Gray Park during the last week of August. He remembered that he'd been in the Battle Mountain Road area in the park when he came across a burned-out Chrysler similar to that belonging to the Johnsons.

Once Frank Baruta got word of this, he and Constable Mike Glas drove up to Battle Mountain Road. It was rough going, as it was a route normally travelled only on horseback or capable 4x4s. At the location described by Krack, they noticed what appeared to be tire tracks angling off into the bushes. From the road, it was almost impossible to see the burnt-out hulk, and it was only because they had a general idea of where to look that they could make out the dull orange outline of the wrecked car.

Together, Glas and Baruta stepped from the police cruiser and followed the tracks to their origin. They stepped over the thick grass and pushed through some wilting bushes for some 150 feet before they were close enough to the wreck to read the licence plate. By now, Sergeant Baruta had the number memorized. He ducked down slightly to read the singed plate number.

"Yeah, this is the one," he said grimly. The vehicle was surrounded by charred earth and there was nothing on it that wasn't melted or disfigured. The two officers then approached together, careful not to step on anything that might be useful in determining how the vehicle caught fire or the whereabouts of the Johnson family. Upon looking in the open windows at the scorched interior, both Constable Mike Glas and Sergeant Frank Baruta froze.

"Mike," Frank managed to say, crouched slightly beside the rusted orange skin of the Johnson car, "secure the area. I've got to call Kamloops GI. This is a homicide investigation now."

Chapter 2 # THE OPENING WHISTLE

September 12, 1982
Kamloops, British Columbia

Located on the second floor of the 30-year-old government building in Kamloops, the detective office was always a busy place. We were forever writing expense reports, drafting occurrence reports, editing and re-sending memos ... sometimes, once we had waded through the bog of bureaucracy, we got to do our jobs — investigating major crime in south central British Columbia. Of course, that didn't appear to be anyone's main concern but ours.

Kamloops was the latest stop in my 20-year career with the RCMP, which had ranged all over central and Western Canada. Three years previously I had been transferred from the hamlet of Powell River, BC, and promoted to sergeant. I had my own office, off in the corner, while the others on the investigation team worked in the general office. There were four of us; Constables Gerry Dalen and Ken Leibel, Corporal Dwight Hoglund, and I were responsible for investigating all the serious crimes in the region, which encompassed the Rockies to the west, Cariboo Country to the north, and the many ranching and mining communities to the south — hundreds of thousands of square miles.

Gerry Dalen was sort of my right-hand man. He was an excellent investigator whose smile and straw-coloured hair could knock a woman off her feet from a hundred yards. I think a lot of it had to do with his being a born and bred cowboy. He was brought up on a farm in Saskatchewan, and had a horse named "Dollar" in pasture back at his place just outside of Kamloops. In fact, the week we began our investigation into the Johnson/Bentley disappearance he was supposed to be taking part in the provincial team roping championships. It was a really big event in Gerry's life, and whenever he wasn't working he was over practicing for the provincials.

Dwight Hoglund was quite new to the General Investigation Section (GIS). We agreed that he looked a bit like a baby walrus, only not quite as cute. He had a mustache that was as wide as he was tall, and more get up and go than all of us combined. While he lacked some of our experience, we loved to sic Dwight on any slackers. We'd just point him in a direction, and everyone in his way promptly sprouted wings. Every now and then, he'd get a wee bit pushy with us. "Fuck off, corporal," Gerry would say with a smile. Dwight would shrug it off. He was pretty easy to get along with, little guy that he was.

Ken Leibel was known as "Reliable" or "Reliable Leibel" for a reason. Ken could be depended on. When Ken said it was done, you knew it was well cooked. He was a premier investigator and one hell of an interviewer, who could turn into a raging bull with the finesse of a priest when necessary. He was pretty soft spoken with the three of us, but shared the same passion for his work as we did for ours. Leibel was a couple inches taller than me, with a tanned and handsome complexion. He had an equal passion for women and the stock market, and when there were problems with either, or one of his investigations — look out! Mr. Quiet Gentleman became the "iceman" until he had things straightened out.

"Ain't putting up with none of that shit, Boss," was Reliable's explanation for doing what he had to do.

Unfortunately, I'd heard a rumour that Ken had been offered a promotion with the Drug Squad in the Interior of British Columbia. Innocently, I tried to keep that from happening. I didn't want to lose Reliable. We were a really tight group of guys, both on and off the job. It took really close friends to help endure what we saw almost every day.

Wanted pictures were all over the general office, but I don't think anyone could see them through the mountains of paperwork heaped on everyone's desk. Messages in and messages out were thinned throughout the day, but never disappeared. Open file folders from all of our investigations littered the dull linoleum landscape of the office. It was a typical cops' workplace, including a few prized trophies on the walls.

We had one electric typewriter floating around the subdivision office, but it never changed hands without a fight with one of the secretaries. Computers? What's a computer? The shoe box we used to file away tips on major crimes was our computer. When someone needed to search for information on a certain crime, they'd simply go to the shoe box. All the cases were marked individually with their own title card, so all we had to do was reach in and grab the appropriate section. It was stupid, but it worked. I looked at it as sort of the "caveman" of the modern card filing indexes.

When I was originally informed of my transfer there, Kamloops Subdivision GIS was presented as a comfort zone for me, somewhere I could kick back and relax. They told me there was the odd homicide, plenty of travel, and the criminals were basically lined up in numerical order to turn themselves in to police.

"Trust me," the staffing officer had assured. When I arrived, hungry for the opportunity to relax after a two-year nightmare in Powell River, it appeared that I'd been had.

The first year I worked in Kamloops GI, we dealt with extortion, robberies, murders, rapes, and the rest of the unspeakables. The Kamloops area was also a hub for homicides involving young women along one of the major highways. These types of murders were the most interesting for the evening news. Being in charge of their investigation, I often used the media to publicize the homicides and ask for the public's assistance in solving them. My investigative philosophy was that we could only work with the information we had, and most of that information would come from the public.

That philosophy had helped me back in Nanaimo when I'd been in charge of a local manhunt for three escaped drug offenders. They had been on their way from Nanaimo to gaol in Vancouver on a chartered aircraft that particular morning when they escaped their cuffs. One had somehow smuggled a knife on board, and the three of them quickly overpowered and beat up the sheriff, Gib Perry. They threatened to cut his throat if the aircraft didn't land back in Nanaimo. The pilot promptly turned around and did as instructed. Once they landed, the three prisoners were released. They stole the sheriff's car, with lights and siren, and darted off into the country.

I coordinated the search from the Nanaimo detachment radio room. I had a personal interest in seeing those three bastards apprehended. There was no reason for them to bring heavies in on Gib, who was quickly rushed to hospital with a number of serious injuries. I think that pissed me off more than the fact that they had escaped. We set up some major roadblocks all around Nanaimo, but none of them were coming up with anything.

Meanwhile, these guys had apparently broken into several different places, looting and destroying property at their leisure. They eventually broke into an elderly couple's residence. The husband was a minister, and both were in their mid seventies. The three fugitives terrorized them and stole some weapons and ammunition. Then they flashed back out to the minister's car and headed into the country, armed and *extremely* dangerous.

Hours passed, and slowly the odds of us finding them were sinking with the setting sun. As the time goes by, your search radius has to increase ten fold. It takes a hell of a lot of manpower to cover a large area like the one we were looking at as the evening came upon us. After an hour of relative silence from the search groups, I was running out of options.

Finally, it dawned on me that one of the auxiliary members, Larry Thomas, worked as a broadcaster for CHUB, a major radio station. We had every auxiliary member helping in this search. "Look," I said, once I found Larry. "How about you call the station and get them to let you ask everyone in the listening area to walk out on their front and back porch to see if they can spot these guys parked on the street or driving around."

Larry was on the phone in seconds, making the request and eventually broadcasting live from the detachment. Five minutes after the broadcast went out, we got a phone call.

"Yeah, I just heard your news broadcast, and I walked outside. The bastards are parked right in front of my house!" The caller explained that he lived down near Departure Bay, so I quickly organized several different cars to move into position on each side of the suspect vehicle. I had a map of the area, and determined that there were only two ways out. I had them blocked off, and knew it was going to be a brutal scene. These guys would be serving 10 to 20 years if they got caught, so they weren't going to give up without a fight.

When the members on the scene tried to approach the fugitives, the driver stomped on the gas and rammed the car into the open. They swerved around the roadblock and headed for the country. Police vehicles hurried after them, lights and sirens swirling through the cool night air. In seconds, radio calls were coming in from the officers in pursuit saying they were being fired upon. Two guys in the back of the minister's car were shooting out the back window, Bonnie and Clyde style. I could only stand there at the detachment, listening to the radio while the other officers were eating bullets.

"Shots fired!" several different call signs cried out. One by one, the Davy Crocketts knocked out the PCs (police cars). The shots were tearing into the radiators, causing the PCs to overheat and withdraw from the chase.

"For Christ's sake," I yelled, "shoot at the bastards!"

Travelling at speeds well in excess of 100 miles per hour, shooting back and forth, the fugitives finally turned off the highway onto a back road. One of the dog men (K-9) involved in the high-speed chase knew the area very well, and relayed their position to me.

"They're heading down the road of no return," he called on the radio, informing me it was a dead-end strip. "We're going to take them down when they come to the end of the tunnel."

"Buckle up," I shouted into the microphone. "As soon as they come to the end of the road, ram 'em!"

The car eventually slowed as it neared the dead end, and the following PC rammed right into the back of it at almost 40 miles an hour. Guns blazing, the officers swarmed around the vehicle. Still shaken from the impact, the three convicts surrendered and were quickly taken back into custody. Instead of serving their original 10-year terms, they would all be sentenced to life in gaol.

After the smoke cleared, the members on the scene discovered that almost 30 police bullets had struck the vehicle, but only one had the velocity to penetrate. So much for government firepower. Gib Perry eventually recovered, and completed his second career as a BC sheriff. I realized that the media could be a very powerful tool for solving crimes. A lot of cops didn't want to admit it, but the more a crime was publicized, the easier it was to solve.

Through my appeals to the media in Kamloops, I was sometimes referred to as "Kamloops' Top Cop" or "Top Homicide Investigator". The public ate it up, but the superintendent in charge of police services wouldn't stomach it. In his mind, *he* was the top cop, and he didn't seem to appreciate my investigative techniques. He made that message very clear one day as we crossed paths in the hallway.

"Top cop, heh?" he snarled. "We'll see about that, sergeant." His glare could have broken a rock. Over the ensuing weeks, I was careful to tread lightly upon his turf. I thought I was in good standing until a surprise expense account audit was launched on my section. It was clear this sucker was going to remain pissed at me for some time to come. There was only one thing left to do. If I couldn't work with him, I might as well work around him.

The highway murders around Kamloops had been happening for a number of years, but had never really been investigated in a coordinated way to any degree. Finally, after yet another homicide landed a young girl's body on the outskirts of Kamloops, I decided to host a "Highway Murders Summit". Originally, we thought we might have to deal with 10 homicides, maybe 15. When I announced the criteria for the summit were young girls murdered or raped (or both) on the highway, where the M/O involved assault and or mutilation of the body, almost 40 cases surfaced across British Columbia and Alberta. The cases involved everything from transvestites to young girls in their early teens. Murders involving women who had had their nipples cut off, bite marks, and objects shoved up their vaginas or their anuses were brought out into the open for the first time.

It was also the first opportunity for 40 investigators to accumulate data jointly and hopefully unearth possible suspects. We pored over gruesome photographs and tapes of the scenes, dead bodies (mutilated and otherwise) for over a week, but that thread of evidence we sought could not be found. In the end, we left with little more than what we had arrived with. You just don't know who's walking beside you on the street.

As expected, the murder summit generated an incredible amount of media attention. Major TV and radio personalities were posted outside our conference doors for the duration, and it was front-page news all across Canada. In the interest of not stepping down too hard on the boss's toes, I suggested that perhaps it would be a good idea if he addressed some of the public's concerns. But the media weren't satisfied with the answers they were getting from the superintendent's office, so I eventually fed them all the blood and guts they were looking for. Of course, front-page headlines about the murder summit with me as the spokesperson further infuriated the superintendent. When he saw me, his face would boil.

Homicides came and went. Some were smoking guns and confessions, while others just stayed unsolved. Those cases that hadn't been concluded were our main priorities, when we weren't racing around trying to keep up with the flood of incoming calls. A good day at the office was when we caught up to some of these sick bastards and had them tossed in gaol for the rest of their lives. On a bad day, the files stayed open.

While in Kamloops, I quietly celebrated the anniversary of my twentieth year in the force. That is a pretty substantial achievement, and a Long Service Medal is presented to those officers who make it that far without breaking the rules or being tried in service court. Usually, this prestigious award is presented at a formal function in red serge. Weeks passed. Months passed, and with them several formal opportunities for me to receive my Long Service Medal. Instead of giving the boss another potential reason to keep me waiting, I just kept hoping I'd be surprised. Finally, after almost six months of waiting, I approached the superintendent's secretary.

"Do you know anything about my Long Service Medal? Has it come in yet?" She could tell that I was genuinely concerned about it. It was obvious that she disliked the situation.

"Mike," she shrugged, "I don't know why, but it's been sitting in the boss's safe since the 15th of December." That was one question answered.

On the brighter side of things, I had purchased a rather extravagant home on an acreage in Kamloops. In the backyard was a 40-foot swimming pool, while inside was a built-in solarium and a hot tub just off the master bedroom. Financially, I was doing all right. I had been purchasing real estate and selling when the time was right. My wife was in senior management with a major banking institution. Holidays abroad weren't uncommon.

One day my neighbour suggested we get involved in a local nightclub called the Brass Rail. It had been put up for sale, and we both agreed that it would be a good investment. The economy was stable, and people weren't drinking any less, so we bought it jointly with our wives. My wife and I were the silent partners, because I wasn't too interested in being told that my involvement was conflicting with my duties in the RCMP.

Then, in the early 1980s, everything came crashing down — except interest rates. They skyrocketed, and the payments we were making on our loan were astronomical. Although the Brass Rail seemed to be crammed with eager customers every night, we just couldn't seem to turn a profit. Heated discussions with my business partner yielded no explanations for the situation.

It also leaked out that I was a silent partner in the Brass Rail, and now the shit was airborne around headquarters. One late Friday afternoon, as I was enjoying a few beers and lounging around the pool, the phone rang. It was the administrative staff sergeant from our local HQ.

"Mike," Dave Bryce began, "the OC just learned that you have an interest as the owner of a bar in town, and he's instructed me to order you back to the office to supply him with a written statement tonight regarding this involvement. He's under the impression that you have violated the RCMP Act by letting yourself get involved in a conflict of interest."

"Well, Dave," I answered, my senses dulled, "I've talked with my lawyer. He assured me that I have not breached the RCMP code of ethics.

If the superintendent wants any further information, he can call my fucking lawyer!" There was a long pause before I got an answer.

"You really want me to say that to the boss?"

"You're goddamned right I do, Dave!" It had seemed like such a great idea at the time. Of course, when Monday morning rolled around, the shit hit the fan in elephant strength and I was standing in front of it.

The superintendent, who was the OC (officer commanding), demanded I rid myself of such evil, and ordered me to find a real estate agent to sell it. He wanted a statement of my financial affairs, and insisted that I should be paying more attention to my work. That's where he was wrong. If I had in fact been paying more attention to the bar, maybe my partner would not have driven the business into the ground.

"Yes, sir," I said. There wasn't much he could have done at that point to make my life any worse. The last thing on my list of objectives was to give him the satisfaction of knowing he'd found a way. "Have a great day, sir."

Everything was coming apart around me. My family life, my financial life, my job. I'd sit in bed, emotionally alone, with all of these thoughts anchored in the forefront of my mind. I couldn't ask anyone for help, and I suppose I wouldn't have even if I'd had the opportunity. It's what women call "a stupid guy thing." My father had told me there wasn't any problem in the world that couldn't be solved with a little hard work. I hoped he was right, because I was soon going to find out.

The partnership fell apart, and I ended up mortgaging everything I owned to keep the business afloat with new management. The bar scene never slowed, but I still wasn't making any money. Interest rates hovered in the 20 percent range, but I soon found out it wasn't the only reason the business was still almost bankrupt. The "friend" I'd trusted to manage the bar in my neighbour's place had also been ruined by the prosperity afforded by the bar scene. Meanwhile the bank started hinting at foreclosure.

Overcrowding led to several charges against the company, and it became a major scandal inside the RCMP circle because I was the owner. They ordered me to stay away from that scene. Then, because my wife was a bank employee, the bank insisted that she assign her equity in the family home to me in keeping with the Bank Act. As soon as her pen hit the paper, the bank took over our home.

It was one of those times in my life where I was all right until I was alone. Alone, simply thinking about how much I had fucked up. In the shower, leaned up against the wall, drowned in my thoughts. On my way to work, driving down the wrong way of life's one-way street.

Back at work, people were still getting raped, stabbed, and bludgeoned to death. Society wasn't going to slam to a halt because I was on the verge of a nervous breakdown. The public was complaining about every unsolved crime, and the upper echelon was ordering me to sell my business. The bank was foreclosing, my wife was drinking, and in an attempt to solve my problems so was I. I was convinced nothing more could go wrong.

That was, until we got the phone call from Clearwater detachment, 70 miles north of us.

"Something you might want to know, Mike, is the Johnson and Bentley families have been reported missing in Wells Gray Park. We're not sure yet, but it will probably be your responsibility in a few days."

Great, I thought to myself. *Here we go.*

Unfortunately, a missing family complaint simply wasn't enough for us to act on. As head of the detective office, however, I wanted to keep track of the developments in the search now being coordinated in Clearwater. The two staff sergeants at Kamloops detachment, Norm Schafer and Dave Bryce, rotated messages back and forth to Clearwater and passed the information on to me. I would relay the messages to the troops when I could.

The second officer in command was keeping us on a very short string. He kept reminding me that we were responsible for serious crime, and the developments in Clearwater simply didn't constitute a serious crime (yet!). Certainly, we talked about it over our morning coffee, and issues pertinent to the disappearance were mentioned throughout any given day, but we were handcuffed until the family turned up either dead or victims of some other horrible atrocity. It wasn't fair, but that was my job.

Of course, the job came with its share of perks as well. We got to wear our own clothes and we had some flashy equipment to get our jobs done. In fact, some of the members from the small detachments we visited regularly to solve any serious crime thought of us as a sort of "Gucci" squad: the boys with all the toys. Because of it, we weren't too well liked among some of them. We were the "big city cops" who'd roll in and stomp all over their turf in running shoes and blue jeans. Then all we'd do was solve their crime for them. In their opinion, it wasn't anything they couldn't do on their own. In my opinion, they were probably right in some cases. The difference was that we had qualifications and expertise in homicide investigation, and we had access to all of the equipment necessary to assess a situation and solve the crime. In their eyes, we blazed across the province wearing sun glasses and leather jackets while they did all the work. One of the hardest parts of our job was dealing with those local RCMP members who weren't too happy to have us around.

While messages were being passed back and forth around the subdivision HQ, rumblings of the missing family could be heard in various corners of the detective office. All four of us were sitting on the edge of our seats waiting for the midnight telephone call. Everyone at Kamloops GI suspected foul play. When a guy doesn't show up for work for the first time in 20 years and when two girls don't show up for school, and nobody is in contact for over a week, foul play is usually the contributing factor. A family of six had seemingly dropped off the face of the earth, but until we got the call it was going to have to wait.

On the morning of the 13th of September, 1982, Dwight, Gerry, and I piled into a PC and headed to a nearby restaurant to discuss the day's objectives over a warm cup of coffee. The fourth member of our team, Ken "Reliable" Leibel, was in Vancouver working on another investigation. We bullshitted about different issues, and had a general belly aching session to get all our frustrations out before the work began in earnest for the day. At the time (although I'm sure it hasn't changed), we had a lot of diplomatic hoops to jump through before we could actually face any given task. Armchair quarterbacks at head office in Vancouver wanted to know everything that was happening on every play. Of course, you couldn't just send them a simple report. Everyone on the way up the chain had to take a peek at it, and in the meantime they wanted their say. If we had written something in the report that in some way didn't appear to cover all the bases, we were usually asked for clarification and then we would have to re-write it. By the time the reports had moved all the way to the top and rolled back down again, they sometimes looked like they had been spray painted with red ink. Everyone wanted things done by the book. Everyone but me.

If I had diligently followed every rule in the book I wouldn't have gotten anywhere. Rules were for fools, but guides for the wise. I knew how to do my job, but the brass insisted on trying to trip me up at every opportunity. I'm not sure if they really understood the problem. The more they got in my way, the less I could accomplish. It seemed pretty simple to me.

That morning, as we were sitting there knee bashing everyone who came to mind, the waitress called me over to the phone. We didn't have cellular phones or pagers back then, so whoever it was on the phone knew where we were every morning at 10 o'clock when we were in town. Gerry moved aside as I slid out of our booth to get the phone. The others promptly slurped back their coffee. It was time to go to work, and my guts quickly shifted to churn mode.

I smiled curtly at the waitress as I picked up the phone, wondering what sort of horror I was going to hear about. Stabbing? Bludgeoning? Shooting? The waitress stripped the tab off the cash register and carried it to the table. The guys put on their coats, mentally preparing themselves for the sight of another life ravaged by violence. We got paid to do it, not to like it.

"Mike, the inspector is looking for you, now!" the secretary from our office told me. "He said, and I quote, 'Tell them to get their asses up here, we have a major problem.' I'm not sure, but it has something to do with some bodies." *Right then! Let's go.*

Five minutes later, Gerry Dalen and I were sitting in the war room being briefed by the superintendent. Sitting beside him was the inspector and one of the staff sergeants. I think it was Dave Bryce.

"We have information that a vehicle bearing the same licence plate number as the Johnson car has been found in a completely burned-out condition in Wells Gray Park. It has been suggested that there are bodies in it."

Gerry and I exchanged looks. They didn't need to tell us much more than that, except to get our butts up to Clearwater. Arrangements had been made for a helicopter from Kelowna to come in and pick us up in an hour, so I darted back home to grab a bag for the trip. Normally, it was a pretty leisurely fifteen-minute drive back home; I made it in seven. I packed a couple shirts, some pants, and a few other essentials. Nobody was home at the time, so I left a note: "I'm out of town. Call ya." I then rushed back to subdivision HQ.

When I arrived, Gerry was helping Dwight pack the car with every piece of extra gear they thought we would need in Clearwater. The trunk was already filled with our investigation kit — flashlights, pens, tape recorders, rubber gloves, plastic bags, and evidence tags. With the rear of the PC sagging, Dwight climbed in and headed for Clearwater.

Not long after he'd left the parking lot, I heard the RCMP chopper approaching from the south. Gerry and I grabbed our "go bags" and headed for the clearing behind the detachment where it would land to pick us up. Both of us were pumped up as we climbed aboard, ducking as the rotor whirled above us.

The flight up to Wells Gray Park in the back of the helicopter was noisy, but Gerry and I were too focused to be bothered. We were submerged in our thoughts, imagining what we might arrive to see. What would we need? What steps would we have to take to preserve the crime scene? What *was* the crime scene? What kind of cooperation were we going to get from Sergeant Baruta's staff? I knew we weren't going to have it easy out there. Normally, if you can get to a crime scene within 24 hours, your chances of finding anything of value are pretty good. As the days and the weeks pass, your chances of figuring out exactly what happened decrease accordingly. The Johnson car had probably been sitting there for almost a month, so we knew we were going to have a hell of a time figuring it all out. It wasn't the big city anymore. We were heading into the bush, where we'd have to play by nature's rules. Those weren't meant to be broken.

Wells Gray is British Columbia's second-largest provincial park, consisting of over one million acres of pristine wilderness. While a majority of the park is covered by a rocky volcanic plateau, the skyline is dominated by large individual mountain clusters separated by glacially born valleys. The northern part of the park is quite rugged and difficult to access. The southern side is the home of the majority of the tourist sites. Raging waterfalls fed by thousand-year-old glaciers cascade over awe-inspiring cliffs, while rolling hills and lush green vegetation are home to over 600 different species of plants and wildlife. Helmcken Falls, probably the most popular attraction in the park, has inspired tourists for decades. Some stand for hours listening to the roar of white water shooting off the Murtle plateau, plunging 500 feet to the river below.

In 1925, the Clearwater Valley Association started a campaign to get the area around Helmcken Falls protected as a provincial park. When word reached the Minister of Lands at the time, his harsh rejection dampened their vigour. Then, a decade later, the Minister of Lands and Municipal Affairs, the Honourable Arthur Wellesley Gray, took part in a tour that eventually led him through the Helmcken Falls area. Accompanied by his nurse and a doctor from Victoria, he was guided across the untamed land to see the splendours of the region.

In order to keep up old Arthur Gray's endurance, he was instructed to drink a mix of orange juice, canned milk, and several quarts of gin, rum, and whiskey at every overnight stop. It is suspected that he was indulging in this mixture a bit more frequently than that. As a result, the Honourable Arthur Gray almost tumbled drunkenly from a foot bridge spanning the Murtle Canyon, and was saved only by his quick-thinking nurse. Rumours later emerged that Arthur Gray was so drunk during his visit, he didn't even remember visiting Helmcken Falls, probably the most spectacular waterfall in all of British Columbia.

Despite these mishaps, an order in council eventually approved the establishment of a park in 1939. It was agreed that it would be named Wells Gray after the honourable Arthur Wellesley Gray, who had stumbled with dignity across its rocky plains. Looking down upon them from my vantage point in the fall of 1982, I wondered how difficult it would be to tackle the terrain below in an inebriated state.

Suddenly, it felt like my stomach was in my throat. I would've been sitting on the ceiling if it hadn't been for my seatbelt. The helicopter leaned over hard as the three of us tried to keep the coffee down. I could see the forest below charging at the window, and knew immediately that we were losing altitude — fast! What the hell was going on?

"We've got company!" the RCMP pilot, Ron Prior, announced as we flew over the boundaries of the park. He'd spotted a media helicopter in the distance, and had moved swiftly down to tree-top level to avoid being seen. Our attention was quickly drawn out the windows. Rotary and fixed-wing aircraft appeared over the jagged northern horizon, probably waiting for us to show them where the crime scene was. Leaning back and forth with the helicopter, the three of us hung on as we darted over the trees and around hills to avoid being spotted by the media aircraft. Like good little reporters, they had obviously been paying close attention to the police scanners. Someone must have mentioned bodies.

Ron had been doing police work long enough to know that avoiding the media at a time like this was critical. Our media "window" wouldn't last forever, but we wanted to get in there without having to worry about being smothered in spotlights as we tried to orient ourselves with the crime scene.

We took the scenic route around the gaggle of media aircraft, and eventually came to Battle Mountain where the car had been located. As I looked out the helicopter window at the wilderness below, I could appreciate the nightmare Sergeant Baruta was having with the aerial grid searches he'd been coordinating. Finally we spotted the site. We didn't get too close to the car for fear the downwash would blow precious evidence all over the mountain. Even from the air the contours of the vehicle were difficult to see. The rusted paint and broken shape blended perfectly into the surrounding foliage. Nearby trees swayed easily in the light breeze, stubbornly shielding the car from view in every direction but straight up.

A couple of PCs were parked on a dirt road that passed not far from the wreck. It was hard for me to tell how visible the vehicle was from the road, but I imagined it wouldn't have been easy to see. Two things were made apparent to me at that point: Whoever did this had a pretty good idea how hard this car would have been to find, and whoever that person or those people were had probably been here before.

Ron brought the chopper down on a clearing not far from where the wreck was located. Gerry and I jumped out and proceeded towards the cluster of activity down the road. The sun was beating down on us, and the humidity, even at that altitude, was choking. I was soon longing for an enclosed, air-conditioned space. To make matters worse, I think every fly in the park came to welcome us, and in seconds we were smacking them off our necks and arms. I'd only been there two minutes, and I was already annoyed with the place. But this was the environment we were in, and we were going to have to adapt to it. Like it or not, I still had a job to do.

It looked like Sergeant Baruta was keeping everyone away from the vehicle until we arrived. I'd worked with Frank before, investigating a murder case in Clearwater a couple of months earlier. A guy had chopped up his wife and set her on a rolling conveyor belt leading to the beehive burner in a mill. We knew who did it, but we couldn't prove it. I'd told the suspect he'd better not leave town without telling us. As far as I knew, he'd done what he was told. There was no doubt in my mind that we were going to be talking to him soon.

Frank and I had worked well together then, and I had complete faith in his expertise. He knew how important it was to leave the crime scene untouched by outsiders. Nothing that was altered could ever be re-placed in the exact same way it was found. Even a small change could foil our perception of the crime and lead us to waste time running down a dead end.

Gerry Dalen and I approached the scene, giving each other the odd hopeless glance. I could see that the Section NCO (non commissioned officer), Norm Schafer, was already there. The coroner was standing by, talking with some of the members of the forensic identification section who were waiting with him. Two members from the dog section were roaming about the woods familiarizing their dogs with the local scents.

A pathologist from Kamloops, Dr. McNaughton, was talking with Herb Leroy, one of our forensic identification specialists who was also our blood-spattering analyst, next to one of the PCs. The pathologist was there to help us sort out the bones. By examining the locations of blood stains, Leroy could help us determine how many times a victim had been struck by a bludgeoning tool. If what lay in front of us was in fact the murder scene, Leroy might be able to help us get a feel for what had happened.

Overhead, I heard the hum of approaching aircraft. *The media are coming! The media are coming!* Almost a century ago in Turkey, my great (great great) grandfather Dr. Charles Kean stood watch in a citadel above the sleeping town of Scutari before the battle of Kars. Upon hearing the thunder of hooves and seeing the glistening of the moon upon bayonets, he cried out the infamous warning: "The Russians are coming! The Russians are coming!" *Here I am,* I thought lamely to myself, *standing on the side of a mountain, listening to the thunder of incoming media aircraft, and seeing the sun glistening upon camera lenses. Great. It's time to go to war.* I would rather have dealt with the Russians any day.

Sergeant Baruta was keeping everyone in order, and doing a fine job of it. His work throughout the past month had been absolutely remarkable. He'd been coordinating the search from day one, and I admired his dedication. In my opinion, he'd gone way beyond anything anyone could have expected of him. When he saw us coming down, his whole body seemed to heave with relief. I think he was glad to hand responsibility over to me.

The first thing we had to do, now that those of us from Kamloops GI had arrived at the crime scene, was establish a perimeter, a grid we would mark off to which nobody but us would be allowed access. I had no idea what I was dealing with, but I knew the perimeter would be at least two or three acres. We then had to establish a base camp. It had to be near the crime scene, but not so close that it interfered with it.

Keeping those things in mind, I approached Frank Baruta.

"Look, Frank," I said, removing my sunglasses and ignoring the ambient buzz of aircraft and mosquitoes overhead, "bring ident in there and take a look. Tell us what we may be dealing with." We had 20 people standing around, and if all of them went storming up to the car looking for bodies, they'd probably destroy any evidence we may otherwise find. They'd push it into the ground, or cover it up, or break anything in their path like a herd of shoppers on dollar day.

I estimated that the car was about 150 feet from the road. Some thin brush swayed restlessly in front of it, camouflaging its rust-tainted skin from anyone travelling past it. You could see it, but you had to be looking straight at it. Frank and Sergeant Harvey Boswell, one of the Ident techs, moved cautiously around the vehicle as we watched.

I noticed more aircraft were arriving every couple minutes. Helicopters flew past with their doors open, while photographers and cameramen tempted death by hanging out of their seats to get the best camera angle. "Doesn't look like there's anyone alive down there!" they were probably saying.

After their examination of the car, Sergeants Baruta and Boswell struggled out of the brush towards Gerry and me. Frank's forehead was dotted with sweat.

"Well, Mike, what it appears to be is a burned-out vehicle," he explained, wiping the sweat from his suntanned face. "There's absolutely nothing left inside. It's completely burned. The shell appears to be intact, and it looks like there's human skeletal remains in the back." Once he had explained the situation as he perceived it, I addressed the two dog men.

"Guys, I'm still not too sure what we have here exactly, but I'd like you to go around the perimeter, say, a couple hundred yards, and look for anything unusual. We've already pretty much messed it up, but look for anything weird around the edges and mark anything you think is out of place. I'll send my exhibit man over to you if you need him." They promptly split up and moved off, their dogs' senses probably still scrambling from all the new smells.

By then the sky was a traffic jam of air activity. Helicopters hovered in place while fixed-wing aircraft wove in and out of them like pylons. It was hard to concentrate with the threat of a mid-air collision a very real concern. All we needed at that point was for a couple of aircraft to come crashing down on our crime scene.

Finally, we moved in towards the car with the forensic identification team, the pathologist, and the coroner. Only the necessary people came in with us. A local constable accompanied the pathologist and the forensic team. We all had full-sized pads of paper and clipboards for recording everything as we saw it. The forensic identification guys were there to take photographs of the scene, bag and label, sift for evidence, and generally help us keep things organized. The pathologist, Dr. McNaughton, was there to give us an idea of what we were dealing with. The back of the car was a horrible, horrible mess filled with burned skeletal remains. McNaughton's job was to help us retrieve those remains without damaging them. I didn't know a femur from a funny bone. If I got in there and started trying to put pieces together, there was no telling what sort of shape I'd come up with. The coroner was there to help us determine how many bodies we were dealing with and officially pronounce death. Normally he'd also have to qualify our assumptions that the bodies were, in fact, dead. However, in this case, there wasn't much grey area there.

While we were walking towards the vehicle, our eyes were mainly searching the ground for evidence. From the road, we had all noticed the tire tracks veering off into the brush. It was pretty clear that the driver had got up a pretty good head of steam and simply swerved around every obstruction until he got stuck. Gerry, whom I'd named my exhibit man, immediately noticed a few small, uprooted trees. He noted that they had been dead for some time, because their leaves were all brown and wilted. His responsibility as the exhibit man was to track all exhibits and make sure photos were taken. He would then record what each piece was, and where it was found.

Gerry's task was enormous, and it wasn't something you could do in a hurry. He had to take his time, ensuring he didn't make any mistakes. Later, if the evidence had to be presented in court, we needed to be able to prove that whoever it was being charged had actually committed the crime. The only way to do that was through evidence collected during the investigation. A cop's memory is as bad as everyone else's, and in court it's only as good as his notes. We had to make sure we recorded everything, otherwise a criminal could walk free because of that one forgotten detail. The mere possibility haunts every crime detective, so they are seldom seen at a crime scene without a pen and a foolscap notepad in hand. Continuity of evidence and exhibits was extremely critical.

Gerry went about his work, gathering evidence. I spotted some broken glass scattered on the ground, probably from a headlight. The Johnsons' car had been described as a cream-coloured 1979 Plymouth. Before me was a piece of rust that looked like it had been there for 20 years. It was sitting upon a perfectly round circle of scorched grass about 20 feet across. I approached from the rear of the vehicle. The back window was gone, and small parts of it appeared to have melted behind where the back seat used to be. The taillights had evaporated, and the bumper looked like it had been sitting in a furnace and had been hammered into its present shape. I looked down at the licence plate to see if maybe we weren't just looking at some abandoned vehicle. The plate number was the same as the Johnsons'.

The tires were mostly burned away, and all the windows had disappeared. The door handles had been vaporized in the fire, and the driver-side door was open about halfway. There was a bunch of stuff up on the roof where the car carrier was supposed to be. I recognized a few melted beer bottles, some canned goods, and some other items that looked like potatoes to me as I came closer. The roof itself appeared to have come under such intense heat that it had assumed a rather concave shape. It looked as if a boulder had been dropped on it.

Five keys were still dangling from the trunk lock. The lock mechanism would have been melted beyond working order, but I tried it anyway. Stuck. *All right, so what kind of surprise am I going to get when I open the trunk?* I filed that away, and proceeded to snoop up the passenger side of the car, careful not to step on evidence.

When I got close enough, I noticed a very distinct odour. A sort of dusty scent emitted from the vehicle, made more pronounced by the fact that it was so damned hot outside. The inside of the car was scorching, and the smells were billowing out the open windows. I'd seen and smelled a lot of dead bodies in my 22 years of service. I'd looked at and investigated them for a living. But I'd never worked a mass murder before. And this was more than a mass murder: Whatever started this fire had incinerated these people. I wasn't even sure I wanted to look in.

But I had to. It was my job. Not only did I have to look in there, I had to figure out exactly what had happened. Eventually, I willed myself to look in. The horror concealed within the vehicle was staggering.

"Holy fuck!" I whispered.

Before me lay a forest of charred bones of every size and shape, fractured and broken. Everywhere. You couldn't even see the floor where the back seat had been. Christ, I thought I could see a ribcage and a hip bone in there. The fire had destroyed everything. The victims had literally been cremated. Not only their bodies, but their entire existence had almost been erased by flames. I couldn't believe that life could have been reduced to so very little.

The dashboard was a sagging ruin. The steering wheel looked like it had been made in a second-grade art class. I guessed there were probably two bodies in there that appeared to have been stacked on top of one another in the back seat. There wasn't any doubt in my mind that the pathologist was going to have his hands full.

"Good Christ," I said, loud enough for all to hear.

Gerry Dalen and I exchanged a hopeless look. *Jesus, please give us some physical evidence.*

Every crime detective approaches a scene praying for some sort of evidence. Without it, the job is almost impossible. To make our situation worse, fire is one of the worst things to deal with. In most cases, everything has been burned, leaving you with nothing — no fingerprints, no hair samples, no clothes. There's absolutely fuck all.

I'd thought briefly about just hauling the whole damned thing to the crime lab in Vancouver. That way, I could get an extremely thorough analysis of the contents of the vehicle, and possibly some explanation as to what kind of material had been used to incinerate it with such finality. I decided against doing that because I knew it would take weeks for the crime lab to get us the information. It was so much faster to let the pathologist go through the car here, picking out the bones and categorizing them first. When we had a good idea of how many bodies there were (the most important information I needed at that point in time), then I'd have a truck come in and haul the wreck out. Before I had the troops turning Wells Gray Park inside out looking for more bodies, dead or alive, I wanted to make sure they weren't actually in the car. I simply couldn't wait three weeks to find out.

At that point it was time for us to take a look at what was in the trunk. I suspected that the perpetrator had probably stored the fuel and some sort of accelerant (there had to have been something to make the fire burn so intensely) in the trunk. I got Gerry to grab a pry bar from one of the nearby PCs so we could open up this sucker.

Careful not to damage anything, we gently inserted the bar between the trunk lid and the frame. With a quick jolt, it was loose. When we opened it up, I got the shock of my life.

I'm not sure if anyone could tell it had really hit home with me, but I was absolutely stunned. I stood there like I'd just been smacked between the eyes with a baseball bat. Staring up at me were two little skulls. One of them was looking straight at me.

The last time I'd seen anything like that was back almost 20 years before. That time, we hadn't had the luxury of a coroner to come in and scoop up the bodies. A corporal and I had to investigate the bodies of a dead family in a house that had recently burned down. Among the victims was a three-year-old child. The corporal wouldn't go near that little body. He couldn't, probably because of the four year old he had at home. In the end, I had to carry out the little frame and prepare it for transportation.

The thought of looking down at it horrified me, even 20 years later, and now here I was looking at the skull fragments of two girls who were about my daughter's age. I really had to check pace there for a moment. For the first time in my service, I understood exactly how that corporal had felt.

It could have been my daughter in there.

The whole atmosphere changed as that trunk opened. The reality struck us with the force of an explosion, then proceeded to suck all of the oxygen out of our lungs to feed its hungry fires. We had been fairly certain the girls were dead before we arrived, but it really didn't hit us until we were looking into those dark holes where their eyes used to be. *What did they see before they died? And what the hell was that sick bastard thinking about as he put these two bodies back here?*

Resting awkwardly on a pile of bones in the charred depths of the trunk, one of the skulls had a prominent hole over the left eye. It looked like she had been shot in the back of the head, and what I was looking at was the exit wound. *What kind of sick, deluded, coward would kill a child?* I had no idea that whoever it was would haunt me for the next couple of years

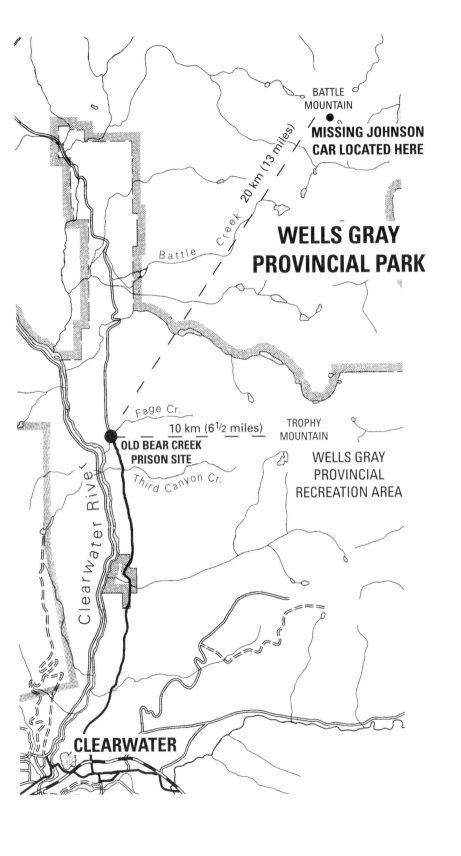

BATTLE
MOUNTAIN

**MISSING JOHNSON
CAR LOCATED HERE**

20 km (13 miles)

Battle   Creek

WELLS GRAY
PROVINCIAL PARK

Fage Cr.

10 km (6½ miles)

**OLD BEAR CREEK
PRISON SITE**

TROPHY
MOUNTAIN

Third Canyon Cr.

WELLS GRAY
PROVINCIAL
RECREATION AREA

Clearwater River

CLEARWATER

Chapter 4 **GETTING UNDERWAY**

Battle Mountain's jagged 7,500-foot peak stands proudly to the north of other tourist havens, including the Indian Valley, Fight Lake, and Battle Creek. All of these locations were named after a legendary Indian battle that took place between the Chilcotin and Shushwap tribes around 1875. As history tells, the Chilcotin band dominated most of the caribou migration route in the region. The only exception was the area around what is now called Battle Mountain, which was controlled mainly by the Shushwap and Canim Lake band.

Around this time the caribou herds were beginning to thin out, and that instigated a battle between the Shushwap and Chilcotin bands. Thirty warriors from each tribe battled to the death near the mountainside, fueled by the need of their bands' survival. It's unknown if the battle itself was a victory for either side, but instead of burying the dead, the bodies were piled upon one another and their weapons thrown in among them. When this was discovered by Benjamin McNeil in 1880, all that was left of the warriors was a mountain of bones not unlike those I'd just discovered in the Johnson car. I knew at this point we, too, were going to have one hell of a battle.

The air space above us was starting to look like a parking lot on Christmas Eve. Everyone in the world had been informed that we'd found the Johnson and Bentley families by the time Dwight Hoglund pulled in with all our equipment. He glanced up at the sky as he stepped out of the car and approached me, probably wondering which one of those planes would be the first to come crashing down on his head.

Hoglund was a real pit bull when it came to getting things done, so it was nice to have him around. He might have been the shortest of all four of us, but with his furry mustache and steely glare he could light a fire under anyone's ass like nothing I'd ever seen. He was always full of energy and he never had any problem getting people busy. I wasn't too keen on having a bunch of Lookey Lous hanging around watching for mid-air collisions, so I promptly got him to run around and get everyone moving. Manpower was a commodity I planned on taking advantage of while it was available. I wanted to accomplish as much as I possibly could before the other members were re-tasked.

Anyone who was standing around had to be given a job. It's important to keep everyone occupied. You don't want someone hovering over your shoulder when you're trying to piece something like this together. We had a thousand tasks to complete, so anyone who wasn't an asset was a liability.

Someone had to go and drain the outhouse at a small campsite down at the base of Battle Mountain, a couple hundred yards down the road. There was a chance the murder weapon had been dropped in there, or perhaps another shred of evidence we could use. That was going to be a really *shitty* job, and everyone who hadn't been doing anything quickly disappeared when I suggested it be done. It was time to say "Junior man prove!" We eventually found our man lurking suspiciously in a bush "looking for evidence." He reluctantly came out of his hiding spot, grabbed a pair of coveralls and some rubber gloves and sulked all the way down the hill to the site.

"Hey now!" someone called out from the trees. Our heads snapped around. A clue? A lead? Anything? "I've got a beer bottle here, a German beer bottle!" Most of us knew better, but there's always that bit of wishful thinking in our minds. "And it's got, it's got *fingerprints* on it!" Well, I suppose it could have been a possibility. A couple of Germans came over, killed these Canadian people, then incinerated all the evidence, but left a beer bottle with their fingerprints on it 25 feet away. We took very good care of that bottle, just in case. I'd seen criminals do much stupider things before. In Powell River, we'd found a murderer's fingerprints under the victim's body, in her own blood. Why not now?

At this point, I was starting to get an idea of exactly how many members were standing around looking at the sky. Time for a grid search. We had to cordon off an area around the crime scene, and search it for any evidence that might be nearby. Once I had everyone who wasn't doing anything gathered around, I passed on the order. In a couple of minutes, they were on all fours scouring the area for shell casings, bludgeoning instruments, contact lenses, thankful they weren't the poor lad down the hill. Anything that hadn't been grown naturally in the bush I ordered them to flag and call the exhibit man, Gerry Dalen, over to have it photographed. Gerry was certainly getting his exercise that day, but he later admitted he was glad he hadn't had to get down on his hands and knees in the mud.

Civilian pilots from Clearwater started volunteering to come out and help us in any way they could. A couple of fixed-wing aircraft were already on their way when Frank Baruta got on the radio and started coordinating the aerial search. He played air traffic controller for a couple of minutes, allocating aircraft to different grids and calling the pilots by name. Frank had been working with those pilots for almost three weeks before the bodies were eventually found. This made him a natural for the task.

Now everyone was doing something. Junior was busy rifling through two weeks of shit, the pathologist was sorting out bones with a local constable in attendance, the coroner was trying to figure out how many bodies we had, Gerry was flagging and recording everything that looked suspicious, the dog men were hunting along the roadside for any irregularities, Dwight Hoglund was hurrying around trying to find people to do things he felt needed to be done, and Frank Baruta was coordinating the aerial search. The stragglers were all on their hands and knees doing a grid search. With everyone out of my hair, it was time to conjure up a plan of attack.

The number one question I needed answered was how many bodies we were dealing with. When I had looked in the back of the car, there appeared to be two of them — probably Jackie and Robert Johnson, the mother and father of the girls. There was no doubt in my mind that Janet and Karen Johnson were the two in the trunk. Dr. McNaughton was still pulling the collection of bones from the front of the vehicle to confirm the numbers. I wouldn't know anything until he was finished, but if there were in fact only four bodies, where were George and Edith, the girls' grandparents?

The other thing on my mind was how they were killed. I had been informed that George Bentley carried a 410/.22 over/under rifle in the cab of his truck, wherever that was. Had the family picked up a hitchhiker and befriended him (or her) for some reason? Had they been robbed in the park and executed? Had the perpetrator used George Bentley's rifle? How many people were involved? At that point, it was impossible to tell. The only thing that was obvious to me was that the pathologist had pulled a hell of a lot of bones from the inside of that burned-out car.

I tried to draw a picture of events in my mind. I was skeptical that one single person could have done all this. There were so many victims that I figured it would have taken at least two people to produce such a horrific degree of destruction. A couple, maybe three individuals go looting the campsite, perhaps when the family is away. Maybe they find George's firearm, or they have a weapon of their own. A knife, a pipe? Another rifle? The family comes back, taking the crooks by surprise, and are quickly executed. After loading the bodies in the car, one or two of them drive it up here, and the other or others follow in the truck. They torch the car, burning all the evidence with it, and now they could be driving the truck anywhere in the country.

What part did the girls play in all this? That was another thing I had to keep in mind. Was everyone killed at the same time? If not, who would have been spared? I believed sex was a definite motive. Why were these people killed? Could they have been killed just for their possessions? They weren't known to carry any vast amount of money. What else was there? The women? The two little girls perhaps? The girls were a possibility, but one that didn't make much sense. Kill the adults for the children? I knew that murder recognized no limits when it came to perverted lust or reason. I remember the night of the annual regimental ball in Nanaimo, a shooting occurred at a bar just next door to where it was taking place. I wasn't at the ball, but I was one of the first detectives at the scene. A teenaged girl was dead and three were wounded, including one person who would be bound to a wheelchair for the rest of his life. The guy responsible for this outrage was being held by the patrons of the bar. I was told that the idiot had just been reading *The Godfather* and had decided to act out part of the novel. He walked into the bar and started shooting people. None of us could believe that a 16-year-old girl had lost her life for no more reason than a killer had been obsessed by a goddamned book.

It occurred to me that there was still another missing vehicle out there. You'd think the Bentley truck would be much easier to find in the bush. After all, it was so much bigger than the car, and it had that camper and an aluminum boat on it. I had no such illusions. If the truck was in the same condition that we'd found the car, I knew it would be almost impossible to spot. I tried to be optimistic, but I was certain if it was still in the park at all, which I guessed it wasn't, it was probably just as well concealed as the Johnson car.

Norm Schafer and one of the corporals eventually found an express bus ticket stub to Kamloops while scouring the campsite area down at the base of the mountain. The name was signed on the stub, quite legibly. Of course, once more that was just pie in the sky. Chances of it belonging to the murderers were slight, but we handled it with extreme care just in case. A couple years earlier one person I knew of in Red Deer kidnapped a safe from a local hardware store. While he was manhandling the safe through the store, his wallet popped out of his back pocket with his picture ID and home address in it. Of course, it isn't always that easy.

During the early hours of this investigation, I more or less stood back and watched the professionals do their work. The pathologist, ident branch, exhibit man, and coroner all worked tirelessly, picking through, bagging, and photographing what little remained in the back seat in an effort to determine exactly what we were dealing with. Oblivious to their surroundings and completely focused on their work, they proceeded to call out the exhibits as they were located, bagged, tagged, and logged. I listened in a trance-like state, struggling to keep my emotions on a professional level.

"Ribs, charred fabric, skull cap and scalp, ribs," and on and on. They were all family men, and it must have been incredibly difficult for them to sift through those ashes. With the well-oiled smoothness of professional expertise, all of them performed flawlessly.

I forced myself to stay composed. I had never wanted to become too emotionally involved in a case. If you treated each and every murder like the tragedy it was, you'd burn yourself out after the first. I'll never forget when I saw my first dead body, back in 1962 when I was stationed in Edmonton. There had been a shooting just outside the city. The suspect had been identified rapidly and while the local force handled roadblocks and questioning, the sergeant I was with decided we should go check the suspect's residence.

We tip toed around the house, peeking in windows with our flashlights. If I'd ever wanted to get shot on my first manhunt, walking around a gunman's house poking flashlights in the windows was probably the best way to do it. Finally the sergeant, who I was trusting with my life, glanced in what must have been the bedroom window.

"Yup, he's in there!" A man of few words! When he said that, my gun almost went off in my bloody hand. I had no idea what was waiting for me as we raced around the house together and booted in the door. I swerved through the halls behind the sergeant, hoping to God he knew where he was going and what he was doing. The suspect was in one of the bedrooms, lying in a pool of blood on the bed with half his head missing. After committing the murder, he'd obviously come back home and shot himself.

The sergeant flicked on the light. "He's dead all right. Mike, you stay here and guard the body. I've got to direct our members in here to deal with it." He turned on his heels and walked out.

I thought he was coming back until I saw the police car drive away. So there's me, in the country in the middle of the night, alone with a dead body. I was sure every time I turned around that damned thing was going to sit up and chase after me. I was scared shitless.

Since then I'd seen hundreds of bodies during my two decades on the force. But unlike before, I was now dealing with multiple bodies, and they had all assembled as one in the charred ruin of the Johnson vehicle.

It was soon brought to our attention that one of the staff sergeants was already conducting a press conference back at the detachment. That was ludicrous, and went against just about every investigative protocol I'd ever learned. It was true that Schafer had been in charge of the search, but once that had been concluded (with the discovery of the Johnson car) the responsibility for the investigation was turned over to me. He had gone way over my head and on his own authority started tossing out information to the public that not even I had been privy to. In doing so, there was a possibility that he had seriously compromised the investigation. There's some information that you have to keep to yourself, and some you can afford to hand out. At this point, it was impossible to distinguish which evidence we'd keep secret and which we wouldn't. I couldn't do anything about it now; the damage had already been done.

The bodies of the victims were soon confined to 50 little plastic bags lying on the grass between the rusted carcass of the vehicle and myself. As the list of exhibits continued, the emotional drain on all of our bodies became more apparent.

"One wrist watch, possible ladies. Two heart-shaped pieces of one locket. Set of rings. A gold band with five stones. A family ring. A gold band with one diamond. A medic alert bracelet ... "

These were people who were not unlike us. Families who had laughed and cried, who had worked hard, who had enjoyed life. Now, it seemed the three generations of that single family had been condemned to extinction, victims of the same society they had come here to avoid.

I wondered to myself how many lives those bags represented. Two? Four? Was it all six? Both Gerry and I looked at one another, and the look he gave me suggested that he was thinking the same thing I was. We were both shaking our heads, swallowing hard, and thinking in concert, *"God, we've got to find this son of a bitch!"* Meanwhile, the seizure of exhibits continued.

"Piece of scalp with hair. A belt buckle. Five teeth ... " Some of the bones they picked out broke apart in their hands. Others were too small to identify. More sketches. More photographs. Piecing the puzzle back together was going to be no easy task for the medical detectives. Nor would it be for us. I knew the public was going to be horrified by our discovery, and they would expect us to prosecute whoever had committed this crime ASAP. We would be held accountable by the media on a daily basis until we could find the bastards who did this.

Were they still in the park? Had they killed anyone else? What was their motive? How did they find this area? Where was the truck now? How would we find it? Where the hell would I find the resources to deal with this? Were we a week behind these bastards? A month?

Slow down, deep breath.

"Mike?" I turned to see the pathologist's sweaty face only a few feet from me. His coveralls were layered in ashes. "I believe I have located six skulls in the car. I'm pretty confident there are six bodies in there."

"Holy shit! There were *four* bodies in the back seat?" I couldn't believe it. My whole body shuddered with amazement. I was also disheartened. Up until that point, I'd maintained a lingering hope that perhaps two of the family had survived and were in the woods somewhere waiting to be found by Sergeant Baruta's search team.

One of the skulls from the back seat (which I later found out had belonged to Edith Bentley) had what appeared to be a bullet hole in it, and there was a very good possibility that the bullet was still in there. The body had been at the bottom, and because fire burns up not down, the pathologist had also succeeded in recovering a very small hair sample. I made a note to organize a search of the Johnson and Bentley homes to collect hair to help match the sample found in the vehicle. There was no such thing as DNA matching back then, so all we could hope for was a match under a microscope. That would help prove who we were dealing with. Dental records would also be checked, and once that was done we could positively identify the bodies. We all knew who it was, but the courts often turned a blind eye to logic. There was no sense going to court trying to convince a jury that the person in the defendant box was guilty when you couldn't prove the dead bodies involved were who you thought they were.

One step at a time, Mike, I'd told myself about a thousand times since I arrived.

"We'll get this down to the lab for X-rays," Dr. McNaughton assured me before he walked off. If there had been hair on the skull, there was a very good possibility that a bullet might still be in there too. With any luck the lab would be able to ascertain the type of weapon used in the murder, and give us some place to start looking. What I had before me was a 10,000-piece puzzle of blue sky. I had just received the first piece.

Now that we had evidence supporting the use of a firearm in this slaughter, it was time to figure out what type of weapon had been used. Was it a 30/30? A .306? A .22? At five o'clock I sent Herb Leroy from our ident branch and the pathologist, Dr. McNaughton, back to Kamloops to X-ray the remains of the skulls they had retrieved. Once we had an idea of what kind of firearm was used, I could involve the media in an extensive publicity campaign. They could advertise that we were looking for assistance, looking for suspects, and pretty much anything else we thought would help us figure out exactly what had happened here.

Once Corporal Leroy and Dr. McNaughton were on their way back to Kamloops, and the skeletal remains were all separated, bagged, and labeled, it was time for Gerry and me to get our hands dirty. We had to get in there and see for ourselves if we could figure out what had happened with what little evidence we had. Both of us had taken several arson courses. Fire, as any firefighter will tell you, has a very predictable behaviour. This particular one had been a real bad ass, but all the burn patterns suggested it had been fueled by a flammable liquid. These six bodies had been almost completely incinerated, and both Gerry and I extensively debated what type of substance would create such an intense heat. We agreed it would be a good idea to contact the crime lab in Edmonton, which apparently had some expertise in the field, and the fire marshal's office. We were interested in contacting anyone who could give us the answers the RCMP arson courses hadn't provided.

Once we'd examined the window mechanisms in the doors, we determined that all the windows, with the exception of that on the driver side, had been closed. The driver-side door was also open, so we concluded there would have been a good volume of oxygen feeding the inferno. The only paint left on the entire vehicle was on the lower right front fender, just above the only remaining evidence of a tire.

The gas cap of the car was intact, so I had more or less ruled out any use of cloth or siphoning of the car's own gasoline to fuel the fire. If you take a cap off to siphon gas, why would you put it back on if you were just going to torch the car anyway? Eventually, the gas tank would have contributed to the blaze, but what I saw was evidence enough that someone had used an outside source of fuel. I thought perhaps a jerry can of gasoline or some other flammable liquid had been used. I made a note to check all nearby gas stations for stolen fuel, and perhaps some information regarding individuals who had recently filled up a jerry can or two.

Despite the extensive fire damage to the car, we didn't notice any sign of collision. That ruled out a confrontation instigated by a highway accident. Sometimes the psychological behaviour we now refer to as "road rage" can have a dramatic effect on a person's demeanour in their vehicle. If there had been any sign of collision, we would have considered a possible highway event. There wasn't any sign, so we pretty much ruled that out.

"Where's the spare tire?" Gerry asked me as I was looking over the front of the car. Where the hell would that have gone? What significance did that have? Did the murderers take it with them? Did the Johnsons leave it anywhere? The visit marked the beginning of a thousand unanswered questions.

At 6:15, the sun was eagerly returning to its nest behind the mountains and our light was quickly following. I decided to leave two officers with the crime scene to protect it from the media, or anyone else who wanted to get in and take a peek. Someone agreed to bring them some food and a thermos of coffee, and the rest of us headed in to town for a fast-food dinner and a war room discussion back at Clearwater detachment.

Although I hadn't had any direct involvement with the Clifford Olson serial murder case, which had ended about a year earlier, I did benefit from some of its investigators' hard-learned lessons. Keeping in mind that it's very easy to armchair detective your way through someone else's investigation, there are always things that can be done differently. Things to keep in mind. We all sit back at some point in our lives and say, "I think I could have done it better." That's because we've learned from someone else's mistakes. Most success is born of a thousand errors. Even if you can avoid those same thousand errors the next time around, you'll encounter a thousand more.

Probably the most noticeable weakness in the Clifford Olson case was that the RCMP detachments involved were keeping all the pertinent information too close to their chest. They weren't sharing any of their data. Instead of one investigation, there were a whole bunch of little investigations going on. All of them had a small piece of the puzzle, and it wasn't until they combined those pieces that the case was brought to a successful conclusion.

If we came up with something that might only be known to the killer, certainly we'd keep it to ourselves. In the interest of maintaining the integrity of the case, that is crucial. However, in the Olson investigation, all the information relevant to the case was being tightly controlled. The public knew very little about the progress of the investigation. Our situation was different in that our greatest asset at this point was the public. Aside from the enthusiasm of my investigators, public knowledge was going to be the determining factor in this case. Unless we could enlist the public's assistance, I knew it was going to be one hell of a rocky road.

Unfortunately, involving the public can open up an entirely different spectrum of problems. Everyone with a phone would have access to our tip lines, and our investigators would have to go check up on every tip. Regardless of whether it was a psychic telling us they had a dream about the family, or someone suspicious of their spouse/parents/kids because they didn't come home one night — everything had to be checked and concluded. That takes a lot of investigators, and given that we had already aroused national attention (stories had aired on national television and the secretary at Clearwater was already starting to take phone calls), the first order of business was organizing the manpower we were going to need.

Looking across the table at Gerry and Dwight in the Clearwater war room, I knew they had a lot on their minds. None of us had ever seen anything like this before. Never mind that we had six dead bodies, but the car had been a burned-out hulk for probably a month or so. There was no evidence that wasn't either charred or broken. The bones were hardly even recognizable as human, and we couldn't yet determine if what we were looking at was the murder scene. I didn't suspect it was, but gut feelings only go so far. The boss in Kamloops didn't want to hear about my gut feelings; he wanted proof. So, remembering what we had learned from the Olson investigation and how we "could do it better," we proceeded to sift through what little information we had in order to find out what information we had to get.

"All right guys, now I realize I'm in charge, but if you're going to agree with me just because I'm the boss, you're fired. Get out. I'm going to need guys who can come up with ideas. I'm going to need guys who are capable of creative thinking, because frankly, we don't have a hell of a lot to work with. We've got a burned-out car, the skeletal remains of six victims, and very little evidence. I need ideas."

"Well, first of all," Gerry began, "we need to get working pictures of the scene developed so that we can look them over, and use them either for show and tells or immediate verification of facts." When the forensic identification guys roll through snapping pictures of the crime scene, it usually takes them a couple of days to get around to developing those photographs. We needed them that night so we could start working with them the next day. We'd also need aerial photographs of the scene, partly to justify the plight of the pilots involved in the air search. When it came down to answering why they hadn't been able to see the car, or why they were having difficulty finding the truck, I wanted the quarterbacks in Vancouver to know why it's so hard to find a vehicle in the bush.

"We'll need to do an aerial grid search of the immediate area," Dwight added. It had already been done, but it had to be done again. Although an aircraft at any given time might have only a 10 percent chance of finding anything of value, after four such flights the odds increase to 40 percent. It was in my best interest to saturate the park with aerial assets. Helicopters and fixed-wing aircraft would have to be allocated to different sectors.

We discussed infra red equipment. It was available, but very costly. The thermal cameras would basically help us see objects through the amount of heat they emitted. Sun-heated metal, for example, would glow brightly in the bush through an infra red camera. Of course, at a certain altitude in certain weather conditions, one bright blur would look like another. Bears, deer, moose and other large mammals would probably be a major source of confusion in the early morning before the metal had a chance to heat up.

"Without infra red cameras," I thought out loud, "I doubt any of our aircraft can find the truck unless they fly directly over top of it. I've seen what the Johnson car looked like from the air. There was no paint, the vehicle was rusted and blotched, and it blended perfectly into the surroundings. To make things worse, nearby trees made the car invisible unless you flew right over it."

While an aircraft can cover a sizable amount of ground in one day, the pilot can't be looking everywhere at once. We're talking about almost a million and a half acres of land, and the truck itself may have been in only one of them. Even with all the aerial assets I could get my hands on, I knew finding that truck in the wooded depths of the park would be harder than finding a tic on a grizzly bear.

There weren't any witnesses, and if there were they'd probably forgotten anything of value to us. We had to figure out how we were going to make anyone who might have seen anything remember.

"Public knowledge is the key," I reiterated. "Everyone who is capable of speech around the town of Clearwater will have to be questioned." We eventually drew up an interview questionnaire that investigators could use on their way around: Where do you work? What is your route? Where were you this day? Any suspicious people? Any weird neighbours? Anything that we could think of that might jog a witness's memory. "Somewhere, someone saw something. The question is, how do we find them?"

"Whoever murdered the families probably knew the park quite well," Gerry suggested. There was a slight chance that they had just stumbled on the location by accident, but we were doubtful of that. "We'll have to get a list of park employees, and treat them all as possible suspects."

"We'll have to question any nearby gas station attendants," Dwight continued. "Maybe they'll remember someone filling a couple of gas cans or a strange-looking character or two trying to bum a ride."

An investigator has to ask a series of normal, down-to-earth, common sense questions: How did these people get in the park and how would they get out? Where did they come in contact with anyone who could tell us where they were? Why were they murdered? Who would have had the opportunity to see them? I knew someone had to have seen them at some point. At one of the grocery stores? At one of the gas stations? The only way to find out was to get original photographs of the families. The investigators questioning the locals in Clearwater could circulate them.

We needed to establish a time line on these victims. This was going to be extremely difficult, because the search and rescue people had already tried and it came up full of holes. There were large gaps between the times and places the missing families had been seen.

"Another concern is that truck." I stopped writing for a moment, looking over at Gerry and Dwight. "Is it sitting on a mountain somewhere in the park rusting away? Is it being driven somewhere?" We knew that it was an '81 Ford, red on top and bottom, with grey in the middle. It was carrying a 10 1/2-foot Vanguard camper, with a mural of an orange sunset painted on the front window. We knew what the boat looked like, and we knew it had a small Evinrude motor. "We'll need pictures of it. I want to refresh the memories of anyone who might have seen them before they died. I want that truck."

Someone could have been driving it around Clearwater, or perhaps heading for the US, or somewhere else in BC. They could have been anywhere in Canada by now. If we were lucky, I figured we might at the very least get an idea of where the murderers were heading, and perhaps how fast they were going.

"We should have the members in Clearwater check into the records of local traffic violations that had been issued within a two-week period." Gerry wrote his idea down before adding: "Have them flag that licence information on CPIC [Canadian Police Information Centre computer]."

"We'll need to organize transportation for the car to the Vancouver crime lab. A flatbed truck with a crane should probably do it." Dwight thought to himself for a moment. "We need a tarp, and perhaps some chains. Maybe a heavy-duty sling."

"News conference," I continued. The media had already saturated the country with Johnson and Bentley news, and I hadn't even talked to them. I knew some of them were trying to get me to do a live interview to describe the situation. I wasn't quite prepared to start dealing with that yet, so I ended up suggesting that the inspector talk with them. The last thing I needed now was to further piss on the superintendent's boots by giving media interviews at the outset of the investigation. He could tell them that yes, we had found bodies, but we didn't know who they were or how many we'd found.

As time wore on, it was quite clear to me that none of us was tired. Adrenaline is an invaluable asset in a situation like that. Everyone was switched on, and we were ready to go all night if we had to. Of course, like every high there is always a low, but we tried to keep those to ourselves.

Within an hour of walking in that room and sitting down, the calls started to flood in. Our discovery had been on the six o'clock news, and everyone was phoning in with information. Actually, one of the phone calls we got was from the guy we believed chopped up his wife and deposited her on the conveyor belt up to the beehive burner earlier that year. I guess he'd taken me seriously, because he was calling to notify us that he was leaving for two weeks. At that point we didn't have a problem with it, so we cut him loose. If we needed to talk to him, he wasn't a hard guy to find. We simply weren't ready to talk to him now.

We had people calling in who thought they recalled seeing the Johnson and Bentley families when they were alive, so we considered getting doctors to put these people under hypnosis where necessary. If we could figure out where the families had been before they ended up on the mountainside, there was a good chance we could find the murder site. If we could find it, I assumed we would also find more evidence.

Where had they been camping? We already knew from Brian and Lynda Bentley that the families both favoured isolated camping spots, generally away from the major tourist hubs. They kept to themselves, mostly, so we were going to have to take advantage of absolutely every tip we received that could give us any idea where they had been. They usually used cash and didn't believe in credit cards. That made them impossible to track through paper trails, so once again we had to rigorously appeal for public assistance in finding their whereabouts before they were murdered.

"We'll need to get phone records from BC Tel for every pay phone in the area." BC Tel keeps a record of all outgoing calls from every phone. We needed to see them all in order to help us determine who was in the park at the time, and where they were calling. I knew that would be an enormous task.

The list grew longer, and it didn't take long before each of us had more than six pages written down. Each idea took up a single line. Our session was abruptly interrupted by a phone call from Kamloops.

"Mike?" Corporal Leroy sounded tired, but I could hear a spark of hope in his deep voice. "We've finished X-raying the skulls. We found the remains of a bullet inside one of them."

"Any idea what calibre it is?" I asked.

"Well, it's in pretty rough shape. As you know, lead vaporizes in extreme temperatures, so we're looking at a fragment here. We've pretty much agreed it's a .22, though."

Whether or not we would actually be able to get any identifying marks off the bullet was another concern. Because the bullet and the skull we were dealing with had been exposed to a significant amount of heat, I was concerned that the outside of the bullet may have been melted clean away, erasing any marks we might find. That was something they would soon find out. They figured it was .22 calibre, and that was good enough for now.

I thanked Corporal Leroy for the news. I knew from experience that I didn't want to be in his shoes. This wasn't an everyday autopsy. Normally, you're dealing with a body. In this case, all they had to work with were the bone fragments and ashes of six bodies. I'd been involved with hundreds of autopsies in my service. The one I remember most vividly was my first back in Peace River in 1963. I'd been named the exhibit man for a case that involved a shooting, and one of my responsibilities was to attend the autopsy. I'd grown up an awful lot, but every cop is nervous about seeing an autopsy for the first time. I'd been gutting deer since I was a kid, so I was confident I could handle it. My curiosity was piqued, and I was anxious to learn as much as I could.

The victim in this case had been really overweight, and I'll never forget seeing that scalpel cutting through three or four inches of fat. The body had been decaying for a couple days, so it had learned to smell like something that cooking show hosts have nightmares about. Christ, I can still smell it today.

"Now, doctor," I said, stepping forward. "I understand he's been shot, and I know he's dead, but what I don't understand is exactly how he died." Dr. Casper looked up at me, and I could see his cheeks wrinkle up from behind his surgical mask.

"Son," he said, pointing at an apron and a pair of rubber gloves on the counter. "Put those on, and come on in here with me." In minutes, my hands were in this guy's abdominal cavity, tracing the channel of the bullet that had ended his life. Dr. Casper also explained the trauma experienced by the body as the bullet hits certain areas. I was put to work weighing the liver, the heart, and a number of other internal body parts I couldn't even pronounce. As bad as it smelled, and as dirty as I was when it was over, I don't think there was an hour in my life I learned more than I had with Dr. Casper.

"They think the weapon used in the murder was a .22," I reported when I returned from Leroy's phone call. "George Bentley carried that .410/.22 over/under with him in the truck, so the next order of business is to have the area checked out for shell casings." Metal detectors were really high tech back then. Hardly anyone could get their hands on one, but I had national attention here. I knew I could get anything I wanted and that included good-quality metal detectors. Dwight spoke next.

"We have to look into the German bottle of beer and the bus ticket. Someone has to go down to a specialty shop in town and figure out what's written on the bottle. We also need someone to look into whoever it was on the bus ticket to find out where he is and where he has been."

"Records," Gerry coughed. "Records of everyone registered in the park. A list of everyone in every hotel, motel, hostel, campsite within — what, say, a hundred square miles."

"We'll need to know the beneficiaries of wills. Any jewelry and other valuables that may have been in the victims' possession and may now be missing. Dental records. Released or escaped prisoners. Similar M/Os..."

As we got more ideas, it was obvious I needed more investigators and some computer time.

Computer time. Back then, getting a computer was an exercise of brute force coupled with some fancy footwork. We're not talking about laptops or desktops. These computers filled rooms, and getting access to them was an arduous task. I hoped that my demand for system time wouldn't get jackknifed on the slippery roads of bureaucracy. With any luck, the administration would review and accept all of my requests without questioning every detail. Of course, the odds of that were only marginally better than winning the lottery a couple of times in a row.

During the Olson investigation, the RCMP had developed a computer program to help detectives process and input information. The data would then be cross referenced with all the other data, and analyzed automatically for a variety of similarities. This would help them determine the value of various sources, and allow them to swiftly rule out any that weren't valid. It was basically an enormous filing card system. The program made an instant dinosaur of our home-grown shoe box, and I was eager to use it. Judging by the amount of incoming information we were already receiving, I guessed it was going to be put to good use.

Someone called in saying they'd found a rifle under a bridge in the park, so that needed to be checked out immediately. One of the local detachment members answered that call for us, uncertain of what he was going to see. Even with the adrenaline fuelling our enthusiasm, everyone was starting to look a little weathered. I felt like I'd been up for days.

My hand was starting to cramp up from all the writing. Gerry and Dwight were having the same problem. Eventually, we would have to compile everything we were writing and send it to Vancouver. They always wanted to know what was going on, and usually not when it was most convenient. One thing that was going to be evident in my report was that we had a lot of things to do, and not a hell of a lot of people to do them. That would quickly change. Whatever I needed, I could probably get. Whatever I couldn't get probably didn't exist.

"We're going to need to make sure that detachments around the province are aware of what it is we are dealing with here." I scribbled down some notes before I continued. "I need every member in British Columbia to have the information, regardless of whether they think they need it or not." We sent the message out as soon as possible: *Six people, they were here and now they're dead. We've got nothing. Help!* That was it in a nutshell. If someone came into their area talking about '81 Fords, or about fires, or about Wells Gray Park, I wanted them to be able to assess and report back to us. It was also important for them to know there were still some very dangerous people out there. No sense having a member pulling over the Bentley truck unaware that the guys inside are cold-blooded murderers.

We wrote down everything we knew, and determined what we needed to find out. We would pass on our requests, and hope that someone would respond to them very quickly. Garages and self-storage facilities needed to be checked. Employee termination records and hunting licences. Everything.

I think about a hundred tips had come in by then. Before we could do anything about them, we were going to need more bodies. I could sure have used a computer, and a metal detector, and pictures, and grid searches, and aerial photos, and records, but they weren't going to happen all by themselves. I needed people, and I needed them fast.

The inspector from our headquarters in Kamloops was present most of the day and evening. He had watched the events unfold, and like us knew the odds of us being successful. He too was a family man, and he was in a good position to understand what it was that the three of us were dealing with.

I ran into him at the coffee machine during one of our breaks. I could tell that he was struggling with the same emotions I was, and there was a very obvious look of desolation on his face. His tone was a whisper of the anger we all felt.

"Now, understand that I'm not giving you a blank cheque, but whatever you need, you'll bloody well get. I don't care if it's manpower, equipment, or money for informants. You call me 24 hours a day. I'll deal with the boss. The eyes of Canada are going to be on us until we solve this mess, and I don't want any screw ups."

"Yes sir!" The inspector's obvious support was more refreshing than the six cups of coffee I'd already had. At the same time, however, he had reminded me that just as we had armchaired our way through the Olson investigation, our peers would be analyzing our investigation. I imagined those detectives would be thankful that it was us living through this nightmare and not them.

The small town of Clearwater, BC, quickly became a centrepiece of media attention. The Johnson and Bentley murders were undoubtedly the most horrendous in Canadian history, and current media technology allowed the country to follow every aspect of the investigation from their couches in front of their televisions. Live satellite coverage fed millions of viewers the gore they yearned for. At the same time, it increased public awareness of our struggle. The message was clear: *The police need your help. This is the number.*

As a result of this media feeding frenzy, there wasn't a room to be had in the Clearwater area. Local businesses (particularly restaurants) flourished, and the residents were immediately bathed in spotlights. In contrast, provincial and private campground reservations were canceled due to media speculation that the murderers were still in Clearwater. There was some panic among the elderly residents who had heard unfounded rumours of a crazed mountain man who lived in the bush. That story spread like a brush fire through the small community.

Wells Gray Park itself was almost completely vacant. The few stalwarts who stayed boasted among themselves that they had the firepower necessary to deal with any threat, be it man or beast. George Bentley had had a rifle as well. We discouraged this posturing, as well as the vigilante attitude that surfaced in the early stages of the investigation.

Like a giant train, the investigation was slowly picking up steam. I was able to second most of the necessary manpower to perform the tasks at hand. The police had just about taken over the town of Clearwater, and citizens seemed relieved by our presence. Sergeant Baruta's detachment was quickly transformed into a "downtown detective office." Members in unmarked police cars were coming and going at all times of the day and night, while the media were camped out in the proverbial front yard. Each TV crew was anxious to air the story of our first big break. They were particularly interested in the long-hair drug squad members sporting bullet-proof vests and sawed-off shotguns. These guys usually worked in an undercover capacity, but had no problem waking up "Sleepy Hollow." Daily briefings were held, and input was solicited from every member present. Our "things to do" list, which was entirely separate from the hundreds of incoming tips, grew longer with each investigative hour.

I had reached deep into the pockets of every specialized unit in our headquarters, but still hadn't come up with enough manpower to handle the volume of investigative information that was coming in every minute. We started working the 16- to 20-hour days that were to become the norm for months to come. We spent them collecting, evaluating, prioritizing, and disseminating the information, but that one positive lead eluded us.

We loaded the Johnson car into a U-Haul cube van using a truck equipped with a crane, and Gerry drove it over to Vancouver. It was important that Gerry retain possession of all exhibits until he could turn them over to the lab. This was for continuity purposes when it came to court. In any investigation, it is important to maintain continuity of the exhibits. You can never tell which particular piece of seemingly unimportant evidence may be crucial to an investigation. A missing link or unaccountable exhibit could break a chain in the investigation and could lead to a "not guilty" verdict on a technicality. There was no way we were going to screw up something like that during the first stages of this investigation. Gerry conducted a debriefing for the crime lab personnel, then supervised the unloading process. The problem was engineering a way to remove the car from the inside of the cube van.

Eventually, two tow trucks were summoned for the task. One was hooked up to the rear of the vehicle and, using its cable and boom, pulled the car out about halfway. Then, the second truck was hooked up to the front of the car (which was still in the cube van) so that when it was pulled out of the van, the car was suspended between the two trucks. Then it was ever so carefully lowered onto a dolly, and then wheeled into the crime lab. The bomb detail went through the car with their fluoroscope, took the roof and the doors off, and literally peeled it down. As they took the layers off, they would take a small grid area and go through each section thoroughly enough to pick out the remaining teeth and small pieces of jewelry.

Once that operation was well on its way, Gerry stopped back in Kamloops for an hour, and then headed to Kelowna to speak with relatives of the Johnson and Bentley families. It was a difficult task, and there were many unanswered questions. Some of them handled it well, others not so well, but it was all that could be expected considering the circumstances. It was an incredibly traumatizing situation, and the family was remarkably cooperative. It was also very hard on Gerry, who, like the cowboy he was, brushed himself off and jumped back in the saddle.

We were soon in touch with our Vancouver headquarters, looking for assistance from the detectives in the elite serious crime unit. They arrived in less than a day, and were promptly put to good use participating in the mundane duties of door-to-door inquiries, researching records, and answering telephones. It wasn't long before they were trading in their shirts and ties for winter boots and warm jackets.

Sergeant Frank Baruta took charge of coordinating yet another massive surface and aerial search of the Clearwater area for the missing truck and camper, while citizens volunteered the services of their vehicles, whether they were ATVs (all-terrain vehicles) or aircraft.

Baruta had the distinction of being a qualified search master. Through his affiliation with search and rescue operations and his attendance at corresponding courses, the detachment commander had a very solid foundation in coordinating our efforts within the park. Frank could very well have done it on his own, but at his discretion he had enlisted the help of a friend to aid in the operation. Between them, they had accumulated well over 30 years of experience.

First, they had divided the entire Clearwater detachment area and some of the periphery into four quadrants on a forest service map. A grid system was employed during air searches of each quadrant, and records kept of which force aircraft had searched what grid at what time on what day. Private pilots, who meticulously logged all of their observations, used smaller maps of each quadrant. To add to this flying circus, a provincial government aircraft equipped with the necessary infra red detection gear was also available for very short periods of time. Its ability to detect a vehicle-sized target submerged in the murkiest waters made it a valuable asset when it was at our disposal.

Ground searches had been underway since the initial complaint back on the 23rd of August. These searches originally encompassed all provincial and private camping sites. With the assistance of some 25 independent logging contractors, federal and provincial services, and civilian volunteers, these searches were quickly expanded to all service roads and skidder trails in each of the four quadrants.

Within that first investigative week Frank was able to beg, borrow or steal for the search police, government and civilian aircraft, logging trucks, four-wheel drive units, ATVs, motorcycles, and inland water transport. Everyone on the ground and in the air had a radio and was in constant communication. When Baruta said he searched an area, we knew that it had been searched very thoroughly.

Armed with a colour composite picture of the truck and camper, as well as a mock-up of the Johnsons' car and pictures of the Johnson and Bentley families, our investigators knocked on every door for hundreds of miles looking for that first thread of evidence.

Meanwhile, the superintendent was calling from Kamloops on a daily basis, inquiring as to what we were doing and looking for results. It was quite clear that he didn't like to be left out of the picture, so we did our best to pacify him with as many details as possible. He demanded (and promptly received) a copy of every message that was sent out asking for assistance or a follow up. I was duly warned not to withhold any information from him whatsoever. *Yes sir, mister superintendent sir.*

He had accused me of withholding information from him in a couple of other investigations. He called it withholding; I called it a need-to-know basis — he just didn't have the need to know every bloody detail. I was there to get the bloody job done, and I usually did.

Finally, we got our first tip on the missing truck and camper. A BC resident who had been vacationing near North Battleford, Saskatchewan, saw the mockup of the truck and camper on TV and immediately phoned our hotline. While we hadn't been authorized to release our own mockup of the truck, the media had used computer graphics to generate a picture of a truck that resembled the Bentleys'. The caller insisted that he had followed that same truck and camper, with the boat still on top and bearing BC plates, into a service station on or about the 24th of August. The witness stated that he had seen two men exit the vehicle, head into the restaurant, and sit down for a meal only a couple of tables away. He believed both were speaking French, and that neither looked as though they belonged to that vehicle. They were shabbily dressed and quite rugged looking. Both were in their late twenties, with unkempt shoulder-length hair. The smaller of the two was described as a blond, while the other, larger male had dark hair. Neither apparently had a firm grasp of the English language. The witness asked himself what these two were doing in such an expensive unit, and couldn't explain the BC plates. He hadn't really thought about it again until he saw the media mockup on TV and realized who he had in fact been looking at.

"Gerry," I said matter of factly, "this could be the lead we've been looking for."

"You could be right, Mike," Gerry agreed, looking over the information I had in front of me. "Actually, it sounds like a tip we received during routine questioning at a restaurant here in Clearwater. A waitress said two scruffy French-speaking guys were trying to put the make on her. Same age, same hair colours. She hadn't seen them since. Shit, I'd better dig that tip up."

"I don't want you to farm this one out," I told Gerry. "I want you to see to it that all of the necessary inquiries are made, and I want them done right away. Commandeer one of the aircraft and get to the complainant yourself.

The complainant lived on Vancouver Island. Gerry would debrief him and get a statement from him to verify his story. If it was genuine, we would need to contact our detective office in Battleford and have them go to the Voyager restaurant to obtain the shift list for the days around the 24th of August. We needed those people interviewed *now*. The cashier or waitresses on duty would have to remember those two. I also told Gerry to stop in Vancouver and pick up the division artist. We would need sketches of these two suspects.

"Bring him back here to see what that waitress can do with him. If it's still positive, you and the artist will be heading to North Battleford." Never one to take his job lightly, Gerry was up and running in minutes. "And Gerry," I said to him before he left, "don't worry about travel authority right now. Just get your ass over there and we'll worry about getting permission later."

"Will do, Mike."

Several hours after Gerry was on his way, we got another big break. A park employee recalled a truck and camper unit parked at the Old Bear Creek Prison site in Wells Gray Park. The employee had only noticed it briefly, and was unsure as to whether or not it fit the description, but assured us that he had indeed seen it within the period of time we had specified. Ken Leibel (who had since arrived from some investigative inquiries in Vancouver) and Dwight were quickly dispatched to the scene, and within an hour had called in to the office.

"Mike, we may have something. You'd better get out here."

The Old Prison Camp site consisted of three acres of clearing where a local "mobile" prison had once stood. Designed to be easily taken apart and put back together again, the prison had been moved years earlier, leaving in its wake a smooth, yet healthy landscape of grass and small coniferous trees. To get there, all you had to do was follow Wells Gray Road across Fage Creek and take the first left. The entrance, however, was now so overgrown that unless you slowed your vehicle right down you'd miss it. I found it after two tries.

When you first entered the site, it was quite easy to tell where the prison buildings had once been. The grass was still flattened, and the area was perfectly set up for camping. There was a fire pit, surrounded by river rocks and spanned by an effective arrangement of tree forks and logs for hanging kettles or pots. Larger logs sitting nearby had been cut in smaller pieces and placed on end. Upon them sat long boards that had obviously been used for sitting around the fire.

As I approached, Dwight was rummaging around the site, and Ken was crouched by the fire pit poking around with a small stick. Off to his right was a square can with a wire through it, and further on were two blocks of wood that one might use to level a camper. Once I'd had a good look around, Ken called me over.

"Look at this, Boss." He rolled over the ashes and exposed three canning lids that were identical to those we had found on the roof of the Johnson vehicle. Poking further, he retrieved three beer bottle caps. "Extra Old Stock," Ken said quietly. Both of us knew that was the same beer that Bob Johnson drank.

"Where did you get the stick from, Ken?" I asked, noticing that one end had been sharpened to a fine point.

"Over on the other side of that bench there, Boss. There's another one there, too." I went over and retrieved the other stick. As I expected, one end was honed to a sharp tip.

The last time those sticks had been used was probably by Janet and Karen Johnson. I stood and looked at Kenny. "They're marshmallow-roasting sticks. Secure the whole area and call out the troops. Do everything you can to avoid the media. We're going to do a hands and knees search."

I immediately suspected that the Old Prison Camp was the murder site, but of course would have to back up my suspicions with solid proof. Within hours, 20 Mounties with various responsibilities were scouring the area with dogs, metal detectors, cameras, and tape measures. While they went about their duties, the sound of rushing water from a mountain creek lured me away.

After walking a short distance through a cluster of trees I was in the creek bed. The water tip-toeing through the stream before me had spent the last thousand years in nature's largest water filter, and was of a refined purity that man could never equal. After a couple of refreshing handfuls and a moment of solitude as pure as the water cascading down my throat, I twisted on my heels and headed back towards the campsite. I made it about two steps before I slipped. Unable to balance in my rugged "go everywhere" cowboy boots, I staggered like a drunk along the rocky beach. When I finally regained my footing, an unnatural reflection off the water drew my attention. I soon discovered the source of that reflection to be four bottles of Extra Old Stock that had obviously been placed there to be kept cold in the summer heat.

I hurried back to the campsite to relay my findings to the other investigators, and to direct the exhibit man and photographer over to the bottles. When I arrived, there was a bit of a commotion around the fire pit. Gerry, who had since returned from his day trip abroad, was sort of in the middle of the crowd, crouched over the pit. As I approached, he looked up at me. The look on his face said it all.

"Fresh .22 calibre shell casings." Gerry stretched to his full height (which was a couple inches taller than mine), and motioned me over towards one of the PCs. "They've found four so far with the metal detector."

"I'll bet my next month's paycheque that this is where the Johnsons and Bentleys were murdered."

Gerry agreed. "The guy I talked to on the Island is certain that he saw the Bentley camper in North Battleford, being driven by two French-speaking males. I just talked to Battleford before I came here, and apparently the waitress remembers them. I guess they both tried to pick her up. She described them identically to the witness on the Island. It's the hottest lead we've got, and we'll have to act on it."

That night at the briefing, I led the parade with an overview of the day's events. Of course, I emphasized the murder scene I believed we had located.

"We retrieved six spent .22 calibre cartridges located around the scene that our lab experts tell us were probably fired from a Ruger. We also found bottles of Extra Old Stock beer in the creek, which is consistent with what Bob Johnson drank. There were also three Old Stock beer bottle caps in the fire pit. We found three lids identical to those we found on the roof of the Johnson vehicle."

The list went on. The marshmallow sticks, the layout of the campsite, seating for six, the blocks for leveling out the camper, the square can with the wire through it (similar to one we'd seen in a family camping picture), the flattened area where the tent was pitched ...

"That, coupled with the two sightings of local residents who believe they saw similar vehicles at the Old Prison site, tells me as an investigator that we have located the murder scene." The room was full of grunting approval as I moved on with the briefing. "There is also a report today that there were two males hired temporarily in the Wells Gray Park area for slash burning during our time frame who fit the descriptions of the two males seen driving what our witnesses describe as the Bentley truck and camper. That tells me that we have to saturate the park area, and show everyone those composite drawings our division artist has compiled with the assistance of the witnesses.

"We're still well behind the eight ball, and we need help. The majority of the tips we have received are from the public, and they are going to be the ones who help solve this thing. I intend to release the murder scene and the composites to the media. Somewhere, somebody must have seen something that is going to—"

"Just a minute there, Mike," the inspector interrupted. "The superintendent is up to full speed on this, and he doesn't believe that you have in fact found the murder scene. At least, he's not completely convinced, so he doesn't want you to release it. Nor does he want us to release the composites. In fact, he's talking about having the investigation return to Kamloops. He doesn't want the investigative office here. He believes you can be more effective operating from Kamloops."

"Ah fuck! Just what I need. How the hell are we supposed to investigate this case 75 miles away?"

"Hey sergeant, I'm just the messenger, but if the boss wants it to return to Kamloops—"

"For Christ's sake! We have other tips coming in from witnesses across the country who think they have seen the truck and camper heading east. Surely to God if we publish the composites along with the truck and camper mockup it'll refresh someone's mind, and maybe give us the key to the bloody farm. There's no way we can follow up the investigation from Kamloops. There's no sense in it. Not now! Jesus, not now!"

"Look, let me see if I can hold him off for a bit. You press on with what you are doing, just don't release the scene or the composites." The inspector stood and proceeded out of the briefing room to return to Kamloops.

"All right, guys. Just forget that bullshit. You team leaders meet with Dalen and Leibel at the crack of dawn tomorrow. You will be given your areas of responsibility that you and your respective squads are account-able for. Treat these inquiries with urgency, and we'll meet tomorrow evening. If anything pops, get back to us ASAP. Oh, and by the way, this isn't the gravy train. You don't have blanket authority for overtime. Beyond your eight hours, you had better be producing at the rate of 150%. And for Christ's sake, keep detailed notes of everything. I know this bug-ger is going to be around for months to come, and we're going to be accountable for everything we do. Get the message?"

Everyone stood, collected their storm coats, and proceeded out the door. Another long, slow day was over. "Guys," I said, turning to Liebel, Dalen, and Hoglund, "let's go for a beer."

Our favourite watering hole was in the local hotel lounge. It was your typical small-town, pub-style lounge that had enjoyed a lucrative existence since the beginning of the investigation. Between the reporters, the writers, and the cops, I guessed that the place was busy almost around the clock.

When we walked in, some of the crew from BCTV were enjoying a few pints off in the corner. Among them was an old friend of mine who had been reporting for that station for a few years, Brian Coxford. I'd had an excellent working relationship with him, and I knew I could trust him to hold information until the time was right. By publicizing the informa-tion I gave him, it generated public interest that often helped me solve crimes. By giving him the breaking news, obviously he got more credit within his circle. We were both using each other, and we both knew it. *Using,* not "taking advantage of." I'd told him right at the beginning of our relationship, "The public is paying our bloody bills, so they are enti-tled to know what they're getting for their money." Not only that, but it helps keep us on our toes.

After the four of us had settled in, I excused myself and headed out on the porch for a cigarette. Only minutes after I'd stepped outside, I was joined by my confidant.

"Hello, Brian."

"Eh Mike," he said. "Haven't kicked that habit yet I see?"

"Quit? Hell, half the time I think it's the only thing that keeps me alive." Between the murders and the bullshit flying around sub/div HQ, I think smoking was the healthiest bloody thing in my life.

"I'm guessing you've got something for us, or should we be heading back to Vancouver tomorrow?"

"I'd hang around a bit longer if I were you," *wink wink.* "It's not for public knowledge at this time, Brian, but I believe we've found the murder scene and we have a couple of suspects who are probably hidden somewhere in northern Quebec right now with the truck and camper." I explained some of the relevant information, details that couldn't jeopardize the case, and told him that he'd have to sit on it until I gave him the green light. I needed the media to publicize this big time, and I knew that he would be a key in getting the national coverage I was ultimately going to need.

"It'll get national attention, Mike," he assured. "If only because of the French connection. I'll keep it under my hat, so long as I get a heads up before the other guys."

"You got it."

The following week dragged on like a bad play. Everyone was working more efficiently now that they'd gotten comfortable in a routine. Information was coming in so fast I'd had to appoint office administrative coordinators to different areas. Check, conclude, check, conclude, over and over again.

We eventually received permission to release the composites of the possible suspects along with the mockup of the Bentley truck and camper, but nothing about the suspected murder scene. I gave Brian from BCTV the immediate heads up, and in hours people in Alberta, Saskatchewan, Manitoba, and even Ontario and Quebec were reporting sightings. Each location was logged and marked on a map of Canada. All of the sightings were identical: Two scruffy males, early to mid twenties, in the possession of a vehicle similar in all respects to the Bentley truck and camper, heading east.

"They're following the Trans Canada Highway, Boss. And by the sounds of it, if they weren't in the Bentley truck, it sure as hell was a replica of it. I'll bet those Frenchmen have that unit buried in some swamp in northern Quebec by now." Kenny was probably right, unfortunately.

As the days passed, we got more and more tips from across Canada. One that we took very seriously was a sighting reported by an apartment manager right in downtown Vancouver. He stated that a truck (without the camper and boat) had been parked illegally in his parking lot, in this specific stall. In his explanation, he claimed the vehicle had no right being there. He wrote down the licence plate number on a scrap of paper he had in his pocket, with the intention of taking the matter up with the apartment owner. It had disappeared the following morning. When the manager saw the truck replicated on TV, he promptly involved the local police who then contacted us with the information. The licence plate number on the piece of paper was 48-36-FY, the same as that of the Bentley truck.

"Is this guy for real?" I thought out loud to Gerry, Ken, and Dwight. "I mean, do we trust him? Does he have credibility? Can we check him out, and will he take the polygraph?" Their "too good to be true" look was as good an answer as any.

It was the lead we were waiting for, evidence that the truck had actually left the park and wasn't sitting at the bottom of Helmcken Falls somewhere. If we could verify it, other witnesses may remember seeing the truck without the camper attached. That lead could change the complexion of the investigation big time.

"Dwight, get this checked out very thoroughly. We need to know about his credibility and his motive. If this turkey is a publicity seeker he could really fuck things up, so we need to get him on the polygraph."

Dwight did end up meeting with the apartment manager, and returned to us with bad news.

"We couldn't polygraph the bastard because he said he has a bloody heart condition." After debriefing Hoglund, it was not clear whether the witness had simply manufactured his sighting or what, but we could find nothing else to substantiate his claim. Did we believe him? Did we have a reason not to? We had to assume that he had in fact seen something, but we were extremely skeptical about the validity of the tip itself.

The media kept the file alive in the hearts and minds of Canada, and we offered them as much information as we could. Unfortunately, after the first few weeks of the investigation had expired, there was very little in the way of breaking news. All we had to offer was the reassuring increase in the number of tips, and that while we were concentrating on finding the Bentley truck commandeered by the two desperadoes, we hadn't decentralized the investigation from the Clearwater area. While a couple hundred tips suggested that the truck was heading east, we couldn't discredit the possibility that it was still local until we actually found it.

Meanwhile, Clearwater detachment continued to act as the hub of police activity. There were usually 20 detectives and support staff in the actual detachment, while 20 others were on constant parade through the streets of Clearwater and nearby homes making inquiries.

Gerry McKinnon, probably the world's longest-serving constable, got a bit tired of the media lounging around on the front lawn of the detachment. His short, sandy hair and wry smile screamed mischief, and he was always digging up ways to make life interesting. I remember one time he bolted out the front door in a panic and sprinted over to a PC. With lights and siren, he roared out of the parking lot with the media in hot pursuit. Twisting and turning, Gerry probably left about 10,000 miles' worth of tire tread on the streets all the way to the coffee shop. We thought it was hilarious, but his tremendous sense of humour was a pretty big reason why he never made corporal.

Being so far away from the investigation was greatly annoying the superintendent, and he made sure he reminded me every day through messages I received via the inspector. Finally, he insisted that the investigation be re-centralized in Kamloops.

"I'm not of the opinion that moving the investigation here will in fact jeopardize the investigation. It can be run just as effectively from here. Pack it up, sergeant. I expect you to be here in the next couple of days."

I disagreed with his appraisal of the situation, and if he had actually come to see the operation we had underway he would have understood. As it was, however, I would have been more productive debating with a brick. The boss was the boss, and there was no goddamned way I that was going to change his mind. I knew we had to stay where we were. You need to be able to feel, smell and touch the heart of the investigation. It may be just a slip of the lip, or another little tid bit of information that changes the direction of the investigation. But, following orders, we moved the entire operation back to Kamloops. There was so much paperwork we needed a pickup truck to move it all. Fortunately, one of the off-duty members had one, and allowed us to use it for the move.

We lost a couple of days because of the foolhardy decision to relocate. Witnesses were still calling Clearwater and those messages had to be relayed to Kamloops. Despite the major inconvenience, things slowly started moving forwards again. Some investigators stayed in Clearwater, busy as they were investigating local tips. Of the ones who returned to

Kamloops, I soon had to redirect them back to the scene, 70 fucking miles away! *How bloody ridiculous is this?*

I was careful to keep my thoughts to myself. One of the superintendent's NCOs had given me a heads up: "Keep a low profile, Mike. One wrong step, and the boss will have you removed from the case indefinitely." It took the greatest powers of my self discipline not to overstep my boundaries when the superintendent and I crossed in the hall. Like a couple of big ships crossing in the night, our brief seconds of exposure relayed looks of contempt and disapproval, fogged by the professional consideration I was forced to display as a show of respect to my superintendent.

"Top cop, eh?" he scoffed.

Oh Christ, not again! "Yes sir!" I said with a smile. *You might think you can wear me down you bastard, but we'll solve this case before I give you the satisfaction.* I often wondered if the Codfather, born and bred in Newfoundland, had ever actually been in charge of his own investigation. Someone said he was a career traffic man before he got his commission. When you get a commission, it seems you're sent on a "Hate Course," where you learn how to hate your NCOs. I must have been looking at the course valedictorian. I knew I'd broken some rules and did things my own way, but it wasn't like I was the detachment slug. I did my job, and I was locking people up.

I looked at his methods through the eyes of a manager and tried to rationalize his actions. He wanted someone to stand before the country and pilot that investigation to a successful conclusion and I believed that someone wasn't me.

It wasn't the first time my superiors hadn't seen things the way I had seen them. I remember one instance back in the late '60s; a man had gone on a shooting rampage in Ladysmith, just outside of Nanaimo. He'd headed to his employer's office and insisted he hadn't received his paycheque for that week. When they didn't yield to him, he drew his .22 and fired several shots into the ceiling, then returned home. The sergeant in charge of the shift quickly delegated us to the scene. He followed behind us.

My partner Bob Schmidt and I drove in with a ghost car, planning our attack as we sped towards the gunman's house. We agreed that we were in no real hurry and that we could take whatever time it took to talk this guy out. He hadn't hurt anyone and was probably more of a threat to himself than anyone else. We set up a temporary base camp next door and made several telephone calls to the suspect's house. He wouldn't talk to us, and each time we called back he'd mutter a few words and hang up. The sergeant was standing there, glaring impatiently at me.

"It's my supper time, so make it quick boys. I want this over with." With that added pressure on our shoulders, Bob and I were forced to devise a plan to get that guy out of the house and in custody. We agreed on a course of action, and headed out for the car trying to get pumped up for the coming drama.

Bob drove right up to the house. He slammed on the brakes, and I kicked my door open so hard it flew back and almost broke my leg. By the time I had myself sorted out, Bob was waiting for me on the front step. With a full head of steam, gun drawn, I plowed into the door. The frame cracked and splintered, and the door flew open. Before I had even stepped into the house, the blast of a rifle sent me ducking for cover. The first thing I saw was the man's body, quivering in a chair in front of the door with a good chunk of his head blown off. Blood and brains were all over the ceiling, dripping down onto the floor beneath me. Some people talk about a smell of death, but there really isn't a smell. When you witness someone being murdered, or like in this case, blowing their brains out, your brain kicks into a sort of half assed shock. Your mind is so absorbed in the event that all of your senses seem to converge on the victim. There's a metallic taste in your mouth, and your hands start to sweat. More often than not your whole body spasms in disbelief. You can't smell anything because you can hardly breath, and all you can hear is your heart pounding between your ears.

The sergeant had heard the blast from next door and arrived on the scene shortly after I walked back outside. Bob Schmidt stormed over to him, stuck his finger right up to his nose and screamed: "Sergeant, you can go home and have your fucking supper now!" Both of us knew that the system had forced this man to take his own life prematurely. We learned something from that mistake, although it was a very difficult one to digest. If the same thing had happened today, we'd have sat outside with the emergency response team and waited the guy out. I guess the RCMP learned something from that mistake too.

After a number of stressful encounters in the halls of subdivision HQ, I was advised that there were certain concerns about my investigative approach to this file. In other words, my credibility was being brought into question. Detectives from the serious crime section in Vancouver soon arrived in Kamloops. There was no doubt in my mind that the super-intendent had requested their presence to administratively check out the file and related tips in audit form. They were there for one reason: to hunt down any fault in the investigation and give the superintendent some basis for replacing me with one of his "yes men." Having investigated hundreds of homicides over the last 20 years, I was confident that they wouldn't find anything.

The audit lasted for over two weeks and turned up sweet FA. In contrast to the destructive effect the audit had on my morale, the serious crime squad did give us a few valuable tips on file management and some good suggestions on other avenues to explore. Those few pointers were very important to me, and personally appreciated. Any good investigator has respect for new ideas and advice from experienced peers. In fact, they were in support of where we had been and where we were going. I wasn't invited to their debriefing with the superintendent, and he never took the matter up with me. I figured he must have been some pissed off when they walked out without giving him a reason to replace me.

Chapter 7 **THE FACTS OF LIFE**

My role from then on, one month after the investigation had begun, was made very clear to me: Stay in the office, let the investigators investigate, and keep the boss fully informed through daily briefings of his inspector. I was instructed not to leave town unless it was an emergency, and not without prior approval from the superintendent. When I was permitted to enter his office and speak to him directly, he always had a huge pile of incoming messages on his desk — every single message that had been sent since the beginning of the investigation. To me, it was like he was saying, "I know everything. Don't bullshit me." The situation was suffocating, and my frustration grew as the investigation wore on.

By this point, time for much needed r&r was down to a minimum. For years boating had been my passion, particularly in Powell River where we had cruised Desolation Sound weekly. Because I'd had so much fun with my larger boat on the ocean, I had bought a smaller boat, Miss Piggy, in Kamloops and had kept it in the Shushwap Lakes. During the first few months of this investigation I was so occupied with trying to solve the crime that I never had a chance to get aboard. As a result of the pressure to solve the crime, my personal life being in turmoil, and every free minute devoted to work, I had totally forgotten about Miss Piggy. When I finally did remember, I had visions of her being crunched between sheets of ice, and lying helplessly on her side like a beached whale. I made a few frantic phone calls to the owner of the marina, who was also a friend of mine, and he assured me that he had taken care of it for me.

"I knew you were busy, Mike," he said chuckling. "I looked after Miss Piggy for you." It was one less thing for me to worry about.

Gerry's life was also in disarray. Outside of the force and his family his greatest interest was his horse Dollar and competing in the rodeos. He was a true blond and blue cowboy, but because he couldn't give the provincial team roping competition his best this year, he declined to even take a weekend off to compete. His total energy was devoted to solving the crime.

All of us were being run into the ground. We were all working at least 16-hour days every day, and our families were suffering as a result. Our wives supported us as best they could, and tended to our homes while we motored back and forth between Kamloops and Clearwater to slave over a growing case file.

On one particularly foul day, December 1, 1982, with exactly 21 years of service, I figured things couldn't get any worse with the superintendent. I'd been thinking about my Long Service Medal for months, wondering what had happened to it and why it hadn't been presented to me. I'd made sure to attend several functions in the event that it would be presented to me in red serge, as is protocol. Finally, I'd had it with waiting. I'd worked my ass off for 21 years, and while it may seem juvenile to someone outside of the force, I felt I deserved the distinction of wearing my medal.

I huffed right up to the super's door. After knocking quite a bit more forcefully than normal, he hailed me in. His office was enormous, its heart a giant boardroom table large enough to seat over two dozen people. He was sitting on the far end of it, looking at me with bespectacled eyes. The look on his face was corrosive.

"What is it, sergeant?"

"Sir, I believe you have something that belongs to me, and I want it."

"Oh?" he shuffled in his seat unbelievingly. "And what might that be?"

"My Long Service Medal, sir. I believe you have had it for over a year, and I think I deserve to have it."

"Is that right?" I stood nervously still as he called for his secretary. Despite my anger, I hoped that I hadn't just gotten her in shit. "The sergeant seems to think we have his Long Service Medal. You wouldn't happen to know anything about it would you?" The secretary rolled her eyes.

"Yes, sir. It's in your safe where you instructed me to put it."

The superintendent didn't even blink. I think it was a true show of force on his part. He was in control. "Would you go get it for me?"

She darted off, and swiftly returned with the presentation box in one hand, and a sheet of paper with the other. "Have him sign for it please." I did. "That will be all," he said to her. After the door was closed, he continued. "Now sergeant, there are a couple of ways to do this. Some of them are formal, others not so formal. Which would you prefer?"

"I'd just like to get my medal, sir." With that, he stood over his desk and slid my medal down the boardroom table to me like he was the shuffle board champ of the Mess. So much for protocol. I had nothing to say, so I took the medal, about faced and proceeded out of the room.

Because the investigation was gobbling up so much of my time, I had things in my personal life I'd been unable to deal with. Christmas came and went. As a matter of fact, it was the first day off we'd had since the beginning of the investigation. New Year's was just another grim reminder that the world was still turning, despite the fact that the investigation hadn't moved in two months. By the beginning of 1983, $7,500 in reward money had been raised for information leading to the truck, and $35,000 for information leading to the arrest and conviction of the person(s) responsible for the deaths of the Johnson and Bentley families. Over 10,000 reward posters had been sent all over North America, smothering police departments, post offices, and just about every tree in the public eye.

Almost 300 people from across Canada told us they believed they had seen the Bentley unit being driven by two suspects. When that many people tell you that they've seen something, you really have no choice. If you don't follow it up, it could bite you in the ass. If you do follow it up, and it doesn't get you anything concrete, at least you know.

People across the country were outraged with the crime, but few understood the real problems we were experiencing despite all of the publicity. Radio programs were both in favour of our efforts and against, from "When are the cops going to get off their asses?" to bouquets for the actual efforts we were putting into it. We were very fortunate to have an excellent rapport with the media. I was able to be completely honest with them, and because of that I was keeping them up to date on a daily basis. They understood what we were going through, and for the most part were extremely understanding of our situation. Mind you, if we screwed up they would be all over us like shit on a blanket.

While the public was actually quite easy to deal with, our problems originated primarily from our own office. "What the hell are you doing? Where are your people and what are they doing? Can you handle it? Are you continuing the search for the truck in Clearwater and how are you doing that?" It didn't occur to the superintendent that there was about four feet of snow in Wells Gray Park. Worse still, the Codfather was keeping incoming Telexes on his desk for days. Then it wasn't uncommon for him to call one of us into his office.

"Did you know about this?" he'd inquire, holding up the latest Telex. He knew we hadn't, because the damned thing hadn't left his desk.

"No sir, I didn't," was the usual reply.

"You're responsible for information like this, aren't you?"

"Yes, sir." We'd bite our tongues, and clench our fists, and grit our teeth, but it didn't help. No matter what we did, there was no appeasing the Codfather.

Overtime and expense accounts were also really big issues with him. If he didn't like the way it looked, he'd put this big red circle around it and send it back to you. I remember Gerry bitching because he'd handed in this one expense account slip, and it kept coming back to him with these red circles around two lunches that he had claimed. He shuffled some things around, and re-submitted it. Those two lunches were circled again.

"Well, fuck it then." Gerry took out the two cheap lunches, and added one expensive dinner that he'd had. We thought he'd get in shit again, but there was no mention of it.

As for overtime, we used to get together and tab up our hours. As we expected, they were astronomical. We agreed that we would saw off half those hours, and submit what was left. No sooner had we delivered them than the inspector approached me.

"Mike, I think you guys went a bit overboard with the overtime." While we were shoveling through the bureaucracy, the public was still screaming for answers.

We had tried just about everything, and we were trying everything else. I had depleted just about every resource, from every department, from just about every detachment across Canada, and we were just as far behind now as we had been when we arrived in Clearwater back in September six months ago. We had used everything: Fish and Wildlife, Department of Highways, BC telephones and hydro, Interpol, hypnosis, and US law enforcement. We had checked every damned pawn shop in BC and Alberta. We had used psychics, infra red, agencies, customs, National Defence, and a search for Bentley possessions in every bloody ditch from Clearwater to Calgary to Edmonton.

One of the most difficult tasks throughout the investigation was following up all of the long distance phone calls that had been made from every phone in Clearwater. Did someone call Quebec? And if so, why?

Thousands upon thousands of records had to be sifted through, and it was a bloody nightmare for our investigators.

We installed anonymous tip lines, checked abandoned buildings, and did more aerial searches. We sent out over 50,000 form letters to people who might have been in the park during our time frame, requesting information and copies of any family photos they'd developed. We checked every parking ticket issued in Canada over this period in the event that one was issued to the Bentley truck. We looked into every prison escapee and used auto part dealers. And on top of it, the phone was still ringing every three minutes. We had 13 clerks inputting information into the computer so it could be stored, retrieved, and withdrawn for comparison purposes. The computer was also very helpful when we had to start all over again and look another way.

By about April of 1983 the calls had started to taper off. We had no further information for the public, and the leads we were looking for to break the case open again simply weren't forthcoming. During our many briefings, we realized that everything was possible. The truck could have been anywhere, including 10 feet underground somewhere in Wells Gray Park. Evidence suggested otherwise, but until we actually found the truck we couldn't know for sure. Instincts were telling us the answer was in Clearwater. Information was telling us it was out east.

Meanwhile, other murders were happening, and we had to investigate those too. My field staff had been cut back to five full-time investigators, but I was able to keep most of the office staff active enough to justify their presence. Some old cases came back to our attention, while people called with information pertinent to newer ones, and then we still had to move forward on the Johnson and Bentley murders. Sixteen-hour days were nothing — like it or lump it. Unless you were out of town, there were no meal expenses or overtime. The wives were frequently bringing dinner in for us.

Also, in early spring we were approached by Global Television out of Toronto. They proposed to film a documentary on the homicides. Bill Elliot, a producer for Global, had contacted me and requested my assistance. I looked at the offer as another investigative opportunity. This film would be shot at the actual murder scene in Wells Gray Park (if I could clear it with the boss). It was one way we could revive the file, and perhaps produce more tips. We were still looking for that one person with the right tip. We needed that one rush, and BINGO!

I soon took it up with the boss.

"Sir, we are at a dead end right now. The tips are not coming in as often as they were, and we are no further ahead than we were last September. Everything so far suggests that the vehicle has gone east, and if we are to continue our inquiries out there we have to bring it to the attention of people across Canada again. I don't know of any other option, except maybe Global's proposal. We've started back at the beginning and come up empty. We've exhausted all of our witnesses." I shrugged. I was at a loss, and with no other option I simply threw myself at his mercy.

"Sounds like a good idea. Let's set it up and see what they can do for us." Stunned that I had his attention, I outlined Global's ideas.

"Sir, they want to reenact the murder scene as we believe it may have unfolded. To that end, we will have to locate and equip a truck identical to the Bentley unit, and a car similar to the Johnson's. We'll need a boat, tent, and we'll have to set up the camp in the same fashion as the families would have." He was nodding in agreement. In total disbelief I continued— "And, sir? If we can reproduce a unit similar to the Bentley truck and camper, perhaps we could drive it across Canada along the same route we believe the two suspects have taken. Perhaps that would help spark the missing lead."

"Perhaps that isn't a bad idea, Eastham. Put it on paper and we'll look at it." I was sure of it now: I was dealing with an impostor. I was dismissed, and immediately went to inform the crew in my office.

"He said it's not a bad idea. I don't know guys — he told me to commit it to paper." Gerry, Ken, and Dwight were gathered around in my office. "All right, get the hell out of here you guys and let me tackle this. I don't think it's toilet paper this time." There were some muttered "Yeah, rights" as the three of them walked out.

The manual typewriter strained under the creative influence of a suddenly vivid imagination. When Global was finished with the truck, we could simply put a few signs on the sides and rear and follow the route our witnesses had laid out many times over. Whoever would drive it across Canada could stay right in the back of the camper, or perhaps lodge at the local detachments or Salvation Army. Gas and some money for food. How could they turn down an opportunity like this?

The following morning, I submitted my memorandum paper to the boss through the appropriate channels. I knew he was in the building, but

I didn't get anything from him. I waited patiently, for days. In fact, I waited an entire week.

Finally, at the end of one day, the telephone rang. It was the superintendent's secretary!

"Are you available to see the boss, sergeant? He wants to see you."

"Yes ma'am, immediately." I ran down the stairs so fast, it actually crossed my mind that I may have forgotten to hang the phone back up. As soon as I arrived at the superintendent's door, I was invited in. He didn't motion for me to sit down, so I stood smartly before him. When he spoke, his tone of voice was impossible to read.

"You and I are going to see the CIB [criminal investigation branch] officer and the deputy commissioner in Vancouver."

The superintendent had that bloody smirk on his face again. *Fuck!* Was this it? Was it the end? You didn't get called to Vancouver to see these two for afternoon tea. I was sure I would soon be receiving my transfer papers to Tuktoyuktuk. Deputy Commissioner Tommy Venner was about the second in command of the entire fucking Mounted Police. This was a guy you didn't get an audience with unless you were already dead. As for the CIB officer, the only time you were in his company was after he'd sent you a scathing memorandum in which he insisted that you were too incompetent to even read the bloody thing and that he wanted to tell you in person with your superintendent present.

When I got back upstairs, Dwight, Gerry, and Reliable were waiting for my news.

"I think we had better go for a drink." We headed across the street to the pub, where I explained the situation. I was not impressed with their reaction.

"Hey, Boss!" Dwight sputtered, strangling a roar of laughter. "Can I have your car if you don't come back?"

Yeah, pretty fucking funny! They were in hysterics. Dwight was a mess, spilling milk all over himself. He didn't drink and didn't smoke. I don't know what was wrong with him.

My mid-life crisis had officially started. D-Day had arrived. I contemplated my likely future. Three years in an isolated detachment in the secluded bowels of the cold north with only the polar bears to keep me warm. The boss must have had my phone bugged, and he'd obviously heard some of my conversations. I wondered which one had pissed him off the most— What the hell was I worried about? He grew up in traffic divisions. He wouldn't have a clue how to wire a phone. Who did he have working downstairs who could wire a phone for him? *Christ ... what else does he know!?* My mind was a cascade of panic and speculation.

When the superintendent and I eventually arrived at the division headquarters in Vancouver, and I knew I was going to have to just buck up and take it. I figured they were pissed about the money. It was by far the most costly investigation in Canadian history, but I could justify every penny under the circumstances. How could they measure the lives of six innocent victims in dollars and cents? I wasn't going to play the lamb in the slaughterhouse, and if I had to, I'd go down with the fucking ship. I'd worked myself into quite a fluster by the time we were standing tall before the deputy commissioner and the CIB officer.

"Good morning, gentlemen," Tommy Venner began. If he was going to bring the heavies down on me, he was being pretty damned polite about it. The air in the room seemed quite pleasant, which was far from what I expected. "Thank you for coming down and meeting with me. I would like you to know that I have followed this case with particular interest, and I have had briefings on a regular basis because this case has captured national attention. It's been quite a manhunt, and today I've brought you here to discuss new investigative techniques that may assist us in the case. This investigation has been difficult, and I understand the frustrations that go along with it. We are here to help, and offer the services and our resources, whether they be financial or further manpower ... "

I wasn't being roasted? My idea of a Third World transfer was banished, and my more logical side took over where my creative side left off.

"Sergeant Eastham will fill you in on our proposal, sir." Holy shit, was I the kid in the candy store now or what?

"Sir," I began confidently, "the most significant factor in this investigation thus far has been the involvement of the media, and the subsequent participation of the public in a massive surge of information. For almost five months, the information was forthcoming. Presently, it's subsided. What we need, sir, is a way to get the information rolling again." I described Global TV's proposal and outlined the rest of my plan, indicating that the Bentley camper unit would eventually end up either in Montreal or somewhere in north west Quebec. He had a few questions, and I answered them as best as I could.

"*Yes.*" The word was a golden one. "The idea certainly has merit. I would like the two of you to travel with our CIB officer to Toronto,

Montreal, and Ottawa in an effort to obtain some support from the Ontario Provincial Police and the Quebec Provincial Police, as well as senior members from the major cities. We're also going to need to get some of our own people over there in on this. If we can get this support I can see this national publicity campaign, proceeding as you described it, being successful. Of course, just what it will bring us remains to be seen. I will leave it to you to establish the parameters and details. You may report through the regular channels, and the chief will keep me updated. Thank you, gentlemen, and good luck."

As we returned to Kamloops, it became clear to me that the superintendent hadn't had any idea why we had been called to Vancouver either. He seemed genuinely surprised that we hadn't been criticized for our failure to have suspects in custody. Much to the contrary, the investigative team had in fact been praised and duly offered the deputy officer's assistance and support. I suspect the boss had thought I was in shit because we didn't have "the beast in the bucket" yet, and there was no doubt in my mind that I would have been the fall man in that event. Fortunately, Deputy Commissioner Tom Venner knew the investigative difficulties, having been a detective inspector himself in Alberta, when I was stationed there in my junior detective days.

Through the course of several meetings in March of '83, Dalen, Hoglund, Reliable and myself discussed what we were going to be doing for Global TV. Before we did anything, we had to collect all of our props. I left that responsibility with Gerry Dalen.

"Gerry, is there any chance you can do this—"

"Well, sure Mike—"

"—in a day and a half?"

"What?" A day and a half was all the time that I'd been given to prove that this idea would fly. As I choreographed the rest of the investigation, Gerry tackled this operation.

In the time allotted, Gerry had to locate a car, truck and camper, boat, motor, tent, and all the details to go with them to match the victims' gear. The camper was an older Vanguard, so his first call was to that company. While they didn't really know how to help directly, they provided a list of dealers in the area Gerry could talk to. The manager of an RV store in Kelowna produced a ledger listing all the campers sold during the time the Bentleys purchased their unit. Going through that, Gerry found a unit similar to the Bentley's that had been sold to a family in Clearwater.

The camper in question hadn't been used in years, and the exterior was extremely weathered. Gerry explained the situation to the owners, and after assuring them we'd clean the unit up for them, it was ours. That was step one.

Next, Gerry had to find a truck to carry it, in particular a red and grey Ford F-150 regular cab long box. He went to a Ford dealer in Vernon, keeping in mind we simply didn't have the money to actually buy a truck. After he laid out exactly what he was looking for, the dealer smiled.

"I've got a truck just like it, but there's one problem." It was probably too expensive for our zero dollar budget. "It's *blue* and grey."

"Well, how much would it be for the truck?"

"Oh hell, we'll *give* you the truck."

We got the truck and paid only what it cost to paint, and even then we were given a hefty discount. The boys at Vernon Ford took very good care of us, and without them there's a good chance this operation would have fallen through.

So we had our truck and camper. Now we needed a boat. The aluminum boat the victims had was quite distinctive in that it was a duller shade of grey and had a pretty deep bow on it. It was unlike anything that Sears or any other manufacturer produced. Through his inquiries with the family, Gerry discovered that George had bought the boat off a man who worked out of his backyard. Apparently, this guy had constructed 12 such boats. Gerry got a list of buyers, and through further inquiries that day learned that one of the boats was for sale.

With no official budget, Gerry paid the 300 dollars out of his own pocket. Now we had the boat, the camper, and the truck. A welder in town manufactured the boat rack, so the next step was to try and find a mural similar to that mounted on the front window of the Bentley camper. Gerry eventually found a store that carried them in Snake River Arizona.

"We've got a couple of them in the back, but they both have an pink tint to them." Unfortunately, the actual mural itself had been discontinued, and there was little or no chance of actually finding one similar in any other respect. But this wasn't necessarily a problem — the change in colour would be an excellent way for us to challenge our witnesses. Adding slight modifications would help us weed out the actual witnesses from the publicity seekers.

Meanwhile, Dwight Hoglund unearthed a cream-coloured Plymouth similar to the Johnson car, and the accompanying roof rack.

With all of our assets put together, Global came out to film the re-enactment.

The men and women from Global were really switched on, and very professional. Gerry and Dwight found they were also a lot of fun to work with. Several professional actors were flown in to simulate the family playing together in a fashion that some witnesses might have remembered seeing. The whole crew knew the business, and most of the investigators just watched in awe as the production was put together, piece by piece. The filming took place around Wells Gray Park, and the scene was actually set up at the old Bear Creek prison site.

At the time Global's re-enactment was set to air, I was in Ottawa with the superintendent and the chief from our CIB office. The trip was business-like and very professional. I was not criticized, slandered, nor was I left out of the loop. We had meetings with senior members of provincial and city police forces as well as our own top brass from each division back east. All were the same: anything they could do to help us pursue the investigation was okay.

In Montreal, of course, we were chided about trying to "hang an innocent Quebecer" when obviously the BC criminal element was more likely responsible. It was all in good fun. The total cooperation of the *Sûreté du Québec,* the Quebec provincial police, was promised, and manpower and media representatives appointed prior to our arrival. Senior brass of our own force in Ottawa seemed surprised at our investigative technique and that we would go so far to solve an investigation.

Unlike the role of the RCMP in contract division, where we are hired by the provinces to enforce all aspects of the provincial and federal statutes, the role of the RCMP in non-contract divisions like Ontario and Quebec in the east is mainly the enforcement of federal statutes and the protection of federal properties. Few Mounties in those regions had investigative experience in homicides, unless they had been transferred there from outside Ontario or Quebec. My opinion of them as a huge bureaucracy who created make-work projects for the government and interfered in the real policing world in contract provinces was somewhat diminished. They were genuine, down-to-earth, good cops who suffered from the same bureaucratic bullshit, just from much larger animals.

Also, because they were in the nation's capital, they were pounced upon in the media every time the force screwed up in the contract provinces. Everybody learned how to weather political storms back there — keep your head down, one hand on your ass, and press on.

A lot of our inquiries had required that we deal directly with different police departments in Quebec. In many cases, there was that language barrier that was difficult to overcome. At times, we would receive reports with the results of tip investigations that were written in French and have to search around to find a member who could read and write our second language.

During the previous winter, I had been able to second a French-speaking constable who had been born in Quebec City onto my staff full time. Claude was a good-looking, six-foot, 25-year-old woman who had done her best to find her way around the western policing world. Coming from Quebec City to the caribou country must have been a total cultural shock for her. Her command of English wasn't the greatest, but she was able to steadfastly pull her weight and she worked extra hard to overcome the language problems.

When it came to receiving mail or telephone calls from French Canada, Claude's contribution saved us literally hundreds of man hours. She had a hell of a sense of humour and delighted in playing jokes on the guys, usually pleading ignorance in French, and suggesting that we should learn the language if we wanted to question her motives. Claude was definitely a "looker" and I always had lots of young and single members volunteering overtime to work on the file, until they found out that she was soon to be married.

Late April of 1983 was taken up planning a major publicity campaign across Canada to coincide with the tour of the mockup camper. We had hundreds of copies of the composites of the two French-speaking men, in English and French, reward posters, and common news releases that we would use at each destination. The planning of this campaign, which would involve a trip across Canada, took about a month. During this time we had to deal with the everyday flow of tips that would come, would have to be assigned, and eventually concluded or left still under investigation because we couldn't resolve them. Our overall focus was to saturate Ontario and Quebec, and have volunteers scour provincial campsites and huge parks.

While all of this was in our laps, Prince Phillip was scheduled to visit Kamloops, and the Queen was heading for Kelowna. As if that wasn't enough, old Reliable Leibel was selected to attend a VIP driving course.

Why in the hell they selected him when we were so busy was beyond me. Just prior to their arrival at their respective destinations, we were advised that Her Royal Majesty's aircraft might be diverted to Kamloops. In that event, I was instructed to be her chauffeur to Kelowna. That would have been great under any other circumstances, but I certainly didn't need that added pressure in my life at that point in time.

Fortunately, I didn't end up having to drive her. Ken Leibel, however, did end up driving the Prince. Old Reliable Leibel had a nasty habit of falling asleep at the wheel, and for some reason I didn't stop worrying about it until I got the phone call that everyone was still alive and well.

Also, throughout the ongoing investigation, the bullshit about my financial involvement in the Brass Rail bar never let up. I was formally advised that the commissioner's office in Ottawa had instructed that I totally divest myself from all responsibility from the Brass Rail, or accept a transfer out of the area. Even though I explained that, formally, nothing was in my name (it was all in my spouse's name), it didn't matter. What the hell did they want me to do? Divorce my wife?

Despite these distractions, things were going a bit better with the Johnson/Bentley investigation. Shortly after the Royal Visit, Deputy Commissioner Venner arrived in Kamloops and personally reviewed the file. To my relief, he was satisfied with our progress, and instructed me to increase the reward for the return of the camper to $7,500.

On May 9, 1983, the great march east started. Cst. Claude Ouelette and I flew to Calgary and then on to Toronto where we held a major news conference on the homicides, and handed out information packages to the media. There was great interest in the truck and camper coming east, and the information that we hoped it would bring. After Toronto, we proceeded to Montreal where similar media events were held. Ouelette did the French versions, while I did the English over a four-day period. Then it was back to Toronto, where the debut of Global's *Citizen's Alert* TV program took place nationally. That broadcast of the re-enactment brought numerous pieces of information into the coordinators in Ontario, and they were flooded with calls from people who believed they had actually seen the truck and camper.

Meanwhile officers Gerry Dalen and Laurie Dewitt set out on their inter-provincial tour with the mockup truck and camper. They were to drive from Kamloops to Montreal in three weeks. There were two reasons for this trip: One was to keep the Johnson/Bentley case in the public eye.

The other was to test some of the eyewitness accounts. That was where the minute differences in our unit were going to come in handy — we would see if witnesses noticed the different tint in the window mural, and the channel iron that made up the boat rack as opposed to the tubular steel used in the Bentley unit. With signs bolted on the sides and rear of the camper asking, "Have you seen this truck?", Gerry and Laurie set out on their big tour.

The trip had come at a very bad time for Laurie Dewitt — he had just quit smoking.

"The world hates a quitter!" Gerry would tell him as the trip wore on, lighting his cigarettes as Laurie chewed on the smoke.

They were on a very tight schedule. Plans had been made for the media along their route to meet up with them at designated points. There, they would conduct a press meeting, and a local member would help them find their way around.

The weather was very cooperative until Gerry and Laurie reached Saskatchewan. Icy road conditions and blustery winds slowed them down significantly. It was not uncommon for the tremendous "sail area" of the camper to push them off towards the ditch. Laurie hung on to the dash with white knuckles as Gerry wrestled the truck and camper along the road in gale-force side winds.

One sighting had been reported from a restaurant along the route. Someone said they had seen a truck and camper parked in their lot, and felt they should report it in. As it turned out, that unit had in fact belonged to an active member from E division who was enjoying some time off.

When the truck and camper arrived in the Toronto area, the weather was gorgeous. For the big press release in Toronto, Gerry and Laurie parked the unit right at the top of the stairs in front of Toronto City Hall. It was a great photo opportunity, and even tourists were snapping away. Some witnesses were in fact picking out flaws in the camper.

"Well, that looks like it," one man said. "But that boat rack was more square."

"Yes, that's it," a woman pointed. "But that mural ... it's different somehow. I think it was orange, not pink."

It was frustrating for us, receiving eyewitness accounts from people like that, but still having to deal with our gnawing belief that the truck was still in Clearwater under a snow drift somewhere.

The Dalen/Dewitt road show was gaining popularity and people were now awaiting their arrival on the nightly news. Claude and I went back to Montreal for further news conferences, then off to Sherbrooke, Quebec, where further media events were held.

There had been sightings of the truck in and around Sherbrooke. I soon found that I couldn't even order breakfast in a restaurant without Claude. I didn't realize that these people simply didn't speak English. After Sherbrooke, we were exhausted, but now had to move on to Quebec City.

While there, we took time for a little r&r and enjoyment of the French culture with the local gendarmes. Man, those guys love their wine! I couldn't keep up with them. I remember this one evening in a local night-club. It's probably the first time I was almost drunk under the bloody table by a female. There's no question I was blurry — so blurry I had trouble seeing myself in the men's washroom mirror. Back to the table, and more good conversation. What impressed me was that these French Canadians spoke English in my presence, which was a courtesy I sincerely appreciated. I was almost nodding off when it happened.

"Sgt. Eastham, she would like to dance with you!"

"HUH?" I blurted.

"She would like to dance with you," Claude smiled mischievously. I looked, and a gorgeous woman of about 30 was standing there with her hand out beckoning me onto the dance floor.

"It's a courtesy in Quebec City," someone said to me. I got up and did my thing on the dance floor to some song I can't remember. I offered the table the occasional glance as this nice lady reminded me how to dance, and the buggers were smiling away at me. *I guess I've still got it, half smacked or not!*

The song came to an end, and I kissed the lady's hand and returned majestically to the table. To my surprise they were all just sitting there, laughing their drunken asses off. I couldn't even get a word in edgewise. Tears were streaming down their cheeks, and I think one guy almost threw up. Every time someone tried to tell me what was going on, everybody else just started rolling up again. I just laughed right along with them.

"Was my dancing with that lady really that bad?" I asked drunkenly.

Claude, bless her soul, stopped laughing long enough to say: "That's no lady, Mike. That's a man!"

They just sat there and howled as I went and washed my hands. When I got back, I made Claude promise me that she would never speak of that incident again. Every time I looked back at the bar, there "it" was smiling at me — whatever "it" was.

The next morning, I asked Claude if my dancing partner really had been a guy.

She responded with that typically saucy French tone: "You made me promise I would never bring it up again, and I won't."

To this day, I don't know if they were just pulling my pisser, but at the same time I'm not sure I really want to know.

We headed back to Montreal, and then to Ottawa for more media coverage. In Ottawa I did a live show with Harvey Oberfield of CTV. The interview went very nicely, until the end. Harvey made a statement about how this had been the most costly investigation in the history of Canada, and asked how I could justify it.

I thought for a moment, and replied with the statement I had used "in house" during the past year: "Harvey, how in the hell can we measure the deaths of six innocent victims in dollars and cents?" I left it at that.

"No further questions." After the show, Harvey apologized.

"I'm sorry about that, Mike. That was one hell of an answer, though!" he exclaimed, giving me a healthy handshake. He wished us the best of luck, and Claude and I proceeded on our way.

The two of us felt like movie stars, what with the TV cameras and reporters following us everywhere. Everyone wanted interviews for both French and English networks. After one such interview, we were treated to lunch at the Chateau Laurier hotel in Ottawa.

After 15 days on the road, we had accomplished exactly what we had set out to do: Quebec and Ontario police were searching all parks within their boundaries, and the public was fully informed about our dilemma. There were hundreds of new tips coming in on the truck and camper, which were being investigated locally by each department and then forwarded to our HQ in Kamloops. When they said they would assist us, they meant it. I was profoundly grateful and astonished at the lengths they went to to help out us westerners.

While Claude and I did our bit with the media, Gerry and Laurie continued with their travels in the mockup. They also had their share of help from the locals. On their way out of Toronto, they got lost. Within minutes, they were surrounded by motorcycle-riding police officers who promptly escorted them to the 401.

When they hit Montreal, I took Gerry and Laurie out for a drink. It was clear they were pretty wiped out after two weeks on the road. To give them a break, some members from Montreal took the truck and camper back to Ottawa. Another member gave them a ride to Ottawa, where they were called out to a possible sighting of the wreck of the truck and camper.

It took two hours to get to the general area, which was way out in the bush. The roads were so bad Gerry and Laurie ended up having to hike another six miles through the mud beneath an umbrella of black flies before reaching the site described by the witness. I'm not sure how the witness figured that a wrecked 18-inch truck canopy resembled the Bentley truck and camper. It was just one more on the list of false sightings.

From that point on, Gerry and Laurie just wanted to get home. They drove back into Kamloops 21 days after leaving on their exhaustive tour.

I had got back from my latest trip out east a few days before them. I returned to an administrative nightmare, and the phone didn't stop ringing. One thing remained constant: we still hadn't found the damned camper!

While I was away there had been an incident where a member of the RCMP highway patrol had encountered a local motorcycle gang of about 50 on a weekend ride coming up the Fraser Canyon. As he approached the oncoming gang head on, it became evident that the lead biker, over in the passing lane, had no intention of moving over to his proper lane. It was a rather arrogant game that the biker ended up losing. Unable to get out of the way fast enough, the cop plowed right through the bike. The gang, choosing to neglect the obvious stupidity of the dead biker, was pretty pissed off about the whole thing.

The brass thought it would probably be in our best interests if we "transferred" this young constable out of harm's way. Would I take him? He can speak French. *Of course I'll take him!* Christ, I would have taken the janitor if I thought I could have used him.

Unfortunately, this fellow didn't last long with us. He was a good worker, but had a lapse of judgment on some things. I remember on one occasion he went through airport security and joked that he had a bomb in his luggage. Regrettably, airport security didn't find that one very funny, so I lost him.

Crime didn't stop just because we were busy. We had our usual homicides and other serious crime matters to deal with. In the middle of investigating possible sightings, developing potential suspects, being audited for expense accounts or overtime, and preparing urgent crime reports, there were other murders that we had to investigate. Some were "smoking guns" as we called them, and some were a little tougher. In one case, a woman shot and killed her boyfriend and his infant child, and the gun really was still smoking when we arrived.

In another case a couple of natives got into a confrontation with a rancher at five o'clock one morning on the rancher's property. As a result, the rancher was beaten to death. The complaint came in as a missing person and it soon developed into a murder. As it turned out, the assailants took the body and propped it up in a pickup truck between them. For the rest of the day they drove around the back country, drinking beer and discussing what to do with the body.

They kept the body with them until the following day when they finally decided to place the victim behind the steering wheel of his truck, and send it off a 500-foot embankment into the Fraser River, "just like the movies." They placed the victim in the truck and started it up. Then they put a weight on the gas pedal, and over the bank it went.

Unfortunately, the body fell out within the first 20 feet down the cliff, and the truck stopped next to the river. Both the body and the truck were visible from the roadway, and it wasn't long before we were at the scene. It also wasn't long before we were on the track of these desperadoes and they were soon in custody. Of course, to get all of the evidence necessary for court purposes we were tied up for a further two weeks. Meanwhile, the Johnson and Bentley investigation continued, without really going anywhere. Then, more than a year after the murders had taken place, we finally got a break.

Throughout the summer of 1983 we had ensured that every public and private campsite in Ontario and Quebec was supplied with numerous copies of information sheets and wanted posters on the missing truck and camper.

And in late August, it happened. We got finally got a call that we could take seriously.

An auto body mechanic in Windsor, Ontario, saw the bulletins and contacted the police immediately. He stated that three or four months earlier, two French-speaking males operating a vehicle identical to the missing Bentley truck approached him. Apparently they had asked for a "midnight paint job" and wanted to pay in cash. They brought the truck into his shop in the middle of the night, and he had a chance to examine it. The camper was missing, and he was later told that they had recently removed it. The witness then began to describe modifications to the front and rear bumpers and the bed of the truck that George Bentley had made to the missing unit.

Furthermore, these two men had asked for advice on how to dispose of two weapons, one of which was a 410/22 over and under rifle and the other a Ruger. Because of the complainant's previous criminal background, he wanted nothing to do with it. He did, however, send the two guys across the border to the US, and gave them a contact person to assist them.

It seemed too good to be true. But it had to be! This guy described details about the truck and camper that had never been released. Everything seemed to fit. The descriptions of the suspects were bang on, the weapon was bang on, and the truck was bang on. Our detectives in Windsor were positive it was the truck in question. Further inquiries indicated that the witness was an old "criminal rounder" with little credibility, but that didn't explain how in the hell he could have fabricated accurate information about the truck and the missing over and under. Nobody outside the investigation knew about these things.

By this time we had almost 1300 people across Canada telling us that the truck "went that a-way" — eastward — and, despite our gut feelings to the contrary, we were basically resigned to that fact. Meanwhile, we were sitting in Kamloops wondering how the hell we were going to explain the aerial searches of the Clearwater and Wells Gray Park area that had continued over the summer.

We were given an address in Detroit, Michigan, where the witness said he had sent the two suspects for the new paint job and to dispose of the weapons. Whenever we received info that had to be investigated in the US, we were supposed to go through Ottawa HQ, who would refer it to Washington DC, who would then make the requests of the FBI or other police department. In our case, we simply said, Fuck 'em — we're not going through that protocol shit — we don't have the time. So we made our calls direct. In the next couple of weeks, messages flashed back and forth across Canada and between us and the FBI. We were preparing to mount a full-scale operation back east when it happened again.

It was a day that I will never forget.

On Tuesday, October 18, 1983, in the late afternoon, I received a call from Frank Baruta in Clearwater.

"Mike, I've just had two forestry workers in here. They say they've found the burned remains of the Bentley truck and camper on an old skidder trail at the 4,700-foot level on Trophy Mountain [which was almost 9,000 feet tall]. They even wrote down the licence number of the truck — 48-36-FY. No shit, it's the real goods."

"Yeah, Frank. What else is new?"

"I'm serious, Mike! I've just sent one of our members with them back to the scene."

"Frank, April Fool's Day was six months ago, so don't bullshit me."

"It's real, Mike — you'd better get your squad up here now!" My heart started pounding. Frank was excited, and he sounded convincing enough. "Believe me, it's true — I've just sent a message to subdivision headquarters. Phone them now if you don't believe me!" Despite his enthusiasm, I was still skeptical.

"No goddamned way, Frank. We're working on something back east right now that may lead us to the truck—"

"Hang on a second, Mike." There was a moment's pause. I could hear the crackling of a radio in the background. "It's confirmed! Our member is at the scene and he has confirmed it! Get up here."

Within minutes, Air III (the force aircraft) was en route to Kamloops. I hurried to the airport, got on board, and zoomed off to Clearwater. Transportation to the scene was arranged and the troops from my office were inbound. Gerry and Dwight were off in Lillooet helping a member on another homicide when they got the phone call. I imagined Gerry was going to be a bit pissed off, because they wouldn't be able to get back until after dark. They'd have to sit around and wait until the next morning which, considering how long we'd been looking, was a real pain in the ass.

From the main highway, it was well over 20 miles up steep mountain grades and then onto a logging road at the top of Trophy Mountain. It was real, and it was incredible.

There it was. There was no camper, no boat; just the remains of a truck that looked like it had spent the last 50 years rusting away. It was on top of a mountain all right. It was so bloody high up I thought I was going to get a nosebleed. It was incredible. The truck was exactly the same colour as the earth surrounding it. No bloody wonder we couldn't find it — it was as if the fire had painted a chameleon like camouflage from front to back.

I was astonished. My mind was racing, yet it was as if I was standing at a fresh murder scene. This time, however, I had prepared for a year in advance for what I was about to discover. The damned thing had probably sat there for the last 13 months, and there was no way it was going to be disturbed until I had the best goddamned investigative and recovery team that I could put together!

It was soon getting too dark for us to work effectively around the truck anyway. That left us with little more to do than sit on our thumbs until daylight the next morning. I checked out the area a bit before leaving, careful not to disturb any potential evidence. Looking under the truck, I discovered that whoever was driving it had got high-centred on a log and couldn't drive any farther. A quick walk a little farther down revealed a huge canyon at the end of the trail.

One thing was made perfectly clear: Whoever drove the truck up there was headed for the canyon, and that had to be local knowledge. There was no way anyone from out of town would have known about that canyon. It also explained the Battle Mountain scene where we found the bodies. Battle Mountain, Trophy Mountain, and the murder scene at the old prison site formed a perfect triangle. There was no question in my mind now that the killer or killers came from the Clearwater area. We secured the scene, left guards, and returned to Clearwater to make arrangements for the next day.

In the middle of a forest and on top of a mountain, blending in with the environment. *Shit, the media and the brass are going to be all over us like the plague!* Baruta was white as a ghost. I tried to reassure him.

"Frank, you and I both know that there's no bloody way anyone would have ever recognized that piece of rust from the sky. Look, let's deal with it tomorrow and get to work. We have a crime scene, and that will lead us to whatever son of a bitch we have to deal with."

Back at the hotel we held a squad meeting. Everybody was astonished. Thirteen hundred bloody people told us it went east, and the goddamned thing was on our doorstep all the time. The media was going to cannibalize us until they saw the scene, and I knew that I would be ultimately held accountable.

"Everybody just get a good night's sleep. Then we're up at six bells and back to the scene." I knew that accounts of the find would be out in no time, so I made a telephone call to my media connection, Brian Coxford. "Brian, we've found the truck and camper in Wells Gray Park. You're going to hear about it first thing in the morning, so get your bags packed." At least this way I would possibly be in some type of control; I knew their audience of over 700,000 people would be demanding answers.

We arrived back on top of Trophy Mountain at daybreak and started setting up a crime scene. Once the areas were flagged off with fluorescent tape and support equipment and vehicles were laid out, we were advised not to touch anything or proceed any further because the assistant commissioner was flying up from our Vancouver headquarters to view the scene from the air. Apparently they, too, wanted to know why the truck had never been located by our constant searches.

Around noon the force aircraft arrived and made numerous passes of the area. We listened to their comments over the radio, and were hardly surprised when they started talking about how easy it was for them to see. It was just another example of the naïveté I was dealing with every day. A helicopter flew them directly to the scene, which was surrounded by 25 people and bordered with yellow fluorescent tape — no wonder they had no trouble spotting it!

It wasn't until after this little show and tell that we were allowed to get back to work. Our teams approached the matter similarly to the

Johnson vehicle, measuring, taping, photographing, and picking up exhibits. An interesting point of reference was that there were a dozen or so seedlings that had recently been planted only 15 feet from the truck on the edge of the trail. Someone had been up here planting trees and hadn't even seen the truck and camper! It was a 7500-dollar find, so we were sure if the tree planters had seen it they'd have reported it to us. The most famous truck and camper of the century and it had been here the whole time.

The other interesting thing was that there was a little bullet hole in the passenger-side door of the truck. That bullet hole could only have been known to us and the murderer. That was the way that particular information was to remain. Nobody from the press was to be allowed close access to the unit. Period.

A couple of things concerned us about the bullet hole at that point. One was that it was awfully large for a .22. Had we been wrong in assuming that the weapon was in fact a .22? Was I wrong in suggesting that the murder scene had been at the old prison site where we found the six shell casings? The lab had confirmed that the bullets found in the remains in the Johnson car were .22 calibre. If that was true, where did this apparently larger bullet hole fit in?

Another thing Gerry expressed his concern about was whether or not that bullet hole had been there the whole time, or if it had been inflicted some time after the truck was torched. That was something we were going to have to find out.

Now that we were standing upon the major missing piece of the investigation, we somehow knew we were going to solve it. There was no doubt in our minds. While we were excited about our discovery, there was another, very ominous air around the scene. Our guts had told us the truck was in Clearwater, but somehow it had eluded us. Instinct told us one thing. Information told us another, and that was very frustrating for us. We were to learn later that our provincial aircraft actually flew within yards of this scene the previous fall when its infra red camera ran out of tape. It subsequently headed home without completing that particular search pattern. That aircraft had never been available again. Had it been, they would have most likely located the truck and camper.

We eventually decided that it was essential to the investigation to also have this complete unit taken to our crime lab in Vancouver. I made arrangements for a flat-bed truck to be standing by at the base of the mountain, and for a Bell 205 helicopter to lift the remains of the truck out. We also tarped it up in an effort to secure potential evidence within the vehicle itself while it was flown the mile or so straight down the mountain to the waiting truck.

The chopper arrived, and the sling put in place, but it was clear there was no bloody way that that aircraft could safely lift that weight without the possibility of losing it en route. I directed that the attempt be aborted, and that another aircraft with a greater lifting power be found. There was nothing available until the following day, and I wasn't in any hurry to make any mistakes. I could see the headlines now: "Mounties Find Truck and Camper, Only to Lose It as It Crashes into Millions of Pieces ... "

We spent the rest of the day going over the scene and very carefully listing every item that we could distinguish in the truck and what was left of the camper. An expert in soil and a botanist were brought in to help us establish the length of time the truck had actually been in that location.

The next day, a Sikorsky helicopter was employed to sling the truck out. Even the larger bird grunted and groaned at that elevation trying to get as much altitude as possible. A helicopter has difficulty generating lift in the thinner air at higher altitudes, and the only reason this bird got the unit off the mountain was "ground effect." A significant amount of lift is created when the downwash of the rotor blades reflects off the ground back towards the helicopter. Without ground effect, we would have been stuck on that rock for another day or more.

Gerry Dalen and I observed the operation from the air in our force helicopter. No sooner had they gained some altitude with the unit, than they started heading down the mountain like a bobsled. *Christ, I hope they can stop that thing when they get to the bottom.* Our chopper pilot was laughing at us, and telling us to relax — those guys knew what they were doing. In about two minutes the truck was in place on the back of the flat-bed truck. Soon it was whisked away to our crime lab.

It was time to find this son of a bitch, and there were no more excuses.

As I expected, the media were all over us. "Mounties Fail to Find Truck Only 1 Mile from Crime Scene," was the headline news that first day. It wasn't until the next day that they got the whole story. The truck was in fact about 23 miles from the suspected murder scene as the crow flies. It was almost 30 miles from the car by road.

O ver the next couple of days we went about drawing up battle plans. Worry and frustration were long gone, and adrenaline had once again set in. As if I wasn't busy enough, looking for manpower, equipment, and answering media questions, the boss chose this time to call me into his office one more time for an update on the current status of my involvement with the Brass Rail bar. Once again, he reinforced the threat that I would be promptly transferred if I didn't follow through on my efforts to divest my spouse of her interest in the "Rail." I just told him I was working on it. I really didn't know how he expected me to sell my wife's interest in the bar while putting all this overtime and energy into probably the most significant murder investigation in the country.

The media frenzy was on again, bringing us numerous tips from the Clearwater area. Several local citizens offered us information on people they suspected, but most of these suspicions were highly speculative and seldom well founded.

By this time, I had 20 local detectives assigned to assist in the continuing investigation. This was soon to be supplemented with further manpower from our Vancouver headquarters. There was no question in my mind that it was a local who had committed the crime.

Once again, we were preparing for door-to-door inquiries in the Clearwater and Wells Gray Park areas. Thousands of square miles would have to be covered again. This time everyone in every household — I didn't care if they were nine years old, or ninety years old — had to be questioned. They were to be interviewed even if it meant six trips back to that particular residence. The interview was to be documented precisely, for record purposes and for future reference, with no exceptions.

The questionnaire centred on the suspect(s) being from the area, and interviewees were to be solicited for their views as to a potential suspect. The investigator's opinion was also to be recorded after each interview and if there was a "gut feeling," the subject was to be pulled for a further interview by another investigator. No stone was to be left unturned. The boss was probably going to have me audited again, looking for that one stone I fucked up on, if only in his own mind.

There were hundreds of things to do. Among them was to review the 13,000 tips we'd received to see if perhaps we had overlooked one piece of information on a potential suspect. That would take another six months, and where the hell was I going to find help to do that one? It was a whole new ball of wax, and our chances of solving this case finally were greater than they had been over the past year or so. *Surely to Christ they won't deny me more help?*

One tip we were working on related to a real pleasant character. When we approached him to put him through the polygraph, we got a very humble "Fuck off, coppers!" He gave our detectives the finger as he walked away. War was declared.

We had enough for an application under the Privacy Act to apply to a Supreme Court judge for a "wire." The application was extremely time consuming for both our investigators and our lawyers, but finally it was approved.

The wire was set in place through surreptitious legal entry and located in a particular position that would best afford us access to the target's conversations. This, of course, was in the kitchen. Unbeknownst to us, the target had moved his child's crib right on top of the wire, and for the next two days all we heard was whining and crying. So much for strategic planning.

At last, our surveillance team caught the suspect driving while impaired. The resulting charge wasn't suitable for court purposes, but he didn't have to know that. We gave him two options: "Either you submit to the polygraph we requested of you within the next couple of days, or you appear in provincial court next Monday morning."

Within a short time the suspect took the polygraph and was cleared. I think he probably got the finger a few times on his way out.

Sometimes the means to gain the end are questionable; however, the shortest distance between two points is always a straight line. You can't always play by the Queensbury Rules.

Our presence in Clearwater was overwhelming for the locals, but it was probably the most friendly town I have ever worked in. Their support and patience were immeasurable.

Telephones were smoking with information coming in. Finally, we got a break in the case. An informant called and advised us that we may want to look at a fellow by the name of David Shearing as a potential suspect. The informant had decided to call after hearing a rumour that Shearing had run over a person out on the Wells Gray Park highway a couple of years earlier and had got away with it. This lead was too good not to give a top priority.

That same day, one of our investigators came in with a slip of paper in his hand. Upon it was written the name *Dave Shearing.*

"Where did you get that?" I asked impatiently.

"Downtown there. I was having lunch, and one of the waitresses just slid me this slip of paper. Why? What's up?"

Members were assigned immediately to answer the question, "Who the hell is Shearing?" In a couple of hours, we had our answer. Gerry Dalen read the information to me.

"Well, he lives a couple of miles from the alleged murder scene. He's about 23 years old and comes from a rather nice family. His father is now deceased, his brother was a sheriff, and mother is alive and well. He's been in trouble before — drugs, assaults, drinking and driving. A bit of a loner, and seems to like younger females, like 13 or 14."

"David Shearing. Didn't we interview the Shearing family at the outset?" The tip was pulled, and yes, we had spoken to the family: *It was terrible; the guilty people deserve whatever they get; no, I didn't see anything or remember anything; I don't know who could do such a thing; I'll call you if I remember anything; best of luck.* David hadn't aroused the suspicions of the investigator; he was just a regular Clearwater Cowboy who liked to drink and fight. The interview was recorded to file.

Routine answers to routine questions. But here was a potential suspect: He had lived in the area and had a criminal record for assault. He drinks and drives, and likes young girls. He had worked in Clearwater, and would have had to drive by the old Bear Creek prison site twice daily while going to and from work.

"Ken, drop everything. We need a major time line on this fellow, and I mean *major.* I want to know everything he's been doing since the spring of 1982 for starters. Stay on top of this and keep me up to speed on any developments."

The next day, another Shearing connection arose. Apparently during one of the door to doors, a woman said to her husband: "Aren't you going to tell them about what Dave Shearing said about re-registering that truck with the bullet hole in the door?" The husband scowled at her, and she left the room.

"I knew better than to pursue it then," the investigator told me. "I let him think I ignored her, but we'll have to go back and interview her when he's not home."

This was the piece of the puzzle that we had been searching for for the last year and a half.

"Pull as many people off door to doors as possible, and get that residence under surveillance now. As soon as the husband leaves, I want that woman brought in and interviewed. Ken, pull whoever you need off door to doors, and get me the Shearing time line right fuckin' now!" It was starting to come together.

"Mike," Ken hesitated. "There's one thing about Shearing I can tell you right now: He's working up in Tumbler Ridge. He's been there for the past few months."

"Who the hell do we know up at that detachment?"

"Isn't Ron German up there now?" Reliable answered. "I think I saw that in the recent transfer list."

"Well, let's smoke up these fucking phone lines!"

Tumbler Ridge was a small logging town about 600 miles north of Kamloops. I had worked with Constable Ron German six years earlier when I had been stationed in Powell River. I remembered him as a real character. He was always smiling about something, and his laugh was infectious. I had never had any problems working with him, and I was sure the guys up in Tumbler were enjoying his company. He loved his job, no matter what it threw at him. There was no question in my mind that whatever it was he was doing up in Tumbler Ridge, he was doing it perfectly.

We finally got a hold of Ron German on about the 16th of November.

"Ron? It's Mike Eastham here."

"Mike!" Ron beamed. "I guess you're pretty busy with that family murder case. Look, I've got a bit of a weird duck up here. He said he used to live in Clearwater, and I figured I could ask him some questions if you wanted me to. His name's David William Shearing."

My heart skipped a beat.

"Well actually, Ron," I said, swallowing, "we're looking at him right now as a possible suspect." I told him we needed to make sure Shearing didn't go anywhere. He told me he'd been watching Shearing pretty carefully the past couple of months, and was confident he could keep him still long enough for us to get out there and interview him. Shearing was apparently heading into Dawson Creek in a couple of days to party a bit

before a court date on the upcoming Monday. Once Ron and I had finished, I hung up the phone and got back to work on Shearing. Constable
German did the same.

Ron German later recounted his first contact with David Shearing, which had occurred a few weeks before I called him. On the 22nd of September, while heading back home from a long day shift, Ron had seen a large yellow Ford pickup coming toward him:

It was missing a headlight, and there were probably a hundred things wrong with it. But I was exhausted, and doing a routine vehicle check was on the absolute bottom of my list of priorities. It was quite normal out in Tumbler to see trucks with one headlight and no taillights, cracked windshields and so on, so making a big deal about it just wasn't worth anyone's time.

As the truck passed, Ron cranked his head around. He saw three heads bobbing through the back window and a bunch of tools in the box. Now Ron became awfully suspicious of that truck. Something about it rubbed him the wrong way. As the pickup slowly turned down the Quadra Camp road to the trailer park, Ron swung around and headed down the dirt road after it.

The truck promptly pulled off to the side when the red and blue dome lights came up behind it. Just so that they didn't know exactly how many cops they were dealing with, Ron fired up a set of huge off-road lights. They were completely blinding, especially at night.

Before Ron even had a chance to open his door, the driver had climbed out of the rusty truck and was heading towards him. Ron noticed that he appeared a bit unstable on his feet. Nothing serious, but he made a note of it. Ron wasn't sure why the driver had decided to walk back to the PC. Either he was a new driver and didn't know any better, or there was something in that truck he didn't want Ron to see. Ron stepped out of the PC and closed the door behind him.

"Hey there, how ya doing tonight?" he asked kindly. There were three of these guys, and he didn't want to piss any of them off.

"Not too bad, officer," the man replied steadily. His curly brown hair sat like a wind-blown nest upon his head. He was a bit shorter than Ron, wearing a black jean-jacket and black pants. His shoulders were broad, but hunched forward slightly. Ron could tell this guy was scared shitless.

"Could I see your driver's licence?"

"Sure," he replied, quickly offering it to Ron. Ron thanked him, and used the million-candlewatt power off the road lights to read his information. *David William Shearing.* Ron handed it back.

"So, where are you heading?" Ron asked casually.

"Just back to Quadra Camp from work," Shearing answered. "Going to go there for a bit, then head back home." His eyes were darting in every direction, and Ron found it very difficult to make eye contact with him. Quadra Camp was a large trailer park filled with every type of living accommodation, from RVs to small homemade shacks. Shearing explained that he was staying there with his friends.

"Okay, then." Ron decided to look the truck over more closely.

The two guys in the front hadn't budged. Normally when a couple of guys get pulled over and the driver is out chatting with the local cop, passengers would turn their heads to check out what's going on. Not these guys. Also, the passenger on the right-hand side had his right shoulder down. It was quite obvious that he was hiding something.

"So what have you got in the back of the truck?"

"Well," Shearing explained as they moved toward the tools, "we've got some impact tools here, a compressor, some wrenches and stuff." Ron looked over everything as Shearing listed it off. He was just about dead on, although there were a couple of other things he didn't mention. Ron guessed there was about 40,000 dollars' worth of tools back there.

It was late, and all the construction workers would have returned home long ago. In Tumbler, guys just didn't work at night. Some workers would come in from Dawson Creek about that time, but these guys hadn't come from Dawson Creek. Ron had the feeling there was something very wrong about this whole situation.

He asked Shearing to sit in the back of the PC and Shearing quickly obliged. Once he was in, Ron secured the door. He wasn't planning on cuffing Shearing, but he wanted to put him where he wasn't going to be a threat if things got tricky. Considering nobody knew Ron was there, he had to take every precaution to control the situation. With Shearing locked up temporarily, Ron could go and find out what the other two were hiding.

He walked around the back of the car, using the blazing off-road lights to hide himself as he moved up the ditch on the right-hand side. He inched carefully towards the truck. His steps were slow and deliberate. Ron knew he'd have to get the jump on these two if he wanted to be effective. As long as they didn't see him coming in around on them, he was pretty sure he'd get a good look at what it was they were hiding. If it was what he thought it was, Ron was going to have to be ready to duck mighty fast.

With his weapon drawn, Ron crept toward the passenger-side door. When he was only a couple of feet away, he could see the two passengers checking in the rear view mirrors. They squinted uncomfortably into the off-road lamps, but kept facing forward. Ron was practically on top of them, looking slightly down into the truck. From there, he could clearly see the hammer of the 30/30 rifle cocked and ready to fire. The stakes in this routine check had just gotten a lot higher. Carefully, Ron moved to the door, sticking his weapon right behind the passenger's ear through the open window.

"Don't even think about moving," Ron snarled. The two of them jumped, but after the initial shock stayed perilously still. The 9mm wasn't the hardest-hitting bullet around, but at that range it really wasn't an issue. "Get your hands on the dash!" Ron ordered briskly. They promptly did as instructed.

Ron carefully reached around with his free hand and opened the door. Stepping around it quickly, he reached in and pulled the rifle out. It had been pointing right out the driver's side door, concealed under the middle guy's bent knees. If Ron had come in on the other side, there was a pretty good chance the guy would have opened fire.

After seizing the weapon, Ron uncocked the hammer and made the weapon safe. As expected, there was a round up the spout. He quickly went back to the car and placed the weapon in the trunk.

With his weapon still drawn, standing a bit to the rear of the truck, Ron ordered the middle guy to step out. He did so quickly, putting his hands in the air as instructed. He was a scraggly-looking character, and didn't appear to be much of a threat. Ron cuffed him and ordered him in the back of the PC with Shearing. When asked his name, he gave it. Later, Ron found out it was false.

Then it was time to face the third guy. This time Ron approached from the driver side, just in case he'd had time to cook up another surprise. Ron could tell by his stern look and his tattoo-stained arms that he'd been in trouble before. Ron ordered him from the vehicle, and he sort of turned away in his seat. It didn't look like he was going to move.

I holstered my weapon. It's not prudent to start grappling with a guy when you've got your gun in hand. After a quiet standoff, I grabbed him right out of the truck. My aggression seemed to take the guy a bit by surprise. He'd hardly had a chance to struggle before I had him bent over the front of the truck and in cuffs.

At that point, I had a bit of a problem. Although there was room for the three of them, I wasn't under the impression that I needed Shearing back there. Once I had all the information I needed on these three, I would let Shearing and the other guy go, and take this tough-looking bastard up to Dawson and book him in for attempted murder.

The third guy was a real smooth character. He gave Ron his name, and when they looked him up on the computer, the guy he said he was actually existed. Then Ron noticed that there were some slight differences — his date of birth was a couple of years off, and he'd spelled the name of his own street wrong. Either way, Ron would get him fingerprinted in Dawson just to be safe. They could then photofax the prints to Ottawa. They'd find out who this guy really was.

Once he had all the information he needed, Ron cut loose David Shearing and his friend, who turned out to be Wylen Laidenen. Before they left, he took down some of the serial numbers on the tools and made a general list of what was back there. He asked Dave where he lived. He replied very broadly, indicating it was about five miles out of town in a hand-built cabin. Ron made a note of that and waved him off:

Once David had pulled away in the truck with Wylen, I drove the two hours from Tumbler to Dawson, and booked the last guy in for attempted murder (the firearm with one in the spout, and the hammer drawn back and pointed at where I was going to stand). Then I finally headed back to Tumbler Ridge for some sleep. I also made a mental note not to pull over any more vehicles that night.

The following morning, Ron German got a call. One of the trailers in the engineers' camp had been broken into the night before, and a bunch of tools had been stolen:

"Well—" I said, trying to silence the voice in my head screaming Told you so! Told you so! *"—what if I told you I ran into some strange characters last night with a truck full of impact tools, compressors—"*
"That'd be them," the man interrupted.

Ron had been working alone in the three-man detachment for the last few days. Constable Mike Johnson was going to be back the next day, so Ron went about his normal routine, keeping an eye open for that yellow Ford truck. When Mike rolled into town, Ron explained the situation to him and the two quickly headed off in search of Shearing. Ron had a bit of an idea where he was, so they split up and started checking every road they could find.

Mike Johnson loved to go out all day in the police Suburban and 4x4 all over hell's half acre. He considered himself a pretty damned good off-road driver, so this job suited him perfectly.
As he was roaring around the bush, I stuck to the nice level roads, looking for places Shearing might have been hanging out. I talked to Freddy Eskrick briefly at the A/C operations shack. He was kind of the town directory, and he could often tell you where everyone was at any time. Fred told me where Shearing hung out, so I checked out some of those places. After a couple of hours, Constable Johnson called. He thought he'd found the spot where Shearing was hiding.
I met up with Mike and with the two of us in the Suburban, we headed back into the forest. I crashed around the inside of the cab as Mike challenged every root and crevasse the road could throw at us.

At one particularly sharp corner, Mike stepped on the brakes and we slid to a halt. We climbed out and moved around the front of the Suburban to take a closer look. It was tough to see through the bush, but the yellow Ford truck was there, and we could see two guys outside digging a hole with a couple of shovels. Their small hand-made cabin sat behind them. There was no siding on it or anything like that, but for a couple guys in the bush, the place looked pretty comfortable.

"That's them." I smiled at my partner. "Now how do we go about this?" We had two options. One of them was to simply walk through the forest. Unfortunately, the bush was so thick that walking through it would have been almost impossible. We'd be lucky to make it within a hundred feet of the two men before they disappeared on the other side of the clearing.

We needed to get up close, and walking simply didn't afford us that luxury. Mike's idea was sound, but a bit on the wild side. He insisted we blaze in with the truck right up to the house, lights and siren blaring, jump out and give chase if the need arose. Even if that hadn't been the better of two ideas, it would have been difficult convincing him otherwise.

I climbed back into the Suburban and double-checked my seatbelt latch. Mike kicked our steed into gear and stomped on the gas. We swerved around the last corner, then roared into the clearing. Wig wags on and the throttle full ahead, we destroyed the peaceful setting like a shotgun blast on a pond full of ducks.

The two guys must have been amazed at the performance as the Suburban scrambled into the clearing like a high-speed cheerleader, pumping its red and blue pompoms with the enthusiasm of a college squad. Swerving towards them, Mike stepped on the brakes and the Suburban slid to a halt.

The two dropped their shovels and bolted off into the bush. Ron and Mike jumped from the snarling Suburban, drew their weapons, and gave chase. In seconds, all four men were crashing through the bush like derailed trains.

Ron picked out Shearing's lanky frame immediately as he bounded clumsily over fallen trees and rocks. The other was Fred White, moving as swiftly as a lumberjack.

This was the guy I had taken to Dawson for pointing the loaded rifle at me the previous night. What the hell is he doing out? *I wondered to myself as we charged at the two runners like horse cavalry.*

"Stop!" Ron yelled as he leapt over logs and cut through the odd bush. "Police!" Mike was right behind him, buzzing through the trees like a chainsaw.

They weren't stopping.

Ron felt like he had been clocking Olympic times, but he didn't appear to be making up any distance on these guys. It was time for Plan B. Ron fired a round over their heads. It bounced off a couple branches and made a pronounced *zing* as it tumbled through the air above them. Undaunted, they kept running. Mike fired a warning shot of his own. His was a lot lower than Ron's had been.

Finally they both got entangled in the thick thorn bushes. The two officers came up to them quickly, but carefully. They didn't appear to be armed but there was no point in taking chances. When Mike and Ron reached them, all four were way too out of breath to struggle.

The officers cuffed the two fugitives and started dragging them out of the bush back to the Suburban. Unlike their previous encounter, Shearing was now full of rage. His eyes were on fire, and he was swearing enough to shame a biker. Mike took hold of Fred White and pulled him along.

"Where's your friend, Dave?" Ron asked.

Dave responded with words to the effect of "Screw you."

"Is he in the house?"

"No."

"Let's go check," Ron said, his skepticism evident.

"You can't force me to go in there."

Well, now I know who's in there, Ron thought to himself. He grabbed Shearing by the cuffs, which were behind his back, and led him in the door. It was hanging open.

"Willie," Shearing called out. "It's me, Willie." Over Shearing's shoulder Ron could see Wylen Laidenen, hiding under a bunk, pointing a .303 at him. When he saw Ron, he promptly tossed it on the ground.

"I'm unarmed!" he insisted. Ron held Shearing in front of him until Mike got White in the Suburban. He came over and took Shearing from Ron so he could move in and take care of Willie. Ron cuffed him and dragged him over to the Suburban.

Once they had the three men nice and comfortable-like in the back, Mike and Ron returned to the shack and took a quick look around. Ron snatched up the .303 and brought it back to the Suburban. He put it in the back after making the weapon safe. Climbing in on the passenger side, Ron knowingly fastened his seat belt and hung on. The Suburban spun around and headed back out the way they came, bouncing around like a dog's nuts. Everyone grunted and moaned as the it peeled around corners and clawed for altitude:

Mike was pushing the edge — he was still pretty wound up after our chase. You get that way, when you're up and on foot chasing after a suspect. It's not always quite what it is on TV, but it's no less exciting if you're actually involved. You get an incredible amount of adrenaline pumping through your system, and you have to be careful to find somewhere appropriate to vent it. The suspect was never an appropriate duct, so now Mike took it out on the Suburban.

After what seemed like an eternity, we finally pulled up to the PC. Mike and I escorted the three men into the back of it. While the Suburban was quite wide and roomy, the PC was like a sardine can. Mike'd stay back and watch the town while I took the three stooges off to Dawson. I would be sure to ask what the hell Mr. White was doing in the back of my PC and not in cells where he was supposed to be.

The ride to Dawson Creek was miserable. It was very hot outside, and the cars back then didn't have air conditioning. The road was very dusty, and it rooster tailed behind us as we drove. I finally rolled down the window a bit to let some cool air in. Putting the fan on re-circulate helped to keep some of the dust out of the open window. That worked great until another car went past the other way, at which point all four of us were eating dirt.

When they finally arrived at the Dawson Creek detachment, Ron booked the three men into cells for possession of stolen property. He also made an inquiry about Fred White. Apparently, the corporal at the detachment had come in just after Ron had left the previous night and asked what White was being held for. Without knowing the whole story, this corporal claimed Ron had no right to lock White up for attempted murder when all Ron had done was find him in the vehicle with a loaded weapon. He gave White a notice to appear in court and sent him on his way.

The drive back to Tumbler was quiet.

It would be six weeks or so after Ron and Mike Johnson's run-in with David Shearing and friends that Ron would get the call from me about Shearing.

In the meantime, Shearing had been released and was supposed to appear in court on November 21 on the possession of stolen property charges. Shearing had been checking in at the detachment every week as instructed, and he always showed up right on time. His pals White and Laidenen had already been shipped off to some prison for a collection of charges, including breaking and entering, armed robbery, and assault. Shearing was still working locally, mainly because he didn't have such an extensive criminal record.

One day in October, Ron stumbled upon Jesse Harrison, the manager of the Quadra Camp trailer park. He was a heavyset fellow who was quite accustomed to dealing with all the rowdies that came into his camp. They were talking about a couple things, and he mentioned Dave Shearing. Naturally, Ron inquired innocently.

"Well," Jesse began, "he owes us about 600 bucks. The last couple times I went to get the money from him, he told me he was going to kill the owner, Joseph Leblanc, and burn the camp to the ground." Joseph had promptly taken some stress leave. He was a city-type guy, who wasn't quite used to dealing with the camp residents. "I've also heard he was a bit weird with girls." Jesse explained how he'd heard different stories about Shearing. Nothing specific, but enough to stick in Ron's mind.

Ron took a brief statement from Jesse, and in it he also mentioned that Shearing claimed he derailed a train. Ron made a note of that, and figured he'd look into it later.

On the 21st of October, Shearing came in for his weekly check-in. Ron was reading in the news that we had finally found the truck that had belonged to the Johnsons. It was a matter of great interest up in Tumbler.

"Look at that," Ron said, glancing at the paper as Dave signed his name. "They finally found that truck and camper."

Dave finished signing before he replied. "Really? Where?"

"Oh, right in the park," Ron answered, scanning the article. "After all that looking, it just sort of popped up on a mountainside. Pretty amazing."

"Yup, bushes are pretty thick over there. Hard to see down on the ground. I used to live near there."

"Really?" Now Ron was curious.

"Yeah, those murders happened a couple miles away from my house. Really a shock to everyone." At that point, Ron made a note: *Call Mike Eastham.*

After our phone conversation, Ron decided to keep a closer watch on David Shearing. He had heard rumours that Shearing planned to leave town, so Ron would do what he could to encourage him to stick around.

On the 17th of November, the day after our telephone conversation, Ron got a report about a missing 3000w homelight generator. Ron and the other man in the Tumbler Ridge detachment, Corporal Wayne Ulander, headed up to Shearing's place to make inquiries. They also wanted to make certain that he didn't plan on missing court on the 21st.

They arrived about 9:30 in the morning and knocked on the door. They could hear two male voices inside. One of Shearing's friends answered the door.

"Sorry to get you guys up so early," Ron smiled. Shearing was pretty used to seeing Ron around by then. He had a friend, Jason Hill, staying with him.

"No problem," Shearing said from the bed. He was sitting there smoking a cigarette. He stood and came over to talk to Ron.

"So, you've got court coming up Monday, heh?"

"Yeah," Shearing said, still quite tired.

"What are you going to do?"

"Well, I'm going to plead guilty to the possession charge."

"You have a lawyer?"

"Sort of." He took a quick pull of his cigarette. "I've got Legal Aid." Shearing told them he was heading down to Dawson for the night the next day, and that he would be back on the 19th. They had general conversation about court, and with that Ron and Wayne left the scene. Walking past the truck, Ron peeked in the box.

There was the generator they had just heard about, sitting there like a trophy on a worn-down mantelpiece.

Under advice from the corporal, Ron left it alone. They went back into town and got some more of their stuff done. They knew where the generator was, and Wayne was pretty well informed as to the situation with us in Clearwater. This is probably why he decided to leave the generator alone. If I wanted them to bring Shearing in later on, they could bring him in for possession of stolen property (PSP), and hold him just long enough for us to get here.

They wrote down some notes, and Ron called me again. I informed him that we would be on our way up the next day. I asked if he could get Shearing in custody and keep him there until we arrived. Ron figured, what with the PSP and the fact that David was on a recognizance, he could probably do it.

Just after noon that day, Ron was following David Shearing's truck. Shearing pulled over immediately after Ron turned on the lights. To Ron's surprise, David's friend Jason Hill was driving, and there was a girl sitting between them. Ron promptly arrested Shearing for theft over two hundred, and headed back to the detachment. When he arrived, he explained what was going on to Wayne Ulander, then took Shearing to Dawson Creek again. Ron was a very familiar face up there those couple of months.

Upon his return, Ron got a call from "Whispering" Jim Struthers, who was a crown prosecutor in Dawson Creek. He was a really great guy who had a very quiet voice and seemed to whisper all the time. Jim would be the prosecutor for Shearing's PSP charge. Ron explained to him why we needed to keep Shearing in custody. When he heard that Shearing was a suspect in the Johnson/Bentley murders, Jim could hardly even speak. He whispered that he'd do his best to keep Shearing in custody. We couldn't ask for much more than that.

I had explained to Ron that we wanted to hit Shearing by surprise. We didn't want him to be held for the murders before we had a chance to interview him. If Shearing was made aware of the situation now, it would give him time to come up with a story. If we could catch him unawares, we would be more likely to get the truth out of him. It was therefore up to the Tumbler Ridge members to try to keep a grip on Shearing using everything but the murders.

Later on that night, Ron got a phone call from Jim Struthers. Ron hoped he had some good news.

"Ron," Jim said quietly, "I'm sorry, but I just couldn't do it. I was there, and ready to insist he be held, but I couldn't. He's out."

Shearing was out of gaol again. Ron knew where he was going, but it wasn't going to be easy getting him back where he belonged without blowing the cover off our investigative team.

November 18th, 1983
Kamloops, BC

While Ron was busy trying to find a way to keep David Shearing within reach, the team and I were planning our northern mission.

I guess it had been a bit of a long shot, thinking that I could avoid the superintendent before I got away to Dawson Creek. A couple of other members had mentioned that he was looking for me that morning. I simply asked where I could find him, then walked the other direction. That had been working for me all day, but I knew I had a problem when the meaty paw tapped me on the shoulder.

"Sergeant," he began, his face heavy with concern. His eyes boggled clumsily behind his thick bifocals. "I don't think it's a good idea for you to go to Dawson Creek." He gave me a pause to argue, but I kept my mouth shut. I didn't fuss. I just nodded. I don't think he'd have been too interested in hearing my opinion just then. "You're too emotionally involved in the case to be of any use to the interrogation. Besides, I've got some work I need you to do around here."

At that point it was a staring contest. I didn't really have a lot to say. I was too busy thinking about how nice it would be to get the hell out of that place. "Yes, sir. Are you finished, sir?"

"Yes, yes," he wheezed as he turned around. "Carry on, Sergeant. We'll speak tomorrow." *Fat chance,* I thought to myself. *I'm outta here.* Satisfied, the superintendent walked into his office and closed the door behind him. I turned and headed straight to my office where my go bag for the trip over to Dawson was waiting.

After many telephone conversations with Ron German and Dawson Creek GIS, I knew that our main suspect would be easy to track whether he was in Dawson or Tumbler. I was actually hoping that he was out of custody and under surveillance because we could use the extra time to prepare for the interview.

Ron German was now confident that our suspect was a creature of habit, and like a bad penny, he would always turn up nearby. There was nowhere for him to go, and we certainly didn't want to give him any reason to be suspicious. Besides, if we arrested him late Friday afternoon for PSP he would be in custody in the Dawson Creek lock up until his court appearance Monday morning. I guessed we would probably need the 48 hours plus with him if we were going get a confession out of him. That meant we had better haul ass up to Dawson early Friday to ensure we would be there by late afternoon. Ron German guaranteed that our suspect would be available for us, and I believed him. That's the way he was.

We had a new team member as well. I had dug up Len Bylo to help us with the interrogation. He had a really great reputation as an interrogator, so naturally I brought him on. Bylo had arrived just after we discovered the truck, and had been a big help when it came to establishing a time line on Shearing.

Leibel, Dalen, Bylo, and I got together in the meeting room once I had my stuff straightened out. I had made it quite clear from the beginning we weren't going to leave that damned place until we had a confession in our hands, and I reiterated that when we all sat down. The other three agreed without question. We had been working the Johnson/Bentley case seven days a week for fifteen months, and it looked like our labours were finally going to pay off.

We were really quite excited about getting the business done and behind us. The resulting media circus would be staggering so we had to keep our egos in check. When it was over and Shearing was behind bars, the reporters were going to jump all over us. That was great, but we had to remember to keep ourselves on track. Despite myself, I was excited. I'd had a lot of weight on my shoulders for the past year. All of Canada was looking for answers, and I'd been unable to provide any until now. We didn't have our man locked up just yet, but we were a lot closer than where we'd been for the last 15 months!

The next order of business was deciding who was going to be working with whom. We quickly agreed that I would work with Ken Leibel and that we would be the first to have a go at Dave Shearing. Detectives Dalen and Bylo would be Team Two. We'd switch every four hours, depending on Shearing's willingness to talk. This decided, Ken and I laid out our travel schedule as accurately as we could, while Bylo and Dalen discussed what Shearing should see and what he shouldn't. The atmosphere was casual, yet professional. Although we were all very tense, we all found time to poke fun at one another when it was appropriate.

Next, we had to figure out how we could get Shearing from point A to point B without anyone seeing him. We discussed which doors we would use, and more important, which we wouldn't. Although I had advocated use of the media extensively throughout the investigation, the information pertinent to the development of a good suspect had been tightly controlled. The stance of the RCMP, and myself for that matter, was unmoving: Involvement of the media during this phase of the operation would be unacceptable. A breach in that protocol would result in a completely smothering situation, and none of us was prepared to deal with that before the interview. TV crews from all over North America would be camped out on the lawn, interviewing and interfering, both inside and outside the detachment. Locals for miles would want to come out for a peek. Worst of all, lawyers of every shape and size would be breaking land speed records to get their hands on the case. I imagined a hundred-car pile up out front of the small Dawson Creek detachment. All the lawyers would be shaking their briefcases out of their car windows, shouting obscenities at one another, arguing about who was going to sue who.

We really wanted to keep the lawyers away, at least until we had a confession. Despite having investigated the case for over a year, we had very little evidence — a burned-out truck with a bullet hole in it and Shearing's alleged involvement in a hit and run four years earlier. "Bring him in with blood on his hands, or don't bring him in," they would say. Otherwise, Shearing would walk out faster than a union worker after a pay cut, and that just wouldn't do.

Finally, after an hour of planning and a couple of administrative delays, we were taken to the airport where we boarded a plane to Prince George. From there, we were to catch another flight to Dawson Creek. Everything appeared to be going as planned until the pilot announced that we were grounded because of the weather conditions. After an hour delay in Kamloops, the small plane leapt into the air, banking northwards towards Prince George. The trip was short, but it was clear to us we weren't going to make the connecting flight to Dawson Creek.

I had wanted to be in Dawson by early afternoon and was pissed when the plane was late in getting us to Prince George. That would mean we would lose critical interview time over the weekend. We disembarked in Prince George, our minds dark with disappointment. Instead of climbing on board another aircraft to Dawson Creek, we were forced into a four-hour drive up treacherous mountain roads in the middle of a blizzard. I think Dalen called the detective office, and in about 20 minutes we had a car there to take us back to the office. I was almost embarrassed, climbing into the piece of shit that was our limousine. It shook like a damned rattlesnake the whole way, and judging by the black smoke pouring out the back, when it came time to fuel up we'd have to ask the attendant to "fill up the oil and check the gas." If those bloody politicians back in Ottawa only knew what they were sending our guys to work in — or maybe they did. I wonder if the austerity program affected them like it affected us.

It took us about 20 minutes to get back to the detective office. The four of us squeezed out of the cursed vehicle, surprised that it didn't fall apart. Life had ridden that thing hard, and we all started bitching about how they should just put the damned thing to rest.

"We can't," the sergeant in charge of the Prince George detective office insisted. "Not until it's no longer serviceable. Oh, and by the way: it's your ride up north, so talk nice." As the four of us growled swear words we thought we'd forgotten, we shuffled back out to the little engine that couldn't. Dalen and Bylo crawled in the back, careful not to snap the rear axle. In minutes, we were rumbling out of Prince George towards Dawson Creek.

The car groaned and smoked as we chugged up and down winding mountain roads to Dawson Creek. We leaned back and forth as Leibel swerved around the tight corners, waiting for the engine to seize. The mood had been shifting steadily since we'd left Kamloops. At first, we had all been excited to get the job done. Now we wondered if we would even make it to Dawson Creek to do the interview at all. One thing after another had gone wrong, and I was starting to think it was a sign.

The pressure on us was extreme, and it didn't help to think that police detectives all over the country would be armchairing our work for years to come. They'd look at the case, analyze it, and pick it apart for mistakes and weaknesses. It was something all of us were expecting, and had learned with experience to work around. Because we would only have Shearing for the weekend without a lawyer, it was important that we get it right the first time around. That meant minimizing the number of mis-

The innocent victims. Above: The Johnsons—Bob, Jackie, Janet and Karen. Below: Janet Johnson, 13, and Karen Johnson, 11

Edith and George Bentley, both in their late sixties, were enjoying a leisurely retirement at the time of their senseless deaths.

Even from the air the contours of the vehicle were difficult to see. The rust-ed paint and broken shape blended perfectly into the surrounding foliage. Nearby trees shielded the car from view in every direction but straight up.

A mushroom picker who recalled seeing the Johnson car in late August had assumed it was just another derelict vehicle until he heard about the missing families. From the road it was almost impossible to see the burnt-out hulk—it blended in very well with the surrounding landscape.

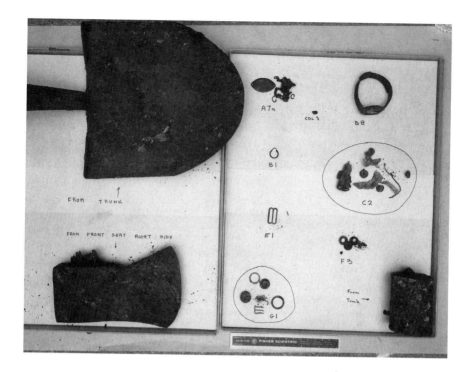

Labels visible in evidence photo: A7a, COL3, B8, B1, C2, E1, F3, G1, FROM TRUNK, FROM FRONT SEAT RIGHT SIDE, From Trunk, FISHER SCIENTIFIC

The horror concealed within the Johnson vehicle was staggering. An evidence photo shows the state of the few objects found inside. When we opened the trunk I got the shock of my life. The backseat (below) was a forest of charred bones. At final count the car held the remains of six people. It was hard to believe that life could be reduced to so very little.

REWARD / RÉCOMPENSE

$35,000 INFORMATION ON PERSON (S) RESPONSIBLE
RENSEIGNEMENTS SUR LE OU LES RESPONSABLES

$ 2,500 INFORMATION ON RECOVERY OF TRUCK AND/OR CAMPER
RENSEIGNEMENTS MENANT À LA DÉCOUVERTE DU CAMION OU DE LA CABINE DE CAMPING

JOHNSON/BENTLEY — MURDERS
Near Clearwater B.C. — August 1982

VEHICLE: 1981 Ford, F.250 — Camper Special —
B.C. Licence 4836FY.

CAMPER: 1971 "VANGUARD" 10½ foot, 6 HP. Evinrude
outboard motor on rear. CB radio call XM12994 on
rear door. "Canadian Auto Association" decal on back.
10' aluminum boat on top.

MEURTRES DES JOHNSON ET DES BENTLEY
Près de Clearwater (C.-B.) — Août 1982

VÉHICULE: Ford 1981, modèle F.250 — Camper Special —
Plaque d'immatriculation de la C.-B. nº 4836FY.

**CABINE DE
CAMPING :** "VANGUARD" 1971, d'une longueur de 10,5 pieds,
moteur hors bord de marque Evinrude 6HP fixé à
l'arrière de la cabine. Indicatif d'appel XM12994,
CB (service de radio général), sur la porte arrière. Auto-
collant de la "Canadian Auto Association" à l'arrière.
Bateau en aluminium de 10 pieds sur le toit.

In August 1982 the bodies of 6 persons were discovered in a burnt car near Clearwater B.C. They had been murdered. The vehicle shown on this poster belonged to one couple and is missing. The camper and truck may or may not be together.

The truck, camper, spare tire, boat, motor and other camping items may have been sold individually. It may have been in the Jasper — Kamloops area between August 1st to 17th, 1982. It could now be anywhere in North America.

Information of the **WHEREABOUTS** or **SIGHTING** is urgently requested.

The reward will be apportioned as deemed just by an official committee comprised of the R.C.M. Police Officer in Charge of the investigation, the Officer Commanding Kamloops Sub/Division R.C.M. Police or his designate and a Crown Prosecutor. The reward offer, expires at midnight 1983 OCT 31.

Anyone in possession of information relating to the murders should contact the nearest police authority or the **Kamloops Sub/Division, R.C.M. Police, General Investigation Section** at **(604) 372-3111. CASE: 82—1454.**

En août 1982, on a découvert les corps de six personnes assassinées dans une voiture carbonisée, près de Clearwater (C.-B.). On n'a pas retrouvé le véhicule qui figure sur cette affiche et qui appartenait à un des couples. Il est possible qu'on ait enlevé la cabine de camping du camion.

Le camion, la cabine de camping, le pneu de rechange, le bateau, le moteur et les articles de camping peuvent avoir été vendus séparément, entre le 1er et le 17 août 1982, dans la région de Jasper-Kamloops, ou alors, n'importe où ailleurs, en Amérique du Nord.

Si vous **CROYEZ AVOIR VU** le véhicule, ou si vous **SAVEZ OÙ** se trouvent le ou les suspects, veuillez nous en **aviser** immédiatement.

La récompense sera répartie de façon équitable par un comité composé de l'officier de la G.R.C. responsable de l'enquête, du commandant de la Sous-division de Kamloops de la G.R.C., ou de son remplaçant, et d'un procureur de la Couronne. L'offre de récompense expire à minuit, le 31 OCTOBRE 1983.

Toute personne possédant des renseignements sur ces meurtres devrait communiquer avec le service de police le plus près ou avec la **Section des enquêtes générales, de la Sous-division de Kamloops, G.R.C.,** numéro de téléphone: **(604) 372-3111. CAS Nº 82—1454.**

SPECIAL WANTED CIRCULAR
NO. 273 - 82-11-22
RCMP IDENTIFICATION SERVICES

AVIS DE RECHERCHE SPÉCIAL
Nº 273 82-11-22
SERVICE DE L'IDENTITÉ JUDICIAIRE, G.R.C.

Canadä

Over 10,000 reward posters were sent all over North America, smothering police departments, post offices, and just about every tree in the public eye. Almost 300 people from across Canada told us they believed they had seen the Bentley unit being driven by two suspects. When that many people tell you that they've seen something, you really have no choice but to follow it up.

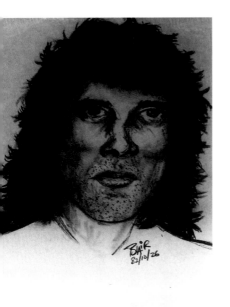

Artists' sketches from witnesses' descriptions of the two French-speaking male suspects. Several people recalled seeing them driving a pickup truck and camper unit similar to the one belonging to the Bentleys.

David William Shearing's name came up in connection with an unsolved hit and run that had occurred in the Wells Gray area a few months before the Johnson-Bentley murders.

takes. If we talked about anything, it was pertinent to the case. We were all fearful of coming home empty handed, but had resolved among us that, come hell or high water, if this son of a bitch was guilty we would know one way or the other.

If we got there, did the business, and came out again with a confession, our peers in the RCMP would be bursting with pride. The rest of police world in Canada would look at us in admiration for about 60 seconds, then say, "Aw, they just got lucky."

The four of us talked quietly about the interview, ignoring the sickly groans emitted from the engine as we made our way farther north. Gerry and Len talked in the back about their routine when our four hours were up. Ken and I spoke briefly about our "good cop, bad cop" routine. I always got to play the good guy because I was so darned good at it. Even I wouldn't want Reliable, playing the bad cop, interviewing me. He had this soft voice, until you pissed him off. When he was pissed, his voice didn't get too much louder, but his eyes could penetrate a steel girder. I've seen grown men reduced to pieces of shit once Reliable got on their case.

When the talking died off, I filled in the gap by describing circumstances in past interviews. I discussed what had worked, and what hadn't. There was a reason for this, of course. I knew Ken Leibel quite well, and I had a vested interest in talking to him as much as I could. Ken had a frustrating tendency to fall asleep while he was driving. I remembered one occasion when he had plowed through a wheat field as he dreamed undisturbed behind the wheel. He'd totalled the car and walked away unharmed, wiping the sleep out of his eyes. I thought Detective Ken Leibel was lucky to be alive. Kenny thought farmers put all their fields in the wrong places.

"How you feeling, Kenny?" I asked, poking him in the ribs to make sure he was still awake.

"Hey, don't worry, Boss," Leibel replied nonchalantly. "I caught 40 winks a couple miles back. I'm all right now." I didn't find that very funny at all. I felt like a cat that had just been tossed in the bathtub. I never knew when to believe this bugger.

Tumbler Ridge, BC

Shortly after eight o'clock that evening, plain-clothed officers from Tumbler Ridge RCMP detachment watched David Shearing and his friend climb on board a bus bound for Dawson Creek. Minutes after they climbed in, the grinding diesel shifted into gear and slowly moved out of the parking lot towards the highway. It was a direct route, so the investigators guessed they had a little more than an hour to get someone in Dawson Creek to take up the surveillance.

When the officers called in, arrangements were made to pick Shearing up for questioning at the Dawson bus depot. Those plans were quickly cancelled. It was discovered that we had been delayed in Prince George. Fifteen minutes after the original phone call, two detectives in Dawson Creek set out for the bus depot. They agreed to watch Shearing until the next morning, when we would be ready to have him apprehended.

The bus roared into the depot right on schedule, and Shearing quickly stepped off, followed by his friend. As the two cowboys lumbered clumsily down the street towards the bars, the investigators followed quietly behind them. Shadowing the two of them as they stumbled from one local bar to another was an easy task. At one particularly sleazy dive, the two men wobbled out with two women. Clucking and burping, the group of four blundered to a local hotel. They checked in, then anxiously moved to their respective rooms, probably anticipating a night of wild sex. Sitting outside the hotel, sipping coffee and munching on snacks, the two officers could only guess at what was going on behind the closed doors. The two RCMP officers grunted about their misfortune, wondering what their wives were doing while they were gone.

"Probably the same thing she does when you're there," one joked, sipping his coffee. "Sleeping."

* * *

When Ken's head started bobbing, I ordered him to roll down his window. He smugly complied, and the interior temperature quickly plummeted below zero. Dalen and Bylo grumbled in the back seat as the cool outside air punished them. I knew it was going to be one of those nights.

Finally the four of us shivered into Dawson Creek and checked into a hotel. We had a big day ahead of us, but we all sauntered over to one of the local bars and had a beer. The trip was over, and Old Faithful had somehow got us there in one piece. We took some time to pick on Leibel's sleeping habits, but mostly just sat there and stared at one another. All of us were in our own little realm, thinking of all the possible outcomes the next day might bring.

"Hey guys, it's my mother's birthday tomorrow. Do you think that we could jointly send her a birthday greeting, like: 'Hey Nan, this one's for you! We got the sucker!'" What would we do if Shearing walked? What would we do if he wanted a lawyer straight away?

A few minutes after we'd drained our beer, we returned to the hotel.

* * *

By three o'clock that morning, the two officers observing Shearing decided it was time for a bit of a stretch. They'd already taken a closer look at the hotel room, and decided the only way for Shearing to exit was through the front door. They were confident he wasn't going to leave. Nevertheless, it was a time for prudence. Four o'clock in the a.m. is a difficult time for any observer. At that time, human reactions are slowest. It's a dark, usually quite cold time of night, especially in November. Nobody has been around for hours, and there's precious little to look at except the moon crawling ever so slowly across the sky. Your body is telling you that you should be sleeping, and every time you look at the clock it gets harder. When the surveillance begins, you tell yourself you're going to get up and walk around a bit if you get tired. The problem is, as the hours tick by and you become increasingly fatigued in your nice warm car on your nice comfortable seat, you want to sleep. You don't want to get up. You don't want to stretch.

But you have to. Close your eyes and there's a chance you're going to open them two hours later, and the hotel room may be empty. With time and experience, a skilled observer will have his internal clock adjusted to living at night. His schedule will be reversed, so that all his sleeping is done during the day. Sometimes, you don't have that luxury. The brain is a hard mechanism to fool, and it would much rather be sleeping than staring at a hotel room at three in the morning after a sleepless night.

The two officers took turns stretching. They never walked too far, just far enough to get some cool breeze down their shirts. One of them proceeded inside the hotel to talk with the man at the desk, careful not to arouse any suspicions.

First, he asked if there was a woman registered with a completely unpronounceable last name.

"A *who?*" the clerk asked, totally confused. The officer repeated himself. "I don't think so. How do you spell it?"

"God, I don't know," the officer lied. "She called me up and told me to meet her here. I'd recognize her name if I saw it."

The man behind the desk scratched at his chin as he looked through the names. He gave up, shrugging. "Here, take a look." He handed the binder over the counter to the undercover officer.

"Oh, here it is all right." Room 202. Jason L. Hill from Salt Lake City. "Thanks a lot, buddy. Wish me luck."

The officer made another phone call to the detachment. Someone there promptly ran a check on this Hill guy. The troops in Ottawa discovered that this Jason Hill had warrants out for his arrest under the name Harwood. Back at the detachment, plans were made to contact immigration.

The hours had ticked past quickly, and as the sun finally started to poke its nose out from behind the mountains, the small town of Dawson Creek came alive. Some folks were out jogging, while others came out walking their pets. It was a bitterly cold Saturday morning, and only the diehards were out that early.

At 6:45 a.m. the two girls trotted out of the room. Shearing and Hill walked out a couple hours later, shunning daylight like vampires. After all, they'd been up all hours drinking and there probably hadn't been much sleeping going on after that. The two friends proceeded to a nearby restaurant and ate breakfast. In no time, they were on the bus heading back to Tumbler Ridge.

"Better call home." One officer picked up the phone and called their detachment with the news. Their new orders? Follow him to Tumbler Ridge and drag him back to Dawson again. Although Shearing was now exactly where we needed him to be, it was simply too early to bring him in. That was mostly our fault. We were going to need a couple more hours to prepare. By the time Shearing was taken into custody in Tumbler Ridge and driven back to Dawson Creek, we'd be ready for him. Arrangements were made for Constable Ron German to head down to the Tumbler Ridge bus depot to make the grab.

I told Ron he would have to arrest Jason Hill, because of the warrants of committal to be executed under the name Harwood. Then he would have to try and talk Shearing into coming back to Dawson with him without actually arresting him.

Ron figured he would need some help carrying out this assignment. The closest member was probably Dennis Piper at Chetwynd detachment. Naturally that was the first place Ron called.

"Dennis, I've got a situation over here," he said. "I've got a couple guys coming into town on a bus in one hour. I've got to arrest one of em, and talk the other one into coming down to Dawson with me."

"One hour?" he asked, hoping he'd heard wrong.

"Yeah."

"Well, I'll get there as fast as I can, Ron, but I don't think I'll make it before the bus." Chetwynd was almost as far from Tumbler as Dawson Creek, down gravel roads. After talking to Dennis, Ron called his boss, Sergeant Ray Cunningham, to see that it was all right. He quickly agreed to send Piper to back Ron up.

With that taken care of, Ron made another call to Al Kjemhus. Al worked with Quintette Security and had just recently entered the RCMP as an auxiliary member. He and Ron were pretty good friends, so Ron knew he'd come along with him if he asked really nice.

"I can't tell you why I need to do this, Al," Ron said to him, "but there's two guys coming in to Tumbler on the bus from Dawson. One of them, Jason Hill, we've got to arrest. He's kind of a half assed, biker-looking guy, and he's got outstanding warrants under the name Harwood. You may have to guard him until Dennis Piper gets here from Chetwynd. The other guy, the primary in this case, is a suspect in a real serious offence." *What a way to break him into the auxiliary program,* Ron thought to himself. "I'm not going to be arresting him. We need to do this as neat as possible. It's got to be quick, and if they want to scuffle, I'll need your help takin 'em down."

Ron understood the need for surprise. If they got in a real bind, then he was ordered to arrest Shearing for the hit and run he'd supposedly been involved in back in 1980, but that was only as a last resort.

Ron picked Al Kjemhus up at home. Once he was in the car they started going through the procedure again. Ron would keep him back behind the car, close to the shot gun. That way, if they did need to draw down on them, Kjemhus was both armed and behind some cover. It was in Ron's greatest interest to bring Al back home to his wife and two children in one piece, so he was wary as to how he involved him. If Shearing or Harwood (a.k.a. Hill) did resist, Al would come over and help Ron, or give chase if required.

While he was immersing Al in RCMP arrest protocol, Ron was also going over his part in the program:

In my mind, I knew I was going to have to be quick at arresting Hill and getting him in the PC without an argument. If you start going back and forth with a guy, your arrest is going to be anything but smooth. Before you make an arrest, you have to be sure that you're going to go through with it. If you hesitate for even one second, it could show a sign of weakness, and that is an ingredient every criminal loves to feed on. I was pretty sure this Harwood would be no different. If you aren't sure the odds are in your favour, you wait until they are. I had Al, and the element of surprise. I was pretty sure the odds were with my side.

With that more or less settled, they moved out to the Dawson highway and waited for the Norline coach to arrive.

At about 1:40 in the afternoon, the bus rolled down Mackenzie and past Ron and Al toward the depot located across from the detachment. They followed a bit behind it, turning to the right as the bus edged into the parking lot. As the bus slowed to a stop, Ron pulled off to the right, about 20 feet away.

Al Kjemjus wasn't at all used to this. Ron could tell he was a bit nervous about the whole situation, and gave him one more confident smile before stepping from the PC. When Ron headed towards the front door of the bus to meet Shearing and Hill, Al stepped from the passenger seat and stood sharply behind the police car. At that point, Ron had to have the utmost confidence in Al's ability to assist him, and his ability to aim that shotgun if things got ugly.

Shearing and Hill were the last couple off the bus. Both looked a bit tired from a long night of drinking. They weren't too pleased to see Ron's stern-looking mug motioning them over.

"How you guys doing?" Ron asked politely. They nodded at him, muttering that they were all right. "Would you mind stepping over to the police car for a minute?" Ron glanced over at Al as they wandered over. He was all business, hovering ominously close to the shot gun.

"You're not gonna arrest us, are ya?" Hill asked wryly once they arrived at the police car.

"Actually," Ron frowned at him, "I'm going to arrest *you*. There's an outstanding warrant out for you under the name Harwood."

"That's not my name," Harwood, alias Hill, blurted out. "It's Hill."

"No it isn't. You're under arrest." Ron promptly searched him, then cuffed him. He didn't resist at all as he was put into the PC. Now all they had to worry about now was Shearing, but that was plenty. He was a prime suspect in one of the most vicious and heinous murders in Canada's history. Ron did know the guy pretty well, but had seen that other, vicious side of him too. He wasn't too interested in seeing it again.

"You don't want to talk to me, do ya?" Shearing asked, ready to head for home.

"Yes, actually," Ron said before he could walk away. Ron quickly asked him about some highway damage he'd come across a couple days before. Some idiot had walked a D-8 Cat from the BC rail service yard to the foot of the trail that coincidentally led to Shearing's cabin. The cleats on the big Cat had torn the road right up, and the Department of Highways was some pissed about that.

"Nah, I don't know anything about it."

"All right, well ... the members in Dawson Creek want to talk to you."

"About what?" Shearing asked, his annoyance evident.

"Other matters," Ron said vaguely. *About how you murdered six people David,* he thought to himself.

"You aren't going to arrest me, are you?" The tone in his voice was getting colder. Ron really didn't want to have to launch the cover story, so he maneuvered around it.

"No, I won't need to arrest you if you come on your own."

"You wouldn't lie to me, would you?"

"No," Ron said truthfully. If Shearing came with Ron voluntarily, he wouldn't have to arrest him; if he didn't, Ron would have to arrest him.

"You did before."

"When?" Ron asked, confused.

"Well, it wasn't you," he admitted slowly.

"Look, I'll drive you down there, and then when they're done talking to you, I'll drive you back up here." That appeared to sit well with Shearing, and took a bit of the stiffness out of his shoulders.

"Well, okay."

The sudden growl of an engine at full throttle tore through the air, accompanied by the sound of flying rocks and gravel. All three men watched curiously as a tornado of snow and dirt swerved into the parking lot behind them.

Dennis Piper had arrived.

He jumped from the car and hurried over. Al's forehead was wrinkled with amazement, and Ron's jaw felt like it had dropped a bit more than six inches. Dennis had made the two-hour drive from Chetwynd in a little less than an hour.

"God, Ron," he laughed as they assembled in front of the PC with Shearing between them. "I've never driven so fast in my life! I think I was airborne half the way here!" Dennis insisted the speedo was up over a hundred the whole way. They had a brief discussion about Hill in the police car, and Ron explained that Shearing was going to come with him to Dawson. Dennis promptly ordered Hill/Harwood into his PC, and Ron settled Shearing in the back of twelve alfa two. Ron and Al then climbed in the front, and Dennis headed back to his car for a slower drive back to Chetwynd.

Ron had to give Al a ride back home before taking Shearing to Dawson. When they arrived, Ron walked him to the door. He was really proud of Al.

"By the way," Ron said over his shoulder as he proceeded back to the car. "You might want to watch the news to see who you helped arrest." Al was probably glued to the TV for the next three days.

Ron and Shearing then proceeded to the office so Ron could make some notes before he forgot anything about Harwood's arrest, or his words with Shearing. Good paper makes good friends, so we all made certain our notes were as accurate as possible. Shearing asked if he could go to the washroom, so Ron let him out of the back and they proceeded into the detachment together.

Back then, Ron had a furry Old English sheep dog named Max. He used to come around with Ron on patrol all the time. Everyone in Tumbler Ridge knew Ron and Max. Max wasn't too fond of being cooped up in closed spaces for long periods of time. Because Ron couldn't take him with him to pick up Shearing, he'd had to leave Max at the detachment. As soon as Ron opened the door, he could smell that the dog hadn't appreciated Ron's ignorance. Shearing pointed out that Max had had a couple dumps on the floor near the bathroom as a gesture of his appreciation.

"I'd better clean that up," Ron said, rising from his chair.

"No, no," Shearing quickly obliged. He scooped up all Max's dirt and dropped it in the toilet. When Dave sat down he gave Max a good pat and a rub on the belly that made his leg do those little spasms. Before Ron had 10 lines written, Shearing made his last friend: a five-year-old sheep dog.

Ron finished writing his notes as Shearing played a bit with Max. Then, off they went. Max jumped in the back this time, and Shearing climbed in beside Ron.

"I guess I've got to wear a seat belt, huh?"

"Yes, David," Ron replied, fastening his own. "You do have to wear a seat belt." They both buckled up, and proceeded toward Dawson Creek. They had a pretty quiet conversation about 4x4s, talking about costs and the advantages of four-wheel drive in snow and mud, the two main elements in Tumbler Ridge.

About 10 miles down the road, they came across a dead moose on the shoulder. Just to keep Dave thinking everything was still casual, Ron stopped the car beside it. The two of them stepped out and went over to take a look at it.

"Jason said he saw this on the way in," Shearing mentioned as they poked around. They hung around for a couple minutes and had a charming talk about road kill. Before long, they were back in the PC and heading north to Dawson Creek again. A bit farther down the road, they came across a pack of coyotes. That sparked a discussion about hunting and guns. Ron mentioned he had a .22 Cooey for shooting grouse.

"Single shot?" Dave inquired.

"Yeah. I'd really like to have one of those pump action ones. That way I could take a couple of shots at once if I had to."

"I've got one," Shearing admitted quickly, "a .22 Remington. It's pretty accurate, and good for hunting deer." As they were talking, Ron got it in his mind to try and get some information of his own. If Shearing knew he was in shit, he was being pretty damned cool about it all.

"It's my dad's rifle," he continued. "Hasn't hardly been used, that I know of." He added that it had some date stamps on it, assuring Ron it was still in great condition. Ron got the impression Shearing was trying to sell him his gun.

Finally they came up to Dawson Creek, and Ron headed in on one of the back roads to the detachment. He parked in the back, and he and Shearing headed in toward the back door.

I was standing at the desk with Ken Leibel when they walked around the corner. I hadn't seen Ron for almost six years, so we greeted each other with friendly smiles. Ken Leibel and Ron shook hands, and we all acted like Shearing was just one of the guys.

"By the way, David, this is Mike Eastham."

Dave's eyes went wide with fear. He'd obviously been reading the paper. We shook hands briefly, and then Ken Leibel took Shearing down to the interview room. Ron then gave me whatever information he had on David he thought might help the interview.

"He's got a really wonderful habit, Mike," Ron began. "If you confront him with something he's guilty of, his head will go down and he won't look at you. His eyes are always darting around, but if he's guilty, they'll hit the ground and won't budge. He told me he's got a .22 Remington pump action rifle. He said he isn't big into hunting, but he also said the rifle was accurate, and worked well on deer, so—"

I was filing this all away, but I guess Ron could tell I had a million things going through my mind. He wished me good luck, and proceeded out the back to take Max for a walk, knowing he'd just apprehended the most wanted man in Canadian history.

Chapter 14 **LAST CHANCE**

Now that we had Shearing in custody, it was time to get to work on him. After all, we couldn't just throw the irons on someone, heave them in gaol, and toss the key. First we had to get them to talk. The tricky part was getting them to say the things we knew were going to land them in gaol. It took some clever footwork to get someone to talk their life away. All of us had years of experience and some interesting ways of getting people to talk, but we weren't always lucky. I knew shit happened all too often.

There were a number of circumstances that would make this particular interview a bit easier. It was a Saturday. If we were careful enough, we'd have Shearing for two days without lawyers crawling all over us. The courts had closed the day before, so all the lawyers would be out curling or drinking or whatever it was they did. Nothing soiled an interview like a lawyer sitting arrogantly in his chair next to the suspect saying, "You don't need to answer that!" over and over again like his nose was skipping over a scratched record. In fact, my first goal was to keep the lawyers away. After the first interview, they could bitch and moan about everything they wanted, but until then we wanted Shearing all to ourselves.

I'd seen cases get thrown out of court for the craziest of things, so naturally every time I walked into the interview room I had to think through every step meticulously. One wrong move and Shearing could be back on the street. It didn't seem fair that something as trivial as not showing my badge when I walked into the interview room could get the case tossed out. I sometimes wondered why they called it the *criminal* justice system. I think somewhere in the bureaucratic circus they forgot about the victims. The criminals had all the justice they needed. The system itself was meant originally to protect criminals against a blatant disregard for their rights and personal safety. Now it had basically turned into a cash grab for every defence lawyer in the business.

Another one of my big concerns was our lack of evidence. We had worked on this case for 15 months, and nothing substantial had surfaced.

But there were two sources of information we considered genuine, and they both pointed at David Shearing. If we hadn't taken them seriously, we wouldn't be up in Dawson Creek on a weekend.

Despite some of our shortcomings, we had our man in custody. That was miles ahead of where we'd been only a month ago. Although we didn't have a hell of a lot to go on, we did have something. If we were really lucky, I figured that something might just be enough.

I'd been going over the proceedings in my mind, shifting into interview mode. I had to be relaxed but professional, strong but passive. It was important not to intimidate Shearing. Intimidation tended to keep people quiet or make them cry for a lawyer. Neither was an acceptable option. As an investigator, I had to adopt the mindset that the crooks were smarter than me, at least until they were behind bars. While that did make the situation somewhat nauseating at times, I never lost sight of my firm advantage. They had to be lucky all the time — I only had to be lucky once.

It was pretty clear in my mind how the interview was going to progress. I'd introduce myself, sit down, and get Shearing comfortable. *Coffee? Smokes? Sure. Have a couple, I don't care.* Once he knew we weren't going to try smacking him around, it was important to establish a "relationship." *Tell me about home. How about Mum and Dad? How about your brother? Your sister?* With any luck Shearing wouldn't even know what he was doing there. If we kept him a bit off balance, he'd be more vulnerable. Because he had only been told he was wanted for questioning about "criminal matters," he would be guessing it was about his court date coming up on the following Monday, or possibly any other number of things he knew that we didn't.

While we sit there talking about all this good stuff, it's important to probe for weaknesses. I'd talk about his life. I'd build him up high and make him feel pretty good about himself, but it was all just an illusion. The more real that illusion seemed to him, the better I'd done my job.

If we were friends, it would be easier to find a chink in that armour everyone puts on as soon as they walk into an interview room. Mother and God were two good places to start. When everything is coming apart all around you, and your world is in flames, every man wants to run home to Mum. Mother comforts, she nurtures. Therefore, she is always a good subject to bring up in an interview. Mothers solve a lot of crime. The emotional ties available through that line of questioning would prove valuable when it came time to creating a relationship between myself and Shearing.

God can be another big help. Those with religious ties always reacted well to God. Religion, although the cause of more deaths than any other reason combined, also solves a lot of crime.

When Mother and God couldn't help, you had to start searching elsewhere. Before you could find other weaknesses, you had to learn about who it was you were interviewing. In order to learn, you had to unlock that safe in which most men hide themselves. That meant making him feel comfortable. If Shearing wanted to talk about Grandma, then I would talk about my grandma. If he wanted to talk about Mum, I would talk about my mum. If Shearing said shit, I'd say shit. I had to develop the illusion that I was just like him, for him to get comfortable. Familiarity is society's way of making you feel comfortable.

Once we'd entered that comfort zone, I'd have to persuade Shearing that we knew a hell of a lot more about him than he was probably prepared to hear. Now, that was a bit of a bluff. We didn't really have a lot of information, but Shearing didn't need to know that. Besides, you could slide farther on bullshit than you could on gravel. He'd be wondering what we did and didn't know, so we hoped he would just assume we knew everything. Although I'd had investigators on his file full time for the past four days and had come up with some pretty interesting stuff, there was nothing really relevant to the Johnson and Bentley case, other than the remark he'd reportedly made about a truck with a bullet hole in the door. While I could bullshit fairly well, it was always important not to go too far. If I bluffed about something that didn't really happen, he'd know that I was full of shit. At that point, the lawyers would come screaming in and the interview would go to hell.

The weight of the interview lurked awkwardly around us no matter where we went. They talk about how Olympic athletes get into that mode where they're all pumped up and so finely tuned they don't think anything can get in the way of them and the gold. The Olympians had their events, and in our minds this interview was our goddamned Olympic event.

The four of us were a team, and as a team we all hoped that together we could put Shearing away. We ate together, talking quietly amongst ourselves about the interview. Shortly after lunch, Dalen and Bylo had taken a peek at the interview room, making certain that it was void of all distractions. The commanding NCO (non commissioned officer) had offered us the use of his office. It was split in half by a couple of neck-high wall dividers. On one side sat the commanding NCO's desk, and a variety of comfortable leather furniture. The walls were decorated with an assortment of pictures, all nicely framed and immaculate. On the other side, investigators had removed everything except a table, three chairs, and a large safe that couldn't be moved even if we had wanted it to be. We would have a couple of leather chairs, with our backs to the wall and a partial view of the pictures and decorations on the other side. Shearing would sit in a small, wooden chair facing us, with his back to the divider. That way, all he'd have to look at was the corner. There was a window that might prove to be a bit of a distraction, but we could work around that.

Satisfied with our interview setting, the four of us got together one last time before splitting off to our separate routines. Dalen and Bylo wouldn't be far away, trying to keep things in the detachment building quiet so as not to disturb the interview. After a couple of good luck wishes and a pat on the back, Ken Leibel and I went our own way. I looked pretty sharp in my "cowboy" uniform. I was wearing a pair of jeans and a jean shirt with a nice leather vest. If I could have nicked a cowboy hat from somewhere, I'd have had it straight away. Shearing was a bit of a cowboy, so we were all cowboys that day. It was another way of bringing some familiarity to the suspect. It would make him feel at home. Comfortable. If Shearing had been a businessman, we'd have been businessmen. Walk like him, talk like him, fart like him — whatever it took, I'd do it. Our objectives were clear: Find the truth and get a statement.

We were standing at the desk when Shearing walked in with Constable German. Ron and I talked briefly between ourselves, while Ken took Shearing off to the interview room. After a quick handshake, Ron turned around and walked back out the door. I turned on my heels and headed toward the NCO's office.

* * *

Ken Leibel was sitting across from Shearing when I walked in. Shearing was sitting in the wooden chair with his back turned, smoking a cigarette. The small cloud of smoke hovered around him. His arms were crossed and his legs were crossed. He turned slightly when I walked in, his white straw cowboy hat low upon his head. He was wearing a brown western shirt and vest that fit him comfortably. His black cowboy boots were scuffed with wear. Cigarette smoke had already started lingering in the small space, and I noticed Shearing had smoked two cigarettes by the butts in the ashtray. I think I had smoked about a thousand before I even got there.

Leibel was sitting close to the wall, on the opposite side of the table. He greeted me with a nod, but we didn't say anything. I could see by his furrowed eyebrows that Leibel was stressed out. I'm sure he could see that I was stressed out a bit too.

"Hi, Dave." I extended my hand for a good ol' friendly shake. We were best friends, after all. Shearing stretched to his full height; he was at least a couple inches taller than me, but shorter than Reliable. *What a monster!* It was a firm handshake, but I made sure my grip was just a little tighter. Our eyes locked. The psychological game between us had begun, and I wanted to emphasize that I was the one in control. Our hands came apart, but our eyes were fixed. Nothing like an old-fashioned staring contest between buddies.

"You can call me Mike. You've met Ken Leibel?" Shearing nodded as he sat back down. "We're detectives from Kamloops." I flashed my ID card, then my badge.

Shearing's whole body shuddered. His lips tightened slightly and he swallowed nervously. His body was rigid, and his arms and legs were still tightly crossed. Getting information from someone in that position was never easy. It's universally recognized as a sign that a person is not at all interested in sharing information. My job was to open him up a little. Before Ken and I could really get down to business, Shearing would have to have his arms dangling by his sides with his legs spread as if he were on an empty bus heading home from a night out. That would make everyone's job a lot easier.

I moved over to my leather chair next to Leibel. When I sat down, I took a closer look at David Shearing. He was a big guy, and it wasn't hard to envision him behind the business end of a rifle. The drooping brown mustache gave him that tough, western look, and his eyes were dark and lifeless. Many people believe they can see the death in a guilty man's eyes; in this case, if that were true, Shearing had confessed without even saying a word.

It was clear that Shearing had had his nose rearranged a few times. It was spread all over his face. His meaty fingers were heavily stained from what must have been years of chain smoking. The cigarette he had dangling from his mouth was shrinking quickly, and before we had a chance to begin he was stubbing it out and lighting another. He gave a new definition to chain smoking. I think at one point he had two or three lit at once.

So this is David William Shearing, eh? I thought to myself. *Son of a bitch.*

I had to write down his general appearance. With that done, it was time to get moving.

"Now, Dave," I began kindly, starting with what I liked to call my "Columbo" routine. "I can be really forgetful sometimes. I'm not very bright and I tend to forget a lot of things, so I'm going to be writing down our conversation and Kenny here is going to help me. You don't mind, do you?"

Shearing shook his head quickly, his arms tightly crossed.

"What's your full name?" Ken and I had to write down everything.

"David William Shearing," he answered weakly. I was expecting this big booming voice. Instead, he was quite soft spoken. I made a note of that.

Everything had to be recorded. Tape recorders were available, but both Ken and I had agreed we wouldn't use one. Sometimes, something as simple as a sliding ashtray sounded like the suspect was being given the beating of his life. Other times a frustrated detective might seemingly raise his voice in a threatening way, which might eventually lead to the suspect walking out on a technicality, happy that the criminal justice system was so forgiving.

A tape recorder was great for keeping track of everything that went on in the interview room, but it could also be used against us. I'm sure lawyers love to get together at the bar on the weekend and laugh about the silly technicalities they've used to get their clients back on the street. Every investigator fights against technicalities in every case, at all times. Say the wrong thing, and Shearing could walk. Everyone in the country would know Mike Eastham fucked it up. The superintendent would be pleased.

"All right," I managed to say with a friendly tone despite a hundred dark thoughts, "when exactly were you born?"

"Uh, April 10th, 1959."

"How long have you been around Tumbler Ridge?"

"Since about the 24th of July."

"Have you got a job in town down there?" My hand was already starting to hurt.

"I did have one up until two weeks ago. I was working for Sun Country Construction, putting up forms for basements."

"All right, Dave. Tell me a little more about yourself." If Shearing cooperated and answered the questions in detail, we'd know pretty quickly that he was getting comfortable. If he was more secretive, it would be a long day at the office.

"What do you want to know?" Shearing hesitated, his arms still crossed.

"Well, tell me about your parents. Where are your parents?" Shearing shifted in his seat slightly and began.

"Dad died of cancer last spring." His tone was sombre. We had been informed that he had been very upset about the death of his father. He'd begun to drink really heavily and had reportedly started getting into trouble within a month of the funeral.

"What about your mother, David? Where is she?"

"My mother still lives in Clearwater ... " He described his parents briefly, speaking proudly of them both. Dad had been a prison guard, and Shearing appeared to respect him highly. Mother had been in an old folks' home in Clearwater for some time, and as David put it, "she's not comin' out of there, I don't think." He hadn't talked to his mother since he'd arrived in Tumbler Ridge.

"Any brothers or sisters?" Leibel was scratching away on his pad furiously beside me.

"One of each. My sister and I don't get along so good." Shearing explained their relationship in slight detail. They hadn't spoken much since he'd left Clearwater. "And my brother Greg — we get along pretty good." Greg Shearing was 37 years of age and currently unemployed. Dave added proudly that Greg had been a sheriff at one point not long ago.

"So," I continued, noting that Mum and brother were two weaknesses I could work on later if need be, "what about you? What kind of things have you done?" And out it came. Shearing lit another cigarette and rattled off his history. He had his grade 12 diploma, and once out of high school quickly signed up for a heavy mechanic course for six months. He was really quite proud of himself for having "graduated college," as he put it. Shearing explained that he'd worked in several different places in the last five years, doing cabinet making and other general labour work in British Columbia. He briefly mentioned his employment with a fertilizer outfit on a farm in Alberta. *That ought to be good for some bullshit.*

"You've done quite a few things in your time, heh Dave? I'm impressed." I smiled at my good friend Dave. "Must be a regular handy man outdoors."

"Yeah," Shearing grunted, taking another pull of his cigarette to finish it off. "I know a lot of stuff." Finished with that smoke, he stubbed it out.

Kenny and I took the time to catch up on our notes. Leibel hadn't stopped writing for 20 minutes. He wanted to get in every word, every detail. We both knew it was imperative. Those notes would later have to be presented in court to indicate what was said and done during the interview. They had to be as precise as possible, otherwise Shearing's lawyer would have him walking out the front door.

"Have you had any past problems with the law?" I knew the answer to these questions, but I wanted to see if he was going to try and bullshit. If I could do it, why couldn't he?

Shearing lit another smoke. His legs were starting to spread out, and his arms were much more loosely crossed than before. "Well, there's been a couple problems. I don't have much money, so I've got to get by." He explained his contribution to several recent thefts, and that he had been apprehended with some stolen property not long before. He had Legal Aid for that case, and he figured he could get off with a simple hand slapping. "I was being really stupid," Shearing admitted. "Some of it was just me, but I had some help from the crowd I hung out with. Not a great crowd, I guess, for that sort of thing."

"Ever done time in gaol?"

"A couple times in Clearwater, just overnight." Shearing's eyes were darting all over the place. I remembered what Ron German had told me about that. *Let's skip the gaol talk, Mike,* I thought to myself. *Let's talk about Mum again.*

"So, Dave. When were you going to head back to Clearwater to see Mum?"

"Well, I'd like to get back home for Christmas, but I couldn't stay. There ain't much work in Clearwater and I kind of like it up in Tumbler Ridge."

"Do you have a car?" Dave uncrossed his arms and relaxed slightly. *Talk about cars, trucks. Whatever,* I thought to myself. *Just open up for me, you son of a bitch.*

"A couple different ones. I just put a new cab on this '72 Ford four by four, but I still need a passenger-side door and some fenders."

That got my attention. The rear bumper had been taken off the Bentley truck, and that bullet hole in the door would have been a pain in the ass to fix without help. *Can he be trying to cover his ass? Has he been looking for a new door and rear fender for the Bentley truck before he burned it? What is going on in there?*

"I've got another Ford, a '75, that I drive right now. I've had a couple other cars, like a 1965 Chevy Belair. That was my first, and it was all right. I also had a '68 Chev, and a GMC pickup."

"Who did you hang out with back in Clearwater?"

"Well, I got along with pretty much everybody. My best bud is probably Allan Smith. I've known him my whole life, but I haven't seen him much the past two years. Anyone else?" Shearing thought out loud, his eyes darting between his hands and the window. "Well, let's say if I walked into the bar in Clearwater, I'd know somebody."

"How about close friends? There's your friend Allan—"

"All my friends are close."

Leibel was writing like he was possessed by some form of scribbling demon. His notes had always been a bit more detailed than mine and it usually took him a little longer to get everything down. Not this time. Deciphering it later proved to be only slightly easier than reading Braille with boxing gloves on.

"So what do you like to do in your spare time? Got any hobbies?"

"Well, I like to play the guitar. Had to learn that on my own, but it was something I'd wanted to learn for a while. I work on my trucks all the time, you know. I like fishing and—"

"Hunting?"

"No," Shearing answered quickly. Too quickly, in my opinion.

"Do you have any firearms?"

"No, I don't have any guns." There was a long pause. Shearing seemed to be looking to me for approval. *Do you believe me?* his eyes wondered. Obviously he didn't know I'd been talking to Ron German. Shearing continued quickly. "I'm not much of a hunter. Just fishing. Spent a lot of time down at Clearwater River, I like it down there. Best damned trout fishing I've ever seen, though, was in Dreyfells Lake. I was there this spring."

"I've fished a few times," I mentioned. *Casting for you, you bastard.* "Caught a couple big ones in my days. Takes a lot of patience."

"Yeah, patience is a lot of the game." Shearing sat up, using his hands now more than before. A good sign, I knew. "That and your lure. You have to have the right lure for the water conditions."

That's real great David, I thought to myself. "Ever married?"

"Nah."

"Any sweethearts? Girlfriends?"

"Well, there was this one girl in Kamloops. Janet Duncan. She's about 20— I'm terrible with numbers and ages."

"How about names?"

"Well, I'm good with faces. Not so good with names." Shearing chuckled nervously.

"Who knows about you David? Who do you talk to?"

"You know, you guys know more about me than anyone. Except maybe my mother and my brother, and maybe Al." *All right, if this does-n't work out, there's the three people we talk to first.*

"We want to get to know you, Dave," I explained gently. "We want to understand you. The more you tell us, the more we'll understand you. We're doing pretty good right now, don't you think?"

"It's pretty good." Shearing knew something was up.

"It looks like you hit the booze pretty hard last night. You drink much?"

"Well, lately yeah. Beer mostly."

Great, I thought to myself. *He's going to tell us he was drunk the night he did it and doesn't remember.* "Any favourites?"

"Well, probably Budweiser."

"Any liquor?"

"If any, probably rye. Silver Tassel or Canadian Club."

"How about drugs?"

"Haven't done much since high school. Tried acid once and didn't like that. It kinda made me ... Well, nothing really. I was just a bit scared to get into stuff like that. Mostly pot back then."

"What about prescription drugs? Have you been taking any medication?" It was important to know this. If he'd been using any pain killers or suppressants just before he was apprehended, the lawyers would argue he wasn't thinking straight.

"No, nothing like that. I don't like taking those kind of drugs. Don't take 'em unless I really have to. Like two months ago or so, I was hitting it pretty hard and fell into a fire pit. Stupid, really. Burned my back and my arm. That was just stupid."

I noticed he repeatedly used the word "stupid". I tucked that little tid-bit in my mind for later use. Shearing continued by explaining his involvement in a truck accident a couple years before.

"This other pickup was spinning around and kind of hit my truck. My legs smashed into the dash, and I fractured my pelvis. I don't drink and drive anymore." *Probably because you've driven over 10 people,* Leibel and I thought to ourselves.

"Was there anyone in the truck with you?" Leibel asked, speaking for the first time. He was usually pretty quiet. As a rule during the interview, I was the kind, forgiving cop; Leibel was the straight to the point, no-bullshit cop.

"Robert Cliff was there with me."

"Ever been to a psychiatrist?" We had to keep him off balance. If it meant changing topics every 20 seconds, I'd change them every 15.

"Well, no," Shearing said, as if seeing a shrink was something done only by weirdoes.

"There's nothing wrong with seeing a psychiatrist, you know. Policemen do all the time. We have a lot of problems ourselves. Alcoholism, depression—" I'd seen both of these in my 22 years of policing.

"I guess I thought of seeing a hypnotist to try and help me quit smok-ing, but I never ended up doing that, as you can tell. I'd like to quit before the end of the year, but I've got a ways to go before then." He enjoyed another long pull. Even his mustache was stained yellow. He was getting a bit too comfortable. Sometimes you had to remind a suspect that at the end of the day, we weren't just there to make the world revolve around him.

"Do you know what we're doing here, Dave?" My tone was louder than before. My energy level was peaked. I was nervous, but excited. My stomach was churning with anticipation, and I knew I was shaking. *Enough bullshit, it's time for me to get it done. He can walk and he can talk, he has emotions. It's time to kick ass.* "Considering the distance we came, we must be here for a good reason." Shearing tried to avoid eye contact, and I could tell he was surprised by my change of tone. He was looking around again, but every time he looked back at me, I was staring straight at him. He'd look down at his feet, but when he came back up for air I was right there waiting.

"No, I'm not sure," he said finally. "I don't have anything to hide, you know. I'm an honest guy."

"We're honest too, David," I answered frankly, looking him straight in the eyes. "We don't tell lies, but then, we won't tell you everything we know either." Now the real work would begin. "We have a job to do. We are professionals, and we're good at what we do. We aren't going to threaten you. We won't beat you, but we won't make any promises either. We can't do anything for you. We're always fair. We won't bring any heavies down on you." I took a deep breath. "I know you're no dummy. You've got the same education as me."

"Really?" Shearing was surprised.

"Yeah. You know you have the same rights as I do? We all have rights. Constable German read you your rights, did he not?"

"Yes, he did."

"Can you tell me what you remember about what he said?"

"Well, he said I have the right to a lawyer, and a right not to talk."

"He should have also said we are investigating a criminal offence, and that you are entitled to a lawyer and to make any telephone calls to get one. You are not obliged to say anything, as anything you say may be used as evidence. You understand what that means?"

"Yeah." Shearing was really starting to cringe. He'd been relaxed, but he was tightening up again.

"It means that you don't have to talk unless you want to. It means nobody can make you talk to us." I stopped to let that sink in, and took the moment of silence to catch up on my notes. "You understand that at any time you want a lawyer, you just say so. If you don't want to answer our questions, you don't have to. Do you understand?"

"Yeah."

"If a lawyer was here right now, he'd tell you not to say anything if you are guilty. He'd tell you to shut your mouth and not talk to the cops. He says that for a reason, you know."

I was slowly herding him into a corner. Now he had to talk. *You're a goner, Dave. I can feel it in my guts and I'm not leaving until you tell me! Now be a good little cowboy and tell Uncle Mike all about it. If you clam up now, we'll both know you're guilty.*

"Yes," Shearing nodded.

Yes? I thought to myself. Most people would be up in arms, howling about innocence and lawyers. This guy knew he was guilty, he just didn't know what we were after him for yet.

"All right, I just wanted to warn you and make sure you understand. It's important that you know where we're coming from. I want to be honest with you. We're always honest and straightforward."

Shearing nodded again.

"Any time you want to leave, you can." Leibel looked at me out of the corner of his eye. I could sense his discomfort. Sometimes, an interview could be like a poker game. If Shearing was good at calling a bluff, we'd be in deep trouble. Telling a subject they can get up and leave was very dangerous indeed. If they *did* get up and start walking out, you had to figure out how to get them to sit back down again, and sometimes that can be a major problem. Leibel shook his head and looked back at his paper to make some more notes. I didn't even want to guess at what he was thinking.

"We are going to be talking to you about a lot of criminal things and I want you to know that that warning applies to all of it. You know you can call a lawyer any time, and that we can't make you any promises. We aren't going to threaten you in any way. Understand?"

"Yeah."

"Anytime we're talking, you can get up and leave. Okay?" Ken's body appeared to shudder so badly I thought the rest of the room would join him. *Have to keep the old boy awake after all,* I chuckled to myself.

"Okay."

"We're detectives, G.I.S. — General Investigation Section. We assist several different detachments of the RCMP in the Southern Interior, such as Kamloops, Merritt, Williams Lake, and Clearwater. We're professionals, and we're very good at what we do." *Don't try to bullshit the troops, David.*

"Are you guys investigating the Johnson/Bentley murders?" *Strike one, Davy boy!*

I wanted to let Shearing squirm a little in silence before moving on. "Did anyone talk to you about it last year?"

"Yeah. Some cop talked to me briefly about it before, last year sometime."

"A uniformed officer? Or plainclothes?"

"Uh huh. Uniformed."

"Do you know Trophy Mountain?" A nod. "How about Battle Mountain?" Another nod. "You know that's where we found the truck and camper and the car?"

"Yeah."

"You know, we have a lot of members in Clearwater. We know a lot more about you than you think." Chew on that one for a minute, big boy.

"Everyone wants to help us, even the shit rats." Nervously, Shearing drew another cigarette. He was squirming, so we had to be careful. If we blew up his skirt too fast he would walk out and our next interview would be with a lawyer giving it the broken record. However, right now things were moving along rather nicely. Both Leibel and I were sweating and shaking like we'd just been in a car accident, and were trying hard to conceal it, but Shearing had been cooperative. That in itself made things a lot easier for the two of us. Now it was just a matter of keeping it on a positive note. "We're getting anonymous calls, a lot of those. Everyone wants to help."

"Yeah?" Shearing was looking around again, his eyes shifting from one thing to another. He'd look at his feet, and then over at the window like he wanted to leap through it. He looked at his hands, then the ceiling. Every time he looked back, I was staring right into his eyes. I just wanted to tease him enough to put him on the edge. I wanted to make him wonder if we were here on the J/Bs, without actually telling him yet. It was a very dangerous manoeuvre because in most cases, the "bad guy" would put a halt to the questioning, and either try to walk out, or immediately call for a lawyer. I was hoping I had read David correctly. If not, disaster was about to hit me in the face like a horse's hoof.

"We've been looking under all kinds of rocks," I carried on in the interest of getting it in Shearing's mind that what he had done was a horrible and repulsive act. There are certain crimes you just did not commit, no matter who you are. You don't kill Grandma and Grandpa, you don't kill Mum and Dad, and you definitely don't kill two little girls. Even the class-one scumbags were helping however they could. "Getting stolen property, drugs, money. Bikers are calling in with all the information they can give us. Bikers!" I wanted to reiterate that one because it amazed me, too. "I want to see if you are an honest guy. I'm going to start back a couple years ago, and see what you will do. Remember, you can leave at any time." Shearing nodded his understanding. I pressed on quickly before Leibel could look at me cross eyed again. "We discovered that a kid was killed that summer on Wells Gray Road." To my surprise, Shearing's whole body appeared to heave with relief. *Gee, is that all this is about?* "It was a hit and run, or criminal negligence, or whatever. The guy didn't stop. I know all about it, otherwise I wouldn't be up here in Dawson Creek on a weekend."

"I know," Shearing admitted.

I leaned across the table again. My pen had started acting up, so until I could get my hands on another one, it was going to be up to Leibel to get what followed on paper. At that point, I really wasn't too interested in breaking the momentum we'd picked up. If I were to get up at that point, there was a good possibility he'd clam up again.

"What happened Dave?" I looked at him as sympathetically as I could. "Tell me what happened." Leibel looked over at me again out of the corner of his eye, wondering if it was going to be that easy. To our surprise, Shearing couldn't get it out fast enough.

"I was driving," he admitted. "I guess you know that."

I don't know anything, David, but you don't need to know that. "Which way were you going?"

Shearing appeared to be in a trance-like state, probably remembering that night. He was driving with a friend after a night of partying when the shape emerged in the headlights. Before he could react, the car lurched.

"What happened?" I asked again during the long pause. Shearing was going to tell me, I knew that. He wanted to get out of there in the worst way, probably under the impression that it would be all over after he confessed to the hit and run. He looked pretty upset, but I hadn't decided whether it was because he did it or because he'd gotten caught. *Fuck you, you son of a bitch,* I thought to myself as Dave chewed over his thoughts. *Squirm!*

"Well, I was driving home, going up to the top of the hill, going about 45 or 50 miles an hour. I saw him on the road, just a shape. It didn't look like a body." Slowly, the words drifted off his lips. "I took my foot off the gas."

"Then what happened?"

"I was scared shitless. I'd been drinking. I knew he was dead."

"How did you know?"

"The whole car ran over him. My whole car bounced, I mean really bounced! He had to be dead instantly."

"Who was with you?"

"You know who was with me!" Shearing snapped.

"Hey, you won't be getting any answers from me, David." *Because I don't have any,* I admitted to myself.

"But I don't want to involve the guy."

"Well that's up to you," I sat back in my chair, raising my hands in the air. Talk about sliding!

"All right, well, you already know — Doug Elliot."

"Then what did you do?"

Shearing thought back for a moment before he continued. "Well, we were scared to go to the police."

"Why?"

"'Cause I'd had a few drinks. I hadn't been drinking that much — I mean, I could still drive, but I thought the cops would think I didn't see the body and didn't try to stop. I just didn't have time. We drove into a turn-off, up the road a bit. We were confused. I didn't know what to do."

I listened as Leibel scratched away.

"We drove around, but there was a piece of chrome under by the door, dragging along the road. I stopped to pull that off." Shearing hesitated. "Shit, what did I do then? Well, we talked about it for a bit and then we agreed that we shouldn't tell the police about it. I was really scared and confused. I drove Doug home, and I went home shortly after." Shearing looked over at me. "I would imagine you want to ask me more questions about that."

"Just a minute." That damned pen just wasn't going to start writing, and now seemed like as good a time as any to get another one. I stood and moved through the divider into the other side of the office and quickly snatched a pen from the desk.

"Who was the guy you ran over?" I asked upon my return, swirling the pen across the paper a few times before the ink came out.

"Dave Carter," was the quick response.

"Did you know him?"

"Yes."

"How did it make you feel?"

Shearing hesitated. "Really confused. I was sad." He paused again. "Well, not sad ... I don't know what. I was upset."

David sure wasn't too upset anymore. *Jesus, don't get so upset Dave, you only killed a guy!* It was pretty obvious to the two of us that Shearing was more upset about being caught than he was about having driven over someone.

"Has it changed your life?" He had to think about that for a couple seconds. I figured any normal human being would have said yes. Without question. "Come on, the straight goods now."

"I don't know. I—"

"Have you had a tough time living with that?"

"Yeah." Shearing sighed. "I've thought about it."

"Have you had nightmares?"

"No nightmares. But I think about it."

"How many people know?"

"I don't know. I thought it was just Doug and I."

"Well, I'm going to tell you. It's no big secret. A lot of people know, except the cops of course."

"Golly."

Golly? I thought. *A guy who kills six people in cold blood says "golly"? What the hell am I dealing with here?* "How do you feel now?"

"The shits," he admitted quickly.

"Well, you've told me and Ken. Does that mean anything to you?"

"Yeah, but I'm not sure what."

"Well, a lot of people feel—" I couldn't find the right word. David got the message loud and clear. "Well, you told me. Do you think you might want to write down what happened that night in your own words?"

"I guess so," Shearing answered, a bit disappointed. He had really thought this was all we wanted him for. The pen and paper were sitting on the table closer to me, so I passed them over to him. We wanted him to write out his own statement this time. He was going to need some practice. Besides, all that talking was making me thirsty.

"Do you want a coffee?" I asked the others, clearing my throat.

"Yeah," Shearing muttered.

"Do you?" I asked Kenny.

"Sure." Leibel took a moment to rest his hand.

"Let's get one thing straight," I turned back to Shearing. When the lawyers pored over the transcripts, they'd probably argue that I had bribed him into confessing by getting him coffee. "I'm not giving you anything. I'm getting you a coffee because we were going to have one. What do you want in it?"

"Two sugars."

I moved around the table and through the divider. It was nice to get out for a stretch. It also gave me some much needed time to gather my thoughts for the next offensive. I headed over to the coffee maker and took three mugs from the shelf above. Once all three were topped off, I dumped a couple sugar cubes in Shearing's mug. I bumped into Bylo and Dalen in the hall on my way back and told them Shearing had confessed to the hit and run. They were very pleased with the news and after a few words, the two of them darted off to reiterate the need for silence around the building.

Both of them had been extremely curious about what was going on. The interview was taking place in one end of the building, and Len and Gerry had taped it off to avoid all outside interference. Unfortunately, not even they were allowed past the tape.

But you could only have held them back for so long. There was an office next door to the interview area, separated by a rather thick wall. It was impossible to hear anything through the wall. The two of them had even gone so far as to try pressing a glass cup up against it. Disgusted with their failure, they kicked around that office trying to think up a way to get in on the action.

Just before giving up all hope, Gerry had spotted a small crack where the wall met the ceiling. Tossing caution to the wind, they pushed the desk up against the wall and climbed on. They found that if you held your head up to the crack just right, you could hear the conversation going on quite clearly indeed. Nobody in the detachment except the senior NCO and the two local dicks knew anything about Shearing, but they had a pretty good idea something big was up when they came in the office and saw Bylo and Dalen scaling the desk with their ears up against the ceiling.

When I walked back into the interview room with the coffee cups in hand, Shearing was crying. It was a bit of a shock for me, seeing this big lug sniffling and pouting as he wrote. *God,* I thought to myself. *What kind of display are we going to see when we throw the Johnson and Bentleys at him?* I put the coffee with the sugar in front of Shearing. It wasn't Mum, but it would have to do.

"Having some trouble?" I asked my good friend Dave. I took another sip. That stuff was so damned hot, I was sure I burned my tongue.

"No," Shearing answered, wiping away tears with the back of his hand before taking a small slurp of his own.

I walked out of the room again for a bathroom break and to grab another pack of smokes while Shearing thought out the rest of his statement. When I returned, Shearing had his head resting in his left hand and his elbow on the table. He briefly reviewed what he wrote, then kept writing. A sip of coffee, review, smoke and write. I sat down in front of him, sipped my coffee, reviewed what I had written down so far, and smoked.

"My stomach is hungry." Shearing shifted in his seat again.

"What?"

"My stomach, can't you hear it growling like that?"

I shook my head. I couldn't hear anything except my heart pounding in my chest. "No, sorry."

"Does my mother know about this?" Shearing wondered quietly.

"No." I looked at my watch: 5:58 p.m. Two hours since the interview started. Shearing took his time and reviewed everything carefully. At times he concentrated so hard I wondered if he was trying to move things in the room with his thoughts. Every now and then, he would look out of the corner of his eye at me. That was a really eerie feeling. Who the hell knows what he might have been thinking.

We stayed silent as Shearing wrote. I jotted down a couple of questions I wanted to ask later on, and spent more time watching Shearing. Watching his breathing. Watching how he swallowed. Listening to him sniffle. I finally looked at my watch again. It had taken him 50 minutes to write out that one page so far. *Jesus.*

"Do you have a tissue?" Shearing asked. He wiped his eyes with the back of his hand before looking up. His nose was out of control.

"Guess what I have in my back pocket," I smiled, pulling out a couple tissues. Shearing took them, blew his nose, then lit another cigarette. "Jesus, kid," I looked at him amazed. "Do you ever smoke!" I popped a cough drop in my mouth, then took the ashtray and emptied it in a garbage bin in the opposite corner of the room. The pleasant swirl of taste in my mouth was like a blast of fresh air.

"Well," Shearing sniffed as I returned to the table, "half of them are yours."

That was a good point. I smiled, and chuckled quietly. Shearing smiled back a bit between sobs, then continued. He had to wipe his eyes clear first.

Ken and I watched Shearing with interest, trying to read what it was behind his dark eyes that had made him kill all of those innocent people. Between the two of us, we believed that the motive for the killings had been sexual. Bylo and Dalen were of the same opinion. RCMP investigators across the country had agreed that sex was a more plausible motive than robbery. If young girls were Shearing's fancy, we all knew that the Johnson girls would have been exactly what he was after.

"How are you getting along there?" I asked after a couple minutes of silence.

"Getting there, I guess. I don't know how detailed you want it."

"It's your statement, not mine. You put down what you think you should put down." I watched him writing. Although he was, in my opinion, a lumbering, big lummox, he was very slow and methodical, dotting all his i's and crossing all his t's. He did, after all, have a grade 12 education. This lad wasn't that stupid.

Shearing ripped the first page off the pad of paper, and numbered it on the top right-hand corner. He also ripped off page two, and numbered it accordingly.

"Well," Shearing stated finally, giving it a once over. "I've described that night anyway, I think."

"Do you want to sign it, or not? It really doesn't matter." At 6:39 p.m., David Shearing signed his name at the bottom of the page. The two of us signed it when he was finished.

"What happens now?" Shearing asked, looking as if he were ready to walk out of the room to freedom.

"We'll have to discuss this." I looked straight at Shearing, who was still sniffling a bit. "Okay, David. You understand everything we've done. I told you when we started that we know a lot about you. We wouldn't be here, especially on a weekend, unless there was a good reason. When we started, we gave you a warning. Anything you say can be used as evidence on everything. I also told you we were investigating the Johnson and Bentley murders, and this is where this all stems from. The warning we gave you still stands. As long as you realize that." Shearing nodded again. He knew he was in a lot of trouble now. "First I want to go over this statement." I read it over slowly, stopping several times to get confirmation on particular words I couldn't understand.

At this point David had just confessed that he had killed someone by running over him. Although it was tragic, the reality was that he would probably get less than two years in the bucket for criminal negligence. His cooperation, writing out his own statement, and tearful remorse would lead some bleeding heart judge to think about giving him two years' probation rather than sending him to gaol. Christ, he could plead guilty to the stolen property charges and this too, and still get squat. Realistically, we were nowhere, other than we had established that he believed we knew a lot about him, and we believed we had established dialogue with him. That would be important later.

"So this is basically it?" I said finally.

"Yes, as I remember it."

"Bet it feels good to get that off your shoulders. How do you feel?"

"Pretty tired," he admitted. He certainly looked the part.

"Have you ever written a statement for police before?"

"No."

"Well, I guess there's a first time for everything, heh?" I chuckled to myself. Cat and mouse. Bring him up, and let him down. Just like fishing, you've got to tease them a bit. I was glad to no uncertain degree I was not the one on the receiving end of these interviews. Admittedly, my life was no straight line either. The bank was foreclosing on my mortgage, I was nearly bankrupt, and saying my marriage was on the rocks was like saying World War II was a bar fight. Suddenly, I was embracing all of those things. I'd have traded none of it to be in Shearing's place. We hadn't even got to the big part yet. "Do you have any questions?"

"I'd like to know what happens next."

"At this point, we have to take that up with the prosecutor."

"Am I going to gaol?"

"I don't know," I lied. *Not for hit and run, buddy boy.* "It could be criminal negligence or hit and run. My job is to collect evidence and take it to the prosecutor. The judge then decides what will happen. Both charges are very serious. I don't know which you'll be charged with. It's not up to us."

"What's going to happen to Doug?"

"Again, that's up to the prosecutor. The passenger doesn't have any control of the gas or brake. You know what happened. You did it, you're the one, in your mind. What happens, happens. All things will work out in the end. It's fate. Do you believe in God, David?"

"No," Shearing answered quietly. *Well, we won't be getting his help on this one.*

"How about your Mum?"

"Not really," his voice cracked. I pushed on.

"She is an honest person," I suggested, "who believes in the principles."

"I believe in the principles," Shearing admitted.

"How do you think this may affect your mother, David?"

"I don't know," he said. "She'll worry."

"But she knows you, Dave. A mother knows. She taught you right from wrong. We are taught responsibility. She knows you understand what you did was wrong. She knows you will take responsibility. That makes you a good person. It's not the people like you we worry about, David. It's the people who don't know they did something wrong, or who don't want to take responsibility for it." I changed the subject as fast as I could. "I did a profile on you, David. Basically you were pretty quiet up until 1980."

"Yes." Shearing couldn't look either one of us in the eye. I was giving him my most intense stare.

"Two things changed your life, David. One was the death of your father." *And you know what the other one is.*

Shearing grunted what sounded like a yes.

"You know, cops go to shrinks for a number of different reasons. Stress, alcoholism ... We're not unlike anyone else. We did a background on you. We know you have fights, we know someone stabbed you in the chin. We know about the guy you threw out the window leaving him without the use of his thumb. We know a lot about you, you know that, and you know what we are here for."

Shearing knew.

"You knew that I had all the details of the hit and run."

"Yeah. Did you talk to Doug?" *Trying to prolong the inevitable, David?*

"I don't tell lies, David."

"Is that the answer?"

"Ah, but David!" I smiled. "Like a lawyer, you should never ask a question you don't know the answer to." Shearing sighed. I offered him another cigarette.

"All right," he reached over eagerly. We both lit up and puffed away. I made a comment about light cigarettes, and Shearing said it was one of his steps toward quitting. At a time like this, I'd have smoked anything I could light. My heart was going 60 miles per hour in second gear, and my whole body was trembling with excitement. I puffed and drank and coughed and smoked, and Shearing did the same across the table from me. Leibel, a non smoker, had been choking and hacking his way through the whole two and a half hours so far. He was probably hoping both of us would have heart attacks.

In fact, I felt like I *was* going to have a heart attack. My chest was pounding and my blood was racing. You can only slide so far on bullshit, I knew. *I've got to jump on this son of a bitch now.* I felt like I was preparing for the race of my life.

David, what do you think about the Johnson and Bentley murders? What do you think of them being killed in your front yard, so to speak?"

"Well, it was pretty bad for the community."

Yeah, and bad for the six people who were murdered too. "Do you know where the car was found?"

"Yeah."

"You know where the truck was found?"

"Yeah."

"You also know where they were killed—" I pressed.

"Bear Creek."

Strike two, Davy! Shearing didn't appear very happy with himself for answering that, and he certainly didn't like the way Ken and I were looking at him once he said it. No one outside of the RCMP had known for sure where the murders had taken place. In any case, we had never made any public mentions of our theories about the murder site. I had suggested from the beginning the families were killed at Bear Creek, but the superintendent hadn't agreed. Instead, he had insisted the murder site was more likely Battle Mountain, where they found the car. *Shove that up your ass, mister superintendent sir!* I thought to myself.

The room was silent. I could feel my heart banging against my ribs. I could hear Shearing's strained breathing. For what felt like an hour, the three of us sat still, looking at each other. Shearing's cigarette burned slowly towards his quivering lips.

"I think I need to speak to a lawyer now," Shearing blurted, breaking the silence.

Instantly I knew were in major trouble. Our case was heading for the big dump unless I could pull it out of the toilet now. Those were the last words that we wanted to hear coming out of David's mouth right now. Get up, pass him the telephone book under lawyer listings, dial the number for him, stand back while he talks to his lawyer, and then listen to what he has to say: *I have just been instructed by my lawyer that I am not, under any circumstances, to speak with you any further. You are advised by my lawyer not to put any further questions to me until he is present. Please place me in the cells until my lawyer arrives...* I had heard it all many times before; that's why there are more murderers on the street than there are in gaol.

Reliable gave me the "I think we're fucked, Mike" look. Remembering that the best defence is offence I said, "David, *I* think you need a lawyer." Leibel almost fell out of his chair! "But I want you to listen to me for a minute. You don't need to talk. You just need to listen to me." I sounded pretty confident, but really I was terrified. We had gotten halfway there, only to hear the "L" word! The look of uncertainty on David's face gave me the opportunity I needed. It was time to diffuse this explosive situation we were in. It was definitely time to slow this machinery down. "But first I'm going to get some coffee. You guys want another mug?"

Yes, all around. *Good, sweat a little you big lummox!*

"I'll be right back." I got up, gathered the empty coffee cups and headed out the door, having a sweat of my own. *All right old boy, now you've got a major situation here.* I needed a couple minutes to reflect. Technically, Shearing had suggested that he should see a lawyer. But he hadn't said, "I want a lawyer right now." He could get up and leave if he wanted to, but he didn't get up and leave, so he was still in the ballpark. Now, how were we going to get Shearing to go lawyerless for another couple of hours?

I stood at the coffee maker, pouring the coffee carefully. I knew I had a problem. If Shearing called in the hounds now, we'd be handcuffed to a conventional interview before I got a confession; I didn't want conventional. I had never been a big fan of conformity, as had been shown throughout this investigation, not to mention my career.

All right. The murder had already happened and lawyer or no lawyer, Shearing was going to have to admit it to himself. He'd had a year and a half to try and forget it, and if he was as good a liar as I thought he could be, he might have tricked himself into believing it didn't really happen. *C'mon Mike! Think!* The minutes ticked past on the clock above me. *That's it!*

I walked back to the room with the cups in hand. Neither Leibel nor Shearing were there. It was no cause for alarm. We'd been at it for several hours, and we'd probably be at it for several more hours if that's what it took. It would be good for them to stretch their legs a bit. At eleven minutes after seven, the two of them walked back in.

"Just had to check the fluids," Leibel explained. When the two were seated again, I leaned across the table towards Shearing. He was visibly upset, shaking uncontrollably and sniffing a runny nose.

"David," I began, laying down my hand. A pair of fives doesn't do well at a time like this. "Stupid things happen sometimes. We all do stupid things. It was stupid, David, but I don't know what triggered you to do it. I know it happened. I just don't know why." I paused for effect. "You do need a lawyer, David. There's no question about it, you need one. But I know what happened, and so do you. The difference is, you know all the details and I don't."

David's lower lip started to quiver slightly, and his eyes narrowed. Defiantly, he avoided eye contact. He tucked his chin into his chest, and crossed his arms and legs. The brim of his cowboy hat hid his expression. I had to strike at the heart of his emotions.

"If you want to cry, go ahead. I want to cry too. It's a delicate subject, David. We have to do it too sometimes. We don't like it any better than you do." Shearing was still looking away, so I couldn't see his face, but his shoulders were heaving. His breaths were short, hesitant. I offered him another tissue, which he accepted so eagerly I thought he was going to take my hand with it. Shearing wiped his nose with the tissue, then honked in it forcibly.

"You know that we know. It's changed you, David. You've been boozing it pretty heavy since then. I know you've been trying to put it in the back of your mind."

Shearing was coming apart. Emotionally, it must have just hit home that he'd lied himself into believing he hadn't done anything wrong. His body had been shaking for so long, he must have been exhausted. David William Shearing had been on the receiving end of almost three hours of interrogation, and had pretty much confessed to the deaths of seven people in his own mind by his emotional behaviour. That was not what one might call a good day out.

"I know that you want to tell us about it. I know that you do. You just don't know how to right now, and I understand. You don't understand why you did it, and I know you think about it." David was not a pleasant sight. Head down, hidden behind his white straw cowboy hat, Shearing was not a happy boy.

"Don't make me involve your mother." *Let's hit on this Mum thing again.* "I don't want to go and search her place, or your brother's place. I know what happened, and I know it was something that got right out of hand." He was now crying so loudly I had to raise my voice slightly. He obviously wasn't even trying to contain it anymore. Shearing had fought a long emotional battle, carrying around the deaths of the Carter boy and the Johnson and Bentley families for years. The load of his crimes sat heavily upon his shoulders, and now it was time for him to answer for them. *Don't even give him a chance to think "lawyer" again.*

"I know you're scared, David. There's a lot of pressure on you about this. Most of that pressure is from yourself. You don't have to talk to us, but you want to tell me. You already told me about Doug Carter. You wrote it down, and we discussed it." I don't think Shearing was even listening. His hand covered his mouth, and his hat covered his eyes.

I'd seen a lot of grown men cry. I knew what it took to make a man cry, but it wasn't what I said that brought a guy to a boil. It was what he was thinking in his head. The guilt that had been trailing him was slowly catching up; I just had to remind him of it. Unlike what many believe, a man is more vulnerable to himself than to others. Others can be ignored. Others go away. Even I'd go away eventually. But after I walked around that corner, he would still have to answer to himself. A man has to look in the mirror every now and then and take stock. The good decisions are always forgotten but the bad ones never disappear. As these build up, the male's self-defence mechanism is to lie himself into a feeling of innocence. Sometimes it works.

Other times it doesn't. Whether Shearing was actually upset about the deaths, or just the fact that he'd been caught was something I still hadn't decided. It was hard to tell the difference. Sometimes, it took being caught for someone to assess his actions and feel guilty or upset. When someone commits a crime, the first instinct is to be nervous: *Am I going to get caught? Did someone see me do it? Who can I trust?* Sometimes, those moments of paranoia are enough to launch people into paroxysms of guilt. Those who can endure this stage are able to deflect their guilt and carry on with confidence.

David Shearing was depressed. He had been on a roller coaster since the beginning of the interview. He hadn't eaten since breakfast, and he had been shaking and crying and sniffling for hours. This was a good time for an interviewer to drive his points home. When a man is broken mentally, you have him in your palm. From that point on, it's a matter of squeezing him just right.

"You knew we'd come for you, didn't you David?" I looked at him from across the table. *Let it all out, David. Go ahead and cry like a baby, then start writing.*

"Yeah." *Strike three!*

"Every time you saw a police car, you wondered when we were coming." Shearing managed to nod between sobs. "It isn't easy David. You can't just shut your eyes and hope we'll go away. We won't. We've been going through this for the past 15 months, and you have been going through it the past 15 months too.

"I know you aren't that kind of person, David. That's why you have to explain it. We've got to do this. I don't like it, but we've got to. When I told you we were from Kamloops, you knew why we were here, didn't you?" Shearing nodded again, his face hidden by the cowboy hat. "There are two ways to do this, David. You could write it out, or we could tape it. You're shaking, though, David. You're upset. I don't think you can write it. I might be able to write it, or we could tape it." Of course, I was shaking too, and I wasn't really sure if I could actually write it either.

"I know you want to help us, David. I know you want to tell us what happened."

David was silent. He wasn't weeping anymore. He wasn't sniffling. There was an uncomfortable silence in the room. I could hear Leibel writing down something, and I glanced over to read it: the word "Silence". I knew I had to keep Shearing talking, even if it was only one-word answers. You let a guy relax for too long and he has some time to assess his situation and think. A well-prepared, energetic, determined individual is very difficult to break down. Good remedies for that are time, isolation, hunger, thirst, and confusion, but none of those were acceptable to the courts. When you had an individual broken down, giving him the time to pick himself up off the ground simply makes your task harder. I only had a couple of ways to get him down where he was, and both of those had long ago expired. I couldn't keep bringing up Mum and brother; they would not have the desired psychological effect.

"I know you're scared, David, and I know that you're worried about us. You're scared because of what you've done."

"I could fucking shoot myself!" His voice was clogged with depression. Shearing looked up, his eyes glowing with anger. "Just go get me your fucking gun and leave me alone with it for a few minutes. I'll take care of everything."

"We don't want you to do that," I said soothingly. I wasn't sure how true it was but— "Your life is still important, regardless of what you did." It's very frustrating to realize there's nobody to blame but yourself. Suicides are often a result of this. Some people say suicide is unreasonable and cowardly, that it's the easy way out. What they don't consider is that human nature automatically seeks an easier way. That is what brought the world remote controls for the TV and automatic garage door openers. Right now, Shearing seemed quite content being depressed. He was mentally and physically exhausted. David hadn't eaten in several hours, and he had been battered with reminders of the deaths of his father, the Carter boy, and the three generations of the Johnson/Bentley families. It was time to move on, and I hoped that if I could build up enough forward momentum, Shearing would just follow along, with too little energy to resist.

"Look, we all make mistakes, and life is quite indifferent about them. The world isn't going to crash to a halt because David Shearing made a mistake. If I had to start all over again every time I made a mistake, I'm not sure where I'd be. Probably still learning to walk. Mistakes are what make us learn." *Thankfully,* I thought to myself, *others are quite content sitting back and learning from another's example. All we need is a bunch of David Shearings running around.* "Do you want to do this 'Question and Answer' style, or would you rather just do this by yourself?" I needed that written confession in his own words in the worst way.

"I don't know," Shearing sniffed.

"David, when did you first see the Johnson and Bentley family?" No answer so I tried again. "Where did you first see them?"

"Shit! What fucking life?" Shearing spat his words all over the table, and me.

"You have a life, David."

"Not anymore I don't." He looked me in the eyes. I returned his glare. His guilt was so evident. The tension in the room was overwhelming. Ken and I were both excited because we knew he was going to confess — we could feel it in our guts. Both of us were shaking from the flood of adrenaline. Shearing was shaking too, feeling pathetic. Hopeless. Worthless. He was reaching for someone to feel sorry for him.

Neither Ken nor I was offering that satisfaction, and that appeared to frustrate Shearing greatly.

"Your life is important, Dave. Important to you and your family. Don't think for one minute that it isn't. We're going to go through this together, Dave. I told you I was going to be fair, and I don't lie." I reached across the table, offering my good friend my hand. Dave hesitated for a minute, then pumped it vigorously. His grip was tight. Once again, I squeezed evenly, but a little tighter. *It's over for you now, boy.*

"All right. Will you tell me about it now?"

"I don't know."

"You know it's gonna come out. I know it. I can't tell you to do anything. It's your decision, but we both know you have to tell me." Shearing was going to tell us. Both Ken and I knew it in our minds, and Shearing probably knew it too. He was folding. If we were really lucky, he might even confess without bringing up the L-word again. "Did you ever think about turning yourself over to police?"

"No."

"Why not?"

"Don't know."

"What's done is done, David. You can't bring back six lives, no matter what. I know you're an honest person. I know you've been drinking. It's not easy to forget something like that. You won't forget." *It's not yours to forget, David,* I wanted to say but didn't. The families of the victims didn't have that luxury, so why should he? "Sometimes people do things, and they don't know why. Crimes of passion, or things that just get out of hand. You can't keep hiding from this, David. It's far too late for that now. Do you think you need help?"

"Yeah," was the quick, honest reply.

"Do you know what made you do it, Dave?"

"No."

"Can you remember it very well?"

"Yeah."

Keep going! Get the forward momentum— "You poor bugger," I sighed. "Let's do it, Dave. It's tough for you, and it's tough for me. Where did you first see the Johnson and Bentley family?"

"Bear Creek."

Finally! Leibel and I exhaled, shaking with excitement. Seven days a week, sixteen hours a day, eating, breathing, sleeping the Johnson and

Bentley murders. We were well on our way to accomplishing our primary objective. My blood was pumping, my heart pounding. The sudden relief of the situation was staggering.

"Do you remember what day it was when you first approached them?" Silence. There was a lot of thinking going on behind that hat. "Daytime? Nighttime?"

"Oh, God!" Dave ducked behind a wall of tears. He'd as good as confessed already. It was time to polish the cannonball.

"It's difficult for us, Dave. Will you help us out? You know you're going to tell us, and I know you will too. I know it's hard for you, trying to decide how you're going to tell us."

"It isn't easy," Shearing agreed, sobbing pathetically.

"There is no easy way," Leibel assured. "You saw them. What time of the day was it David?"

"I gotta think for a while." Dave immersed himself in thought, then quickly surfaced with curiosity. "What happens if I tell you?"

"Well," I started matter of factly, "you will be charged with murder. You'll be in custody, and we would obviously have to have you checked out by a psychiatrist to see why you did it."

Shearing nodded.

"Where is the gun, David?"

"At the ranch."

"Is it the pump?" I remembered the .22 Ron German mentioned.

"Yes."

I was so excited, I was talking faster and Leibel was struggling to keep up. "And the boat and motor?" *Push push push...*

"At the ranch."

"Where on the ranch, David?"

"I can draw you a map." I slid him the pad of paper and a pen. Dave wiped his eyes again before starting. He drew a rough map of the area, explaining the details. As soon as he'd drawn that map, he had as good as confessed, though getting it accepted in court as evidence was an entirely different matter.

"Is the boat under anything, or concealed?" Leibel wondered.

"Yes, it's under some bushes."

"Where's the equipment that came with the boat? The gas tank, and life jackets?"

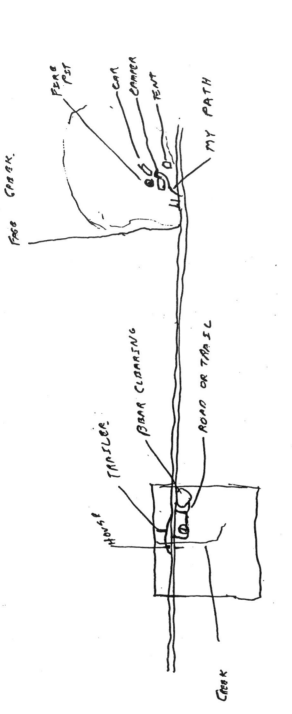

Map drawn by Shearing during the interview indicating where he had left some of the victims' possessions.

"Underneath it." When he was finished drawing, he signed the bottom.

At that point, I knew it was going to be a long haul and decided to leave the room for a jug of coffee.

We'd done it, I realized, as I closed the door behind me. I had Shearing in the palm of my hand. We were a breath away from getting some closure on a year and a half of work. We'd spent thousands of man hours, hundreds of thousands of dollars searching for him. I'd taxed every man and woman to their limit. We had ruthlessly pursued every tip, looked under every filthy rock and between every tree. I'd been down on my knees, crawling about the bush looking for that one piece of evidence. Finally, it had appeared. The elusive truck and camper we'd searched for across the country popped up right under my damned nose! Helicopters had passed the area several times, one with an infra red camera that ran out of film one hundred feet from the location of the truck. Hundreds of thousands of dollars up in smoke—

That wasn't really true. Having organized such a determined search was a victory in itself. The fact that it turned up nothing conclusive was its greatest success. The truck hadn't gone out east after all. Instead it had been quite happily rusting away on the mountain for over a year. Simply processing almost 13,000 tips and organizing 30 filing cabinets' worth of paper work was a success, proving to the rest of the country that we could do it. Choreographing the search through detachments all over the country, we had proved a point. Regardless of the media attention that had been the backdrop of the investigation from the start, the RCMP proved it was an institution determined to serve and protect the citizens of Canada.

I went back to the room, moving around the dividers into the interview area. Leibel was supervising Shearing, who appeared to be drawing another map.

"All right," Shearing began, "this is where they were."

"Where did you come in? The main gate?" Ken asked.

"No, the fence over here. I came to the campsite through these bushes here." He pointed.

"Who do you shoot first?" I inquired.

"I don't remember," Shearing admitted.

"These four over here?" I asked, pointing. Shearing nodded. There were four circles around the fire and two slightly right, in the tent. He had the basic layout of the campsite. The fire, the tent, and the truck were

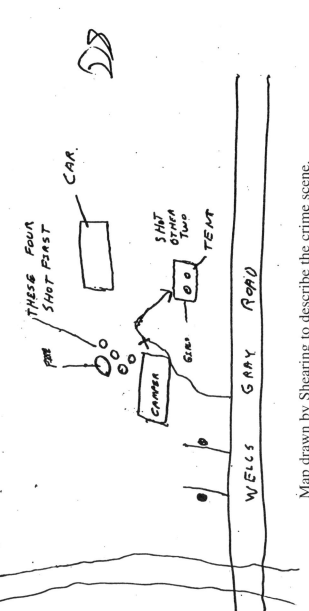

Map drawn by Shearing to describe the crime scene.

labelled. As indicated on the map, Shearing approached from behind the truck, and fired from a position between it and the tent. The tent was slightly right of the truck-camper combination. "Then I shot the two in the tent." He marked it down on the map, and initialled it "DS".

"What then?"

"I put them in the car. The adults I put in the back seat. The two girls I put in the trunk."

"Then?"

"I drove the car down to the clearing, and parked it there. I then went back and got the truck, and parked it there too."

"When does the bullet hole in the truck show up?"

"What?"

"The bullet hole in the passenger-side door. It wasn't done with a .22."

"It wasn't?"

It was my turn to be confused. Ballistics insisted the hole they found in the door was made by something slightly larger than a .22.

"How many guns did you have?"

"Just the one."

"This was at nighttime, that you drove the vehicles?"

"Yeah, well, yes."

"You took the truck to the bare clearing?"

"Yeah, down here," Shearing pointed to it, but ran out of page. "Do you want another map?" I nodded, and Dave quickly started working on another map. While he worked on it, I could feel my stomach churning. It had been quite some time since we'd eaten too.

"Do you feel like having something to eat?"

"I don't know," Shearing answered, still drawing. He continued as if I hadn't said anything. When this kid was thinking, there wasn't anything that could take his mind off it. I imagined that this same concentration had swallowed David up whole as he planned the murders. Lurking only a few feet from the campsite, his shadow was a fountain of darkness cascading over the flickering light of the camp fire. As the family of shadows surrounded him, their dark contours dancing around his silhouette, the seventh shadow stayed still, busily planning an execution, to the tenth degree of perfection. "I parked the vehicles here."

"How far is it between here and here?"

"Three or four hundred feet."

"How long did you leave the vehicles there?"

"I left them there, I think it was the next day I came down and started sorting through the tools and stuff. I wanted to keep the key for the camper, I don't know why. I'm not sure if it was that day, or another day I drove the car up to Battle Mountain—"

"Okay," I stopped him for a minute. Step by step. Most important, I had to keep strict control. "What tools did you keep Dave?"

"A plastic sort of tray full of wrenches and stuff."

"Like what?"

"Well, wrenches and pliers. A bunch of tools."

"Where are these now?"

"Probably some might be in my shed by my house."

"What colour was this plastic tray?"

"A bright colour. Orange I think." I signed the third map, and Shearing initialed it "DS".

"What else was in there?"

Shearing thought for a moment, jotting down a few items. Included in this list was the mention of a compass. In brackets, he added that it was in the cabin there in Tumbler Ridge. He remembered three other items, but didn't remember the rest. I made a mental note to ensure German was given full particulars in order to secure a flawless search warrant to look for this compass. I knew full well that if the statement was tossed out of court on a technicality, we would have to rely on corroborative evidence to support our efforts towards a conviction on six murder counts.

"What else do you have at your house, or at the ranch?"

"The camera."

"Where is it?"

"The house."

"What about the film?" Leibel asked.

"I tossed it away."

"Where did you throw it?"

"In the camper, I think."

"What else is there?" I persisted. The more information he gave, the better it would look in court. *Polish that cannonball,* I thought as I scribbled down everything I could.

"I don't remember."

"Fishing equipment?"

"Didn't keep it."

"Spare tire?" Shearing thought back for a moment.

"Now what the hell did I do with that? It may still be down by the boat."

"Anything else you can think of?"

"Not really," Shearing said. Now I could hear Dave's stomach rumbling from across the table. I wondered briefly if Shearing just wanted to get it over with. At this point, Shearing appeared a bit more relaxed. He had faced the major hurdle of admission finally, and it was as though he was imagining himself at the scene, reliving the experience. There was no emotion shown when he was thinking, as if the same methodical smoothness that had taken over him then was again interfering with any feelings of compassion a normal human would have. I don't think that a gun shot beside his ear would have deterred him from his train of thought.

"Do you want to do us a map of Battle Mountain, then Trophy Mountain, where the vehicles ended up?" Shearing nodded, and started to draw the fourth map. I took that time to fill his mug with coffee. Leibel dropped two sugar cubes in the cup for him as I lit another cigarette.

"All right," I began again, having sipped away some of my coffee. "Insofar as the car is concerned, what did you do?"

"I stopped and walked over to the area I wanted it, to see if I could get it through there. I decided it would make it and went back to drive it in there."

"What else did you do?"

"I had to move some logs, and a couple rocks."

"Did you have anything when you went in there?"

"A flashlight."

"How about an ax?"

"I might have, but I don't think so."

"Did you chop anything? Any trees?" *Any bodies?*

"I don't remember."

We were sure an ax had been used to cut down a small tree prior to setting the car and victims afire. In the back of my mind, I was also wondering if we were dealing with some kind of macabre ax murderer here.

"Then what?"

"I drove it in."

"Did you get stuck?"

"Yeah, on some logs."

"Then?"

"I poured some gas inside the car, and in the trunk."

I don't think it ever even dawned on him that by lighting that fire he'd almost extinguished a whole family's existence. Those two girls in the trunk, and the decaying bodies of their parents in the back, and here he was explaining it to me like a shopping trip.

"Did it explode when you lit it?"

"You mean right away?"

I nodded.

"Well, it just went *womph.*"

"What did you do with the keys?" I recalled they had been left in the lock on the trunk.

"Jesus, I don't know."

"Did you leave any doors open?" *Driver side,* I thought to myself.

"Yeah, I think I left the driver-side door open."

"Okay, so you're there. You get stuck and get out of the car. You open the trunk and where was the gas?"

"I don't know."

"Where did you put it first?"

"In the front."

"How did you light it up?"

"A piece of paper, or birch bark."

"It would've been pretty dark at that time, heh?"

"Yeah," Shearing nodded as I motioned for him to initial the map. He did straight away— "DS".

"After you lit the car on fire, where did you go?"

Shearing took the map and marked where he stood with an X slightly to the right, towards where the road would be.

"Then what happened?"

"I watched it burn for a while, then headed back." *What the hell were you thinking, you sick bastard, while the fire was swallowing up their bodies? Standing there, in the glow of the fire, listening to the crackle of the inferno...*

"All right. How about Trophy Mountain. Do you want to mark down what you did with the truck and camper?"

Shearing nodded again, and started to work on yet another map. It was labelled #5 for evidence purposes. A couple days after torching the car, he drove the truck and camper unit up Trophy Mountain road (Route 80). After ducking it into the bushes and getting stuck again, he set it afire using a full jerry can of fuel. He watched it burn with idle curiosity, then turned away and proceeded home. I had him draw the interior of the cab, including the front of the truck, the dash, steering wheel, and behind the seat.

"Were you drinking when you did this?"

"No."

"What about the camper? What do you remember about the camper?"

Shearing drew it on another sheet of paper. The first thing he drew in the camper was the *bed!* It was purely subconscious on his part, but my alarms went off immediately. Shearing had just proven to me that he had spent more time in that camper than he was letting on. I didn't press on that. We could explore that later. Totally unaware of what he'd done, Shearing continued to draw the location of the books, closet, table, sink, clothing, and food.

"There was a bunch of stuff on the table," Shearing added. I asked him to pencil it in respectively.

"Other than the compass you mentioned earlier, is there anything else that you took from the camper to Tumbler Ridge?"

"There's the tools in my truck."

"No, in Tumbler Ridge."

"That's what I meant. Do you mean my cabin?" I nodded. "No."

"Where is the gun?"

"In the rack at my house, in the front room."

"What kind of gun is it?" Leibel asked from behind his rapidly filling pad of paper.

"An old .22 pump action."

Now that we had everything we needed, the tension among us all began to ease a bit. Leibel and I could sit a bit more comfortably knowing that Shearing had supplied enough information to corroborate certain circumstantial pieces of evidence and present them in court. We would obtain legal expertise in the preparation of search warrants for Tumbler Ridge and the Wells Gray Park. Even if his verbal statements were tossed out of court, we were certain there was sufficient evidence at the Ridge and at his residence to tie him into the murders. The personal belongings of the children and the family would certainly put him at the scene. The crime lab would be able to link the weapon to David's residence and to the murder scene. Now all we had to do was ensure we could somehow prove he pulled the trigger on those six people in the event his verbal statement was thrown out of court.

"Now, you can either write out the statement like you did the other one, or you can talk and I'll write everything down."

"All right, sure." I checked my watch; it was about 9:25 p.m. We'd been at it for over five hours. Leibel had a pretty heavy case of writer's cramp. I grabbed the pen and paper.

"Don't go too fast," I asked, and put the appropriate header on the page. Carefully, Shearing outlined the entire sequence from beginning to end.

He'd spotted the truck and camper on his way home from work one day in August. That evening, he decided to take a short walk through the bush, and found himself heading for the campsite he'd seen earlier that day. Moving around in the bush to a spot where he could look down on the camper, Shearing watched with idle curiosity. While crouched, he thought one of the campers had seen him, so he proceeded back across the field and hid out in some available shrubs. He waited there for a couple of minutes to make sure nobody was following him, then proceeded home.

The next night, he went back with the .22. He followed the same path, only this time he walked straight out into the light of the fire and started shooting. When the four people by the campfire were down, he proceeded to the tent, crouched, and shot the two girls. He quickly loaded the bodies into the car, segregating the two groups. The adults were put in the front and the two girls in the trunk. Shearing collected everything that was lying around the campsite and stuffed it in the camper. It wasn't long before the car and the truck and camper were parked a couple hundred feet from one another in the clearing. The next day, after rummaging through the effects, he took the car up Battle Mountain and torched it. A couple days later, he returned for the truck. Moving it up Trophy Mountain and veering off the road, he got stuck, so he torched the truck in place.

"Is there anything else you want to add?"

"Well, there are a couple other details, but they are pretty much covered in the maps."

That's it? That's all there is? — "I stalked them a couple of nights, went down, shot the six people, loaded the bodies, stole some property, drove the vehicles out into the night and torched them and the bodies. The end." *Bullshit! There's no way this is the end of the bloody story. This guy is far from that callous. The end of his story is totally unbelievable. His descriptions of the events as they unfolded defy common sense.*

"Is that all?"

"Well, now I know I done wrong." *Now? Jesus!*

I marked down the time — 2145 (9:45 p.m.) — and then stretched, leaning way back in my chair with my arms stretched above me. Leibel stood and shook out his legs. Shearing stayed idle. It had been almost six hours since we had begun the interview.

We had almost everything we needed, but we still had to be careful. Both Leibel and I were so hungry we would have eaten mud if there'd been any in the room. We were eager to move on. However, our eagerness could be the difference between landing the bastard in gaol and having him set free on a technicality. The two of us had to remember that it was important now more than ever to proceed with caution. All we needed was to see Shearing walk free because of some detail we'd overlooked in haste. Reviewing the statement orally, Shearing stumbled over my chicken scratches. I then read it over again out loud, line by line, using a sheet of paper to mark my spot. Leibel took this time to jot down some questions of his own, and once we were finished reviewing the statement, he handed his queries to me.

"David," I began, reading the paper. "Did you have any blood on your clothing?"

"No, just on my hands." I jotted that down, a bit suspicious.

"Another thing: There's some pretty big distances here, for walking. I'm wondering if you had any help."

"Nope," Shearing answered, almost proudly. "It was just me."

Boy, good for you David! I read further down the page. "The one other thing that bothers me here, David, is that hole in the door. It was bigger than a .22. What type of .22 shells did you use?"

"Long rifle. That was all I used, was the .22."

Satisfied, I put my pen down and stretched again, leaning way back in my chair. There were a few issues that had risen in my mind that we weren't going to address today. The most prominent was simple arithmetic. We'd only found six shell casings at the campsite. If Shearing had, as he suggested, hit the door with one round and required two bullets for one of the victims, then we were two shell casings short. Something else happened that night, and I was pretty sure what it was.

"Well, David. It's been quite a day."

"Yes it has," David William Shearing agreed, sighing deeply. He'd just talked his life away.

When we were done with Shearing, Leibel took him to cells and I went out to find Ron German. He was still kicking around the detachment, writing notes and taking Max for walks. It was imperative at that point that everything regarding the arrest be accurately recorded in his notes, because we knew that eventually someone was going to be looking through them to find a way to get Shearing released. I met Ron in the hallway. He could tell by my grin that we'd got our man.

"How'd it go, Mike?" he asked me right away.

"Well, not the toughest interview I've ever seen, but damn I'm glad it's over." We shook hands, smiling away. It was a huge load off both of our shoulders. "Look, do you think you could stay in cells here with him tonight?"

"Sure," Ron said quickly. He was always eager to help, no matter what he was asked to do.

"All right, that's one thing taken care of." I also had to arrange transportation for our trip to Clearwater in the morning for the re-enactment. I headed for a phone to set up our trip, and Ron headed for the cells.

I made one quick call before I got down to business. My mother was not unlike any other mother when it came to worrying about her son. Although I was now 42 years old, I was still her "baby" and she worried about me. Reading the newspapers, and watching TV made her anxious about my health. She was forever telling me to be careful in my job, and asking, "How can you stand to deal with all of those terribly horrible thugs and murderers?" Her birthday was very special to me, because she was a very special mom. At the last minute, I'd had to cancel my plans to be at her birthday celebration so that I could come to Dawson. By now it was well after 11 p.m., but I knew she'd still be up watching the news.

"Hey mom, happy birthday." She was so happy to hear from me. "Sorry for phoning so late, but I've been busy up in Dawson Creek for the past couple of days. Just wanted to call and let you know that I hadn't forgotten you on your special day." We chit chatted briefly, and I told her I would be over to see her on Gabriola Island the following weekend, I hoped. "By the way, Mom, I have a very special present for you, but you won't get it until 6 p.m. on Monday night."

"Why 6 p.m.?" She asked.

"Well, watch the news on BCTV at 6 p.m., Mom, and you will understand."

"Did you catch him?"

"Six p.m., Mom. Watch it." We said our long goodbyes, then I called Kamloops to talk to Vic Edwards who was second in charge of our headquarters. I knew he would be expecting our call at any hour of the night. I also knew he would get the message of our success to the superintendent and would put out any fires the boss might have lit as a result of my hurried departure from Kamloops the day before. The news was well received. At that point, I didn't give a rat's ass if I was in trouble or not. We'd done the job we had set out to do and I was confident we could tidy up the rest of the investigation the next day.

The third call I made was to our regional Crown Counsel and head prosecutor in Kamloops, Bob Hunter, one of the best in the business. I filled him in on the day's events, and received further legal instructions on how to wrap the case up. Hunter was delighted with the news. He said he would be in his office on Sunday evening to prepare the information charging David with six counts of second degree murder. Hunter also told me that while I was getting "warm," I still needed a hell of a lot more evidence than I had to support the first degree murder charges I had in mind. We needed to prove it was premeditated, planned and deliberate. It all came down to whether or not we could show David had in fact observed the family, left, and then come back again. Proving premeditation in a case where the accused doesn't know the victims is almost impossible, but you can bet I was determined to try. I would also try to find evidence of the sexual assault I felt sure had taken place. This kid was going to do 25 years to life, period!

Back at the cells, Ron German was helping David Shearing cope with the aftermath of his confession:

I found Ken Leibel and Shearing sitting in the female cell. All the cells were the same, but they were marked so that you could keep everyone separate if you had a whole cluster of people in at one time. I went into the cell and quickly shook hands with Shearing. He looked like he'd just climbed a mountain, but I think he was relieved to see me. I wasn't too sure if he knew I was going to be staying with him that night. Leibel searched him for drugs or weapons, while I proceeded to fill out the C-13 prisoner record.

Once I had that finished, I headed off to get some blankets and a towel for Shearing. With everything I figured he'd need for the night, I returned to the cell and left the blankets on the bottom bunk. He was washing his hands, so I draped the towel over his shoulder.

"Thanks Ron," he said to me quietly.

"Hey, no problem," I said, patting him on the back. "If you need anything else, just let me know."

"Okay, thanks."

There was a chair just across the hall, so I slid it over to Shearing's cell and sat down. It didn't take him long to finish washing himself, so once he returned to his cell I locked the gate. Soon he was crawling into the small bunk.

"How long you going to be staying in Dawson, Ron?" he asked me once he was comfortable.

"Until tomorrow," I said. "We just want to make sure you've got someone here if you need anything."

"Well, I really appreciate it. I guess there'll be someone with me for a while."

"Probably." He was quiet for a few minutes. I could only guess what he was thinking. I spent a lot of time looking in at him, wondering what was going on in his mind. What did he remember about that night? What did he think about sleeping in a prison bed for the rest of his life?

"How long are your transfers for?"

"Pardon?"

"Well, how long are you going to be in Tumbler?"

"About two years. Generally in a place like Tumbler you serve two years. After that you can pretty much pick where you want to go. It costs a lot of money to transfer members. Let's say I found a place I liked, they'd probably let me stay there as long as I wanted, depending on where it was."

"Do you like it in Tumbler?"

"It's all right there," I admitted slowly. "But I couldn't see myself staying up there more than two years."

"I liked it up there, a lot," Shearing stated, rolling over on his back. "But I guess I'm going to be seeing the inside of these for a while." His voice was starting to strain. "Maybe even a padded one."

"You think so?"

He didn't answer for a couple seconds. "I guess I've got to go into a 30-day psych remand."

"Yeah," I nodded, "they do that for all cases like this." I really didn't know a lot about that, but it stood to reason. Just looking at the circumstances of the case, it was clear that Shearing was a bit messed up. Of course, just looking at him, I wouldn't have known he was victim of very dangerous psychological problems.

"I guess I'm going to have to look at black blotches and tell 'em what I see."

"Yeah. It's a tough job to figure out what's in the mind. Really though, maybe it'll be good for you to go in there and have someone talk to you about what's in your mind. Maybe it'll help you understand yourself a bit more."

"Maybe," he allowed. "What's the chance I could get some of my clothes from the cabin?"

"I'm sure I could make some arrangements get some of your stuff."

"There's a couple of kit bags in there under the bed and stuff. Those belong to Doug and Willie, but the rest of the stuff is mine."

"All right," I was writing everything down, but I made a special note to myself to arrange to go get Shearing's things the next day.

"Could I have a cigarette?"

"Sure," I said. He had some in his cell, but didn't have a lighter. I lit his cigarette for him, and he sort of stood by the cell wall between us.

"I guess being a cop is pretty hard."

"You could say that. A lot of people don't understand how hard it is, without actually following us around and watching what we go through. I guess after a while you get used to it, and it almost seems normal."

"How long have you been a cop?" Shearing sat down again on the bottom bunk.

"About seven years," I said after doing some quick arithmetic. "I was in Powell River before I was transferred over to Tumbler. That's actually where I met Mike Eastham." His head was drooped over, and he wiped his eyes but I couldn't see any tears from where I was sitting.

"I've got to stop thinking about this."

"I bet you've got a lot on your mind. Do you want a tissue or something like that?"

"No, I'm all right." He paused. "I bet this will keep the papers happy for a while."

"Yup, so long as they've got their story and make money, they'll be happy."

"Will my family be notified before it gets out in the papers?"

"Well, it will be a couple days before the papers get any word of it. I'm sure you can tell your family on your own. You can probably make any arrangements you want." He sighed deeply. I stood for a minute to stretch my legs, and headed over to see if I could turn the lights off. I couldn't. I was also disappointed that I couldn't turn the heat down a bit. When I returned, Shearing was still sitting on his bunk.

"Do you fish at all?"

"What?"

"Fishing? We talked a bit about hunting before; I was just wondering if you fish."

"Well, not too much. I used to when I had more time."

"There's some good rivers near Tumbler for fly fishing," David was fighting off tears. "I used to fish all the time in Clearwater too. I loved fishing." He wiped his eyes clear again, sniffling. "Shit." David laid down on his back, hiding his face from me. "I guess I won't be as hated as Olson is. I know a lot of people wanted to kill him."

"He's a different kind of person than you, Dave."

"Yeah, but I bet there's people out there who want to kill me too." He was probably right, but I skipped over that topic. He was depressed enough.

"Isn't Olson out east now?" I asked.

"I think so. They gave him his own trailer and stuff like that. I guess they're not used to having someone like that in cells. I sure hope the cells in Kamloops are better than this."

"Actually," I replied. "I think they're just like this." Shearing didn't like that at all. He pouted a little bit more, stood up and moved over towards me again.

"I'm going on my first plane trip tomorrow, down to Kamloops on the police plane. You ever been on it?"

"Yeah, a couple times. It's a nice aircraft."

"What's going to happen to me when I go to court?" he asked, this time looking straight at me.

"You mean security wise?" He nodded, sitting back on the bunk. He was really uncomfortable in there, and alternated standing and sitting every couple minutes. "Well, I'm not too sure about that, Dave. There will probably be extra security around the court house to make certain you don't get hurt."

"Will it be open to the public?"

"That's up to the judge, but I'm pretty sure it will be."

"This is going to be tough on my family," he said softly, closing his eyes. "I'm not sure how I'm going to tell them."

"Well, you tell them that you did something very wrong, and you've taken responsibility for your actions. You confessed and cooperated because you understand what you did was really bad."

"I wish it were that easy," Dave thought out loud. I was glad I wasn't in his position. "What's going to happen to that moose we saw on the highway?" Obviously he was trying to keep his mind off it as much as he could. He had a long road ahead of him.

"Well, if the department of health determines the meat itself is salvageable, and still good, it gets sent to the old folks home."

"That's good that they do that." Dave sighed again, crawling under the covers this time.

I looked at my watch. It was 2:35 a.m. Jesus, had we really been talking for three hours already? "Did you know what was going on when I picked you up, David?"

He rolled over in his bunk and looked at me. "No, I didn't have a clue."

Exhausted, his breathing settled to a deep, throaty whisper. In minutes, he was asleep.

The next morning, Ron got David Shearing ready for the flight to Clearwater, where he would re-enact the murders for us. Len Bylo and Gerry Dalen came by to give Shearing his secondary interview. They had general conversation with Ron about the previous evening, but he didn't have any real exciting news to tell them. Dave hadn't tried escaping, or hanging himself, and had all in all been a good boy.

About an hour later, once Gerry and Len had completed their session with Shearing, Ron escorted him to an unmarked PC for his ride to the airport. Ken Leibel and I were going up in one vehicle, and Len and Gerry were going to be driving with Shearing. Before Shearing crouched into the car, he turned and looked at Ron.

"Thanks Ron," he said, making a Herculean effort not to cry. "Thanks for staying with me last night." They shook hands quickly, and he crawled into the back seat of the PC.

"Bye David. Good luck." Gerry closed the door and after a few words turned and climbed in the driver's side.

Soon our little procession was moving through the streets towards the local airport. We met up with the others at the airport, after stopping by a McDonalds to pick up breakfast. There was a King Air aircraft waiting for us.

I greeted David as warmly as I could. He still looked a bit tired to me, although I could see by his inability to stand still that his coffee buzz was starting. There wasn't a lot of concern on his face at this point. He'd told us pretty much everything. Now it was just a question of showing us what happened where. Leibel and I were pretty much sitting on the sidelines for this procedure. We had already had our turn, so now we would sit back and let Gerry Dalen and Len Bylo work their magic.

I knew that the re-enactment was critical; in fact, just as important as the actual confession. In those days, we could ask a suspect certain questions during the re-enactment, like "Show us the gun you used to kill these people," and his subsequent pointing to it in a photograph would usually be admissable in court and could be fairly powerful evidence.

Our heads bobbed slightly as the aircraft began its slow taxi towards the runway. Everyone was ravenous, so I promptly passed around my rations of Egg McMuffins. The sound of wrappers being eagerly ripped from the warm sandwiches was quickly muted by the engines as the pilot spun up the turbines. We'd made very short work of breakfast, and Kenny quickly started scolding me about only getting them one each.

We chatted among ourselves. The pressure was off now, although the job wasn't over yet. Bylo and Dalen were facing one another in their chairs, and Shearing was close by but we never talked about the murder. Dave pretty much kept to himself. I'm not too sure how he felt about us. I think my plan to make him think we were good friends had worked well. He was comfortable with us, and I suppose we were about as comfortable with him as could be expected.

The flight to Kamloops was about an hour and a half. The ride was smooth and actually quite pleasant. Once there, we waited to board our next plane that would take us up to Clearwater. Shearing wanted to light up a smoke, but because the signs clearly stated that there was to be no smoking in the hangar area, we headed back into the hangar office.

By the time he was butting out his smoke, the Beaver had arrived to take us up to Clearwater. We all squeezed into the small aircraft and took our seats. The flight to Clearwater was a little less than half an hour, but turbulent — it felt like we'd been strapped to the back of a duck. When we finally got back on the ground, Shearing had less colour than a corpse.

As instructed, the area around the airport was being tightly controlled. In order to avoid swamping David with questions, I had called ahead and ordered that everyone stay clear of the aircraft when we arrived. A gaggle of detachment members were gathered a hundred feet away, gawking like a busload of sightseers at Helmcken falls.

"So," I asked Shearing as we disembarked. "How'd you like your flight up?"

"Well, the first plane was pretty nice. I liked that. But do we have to go back on that little one?"

Sergeant Boswell met up with us at the aircraft and explained that Shearing, Dalen and Bylo would ride in the brown Ram Charger, while Reliable and I would follow in the green Plymouth. He also mentioned that he would be taking photographs as Dalen and Bylo got Shearing to point out areas of interest. Before we mounted up, Len came over to talk with me

"We're going to start over at the truck," Bylo explained. "Then we'll head over to the murder site. It might be a little difficult to pick out. He committed the murders in August, so there wouldn't have been any snow on the ground." There wasn't a lot of it there at the airport, but I assumed it would get thicker as we headed four thousand feet into the mountains.

"All right," I nodded. "We're right behind you Lenny." I quickly proceeded back to the car where Leibel was waiting behind the wheel. I climbed in the passenger side, and he put the it in gear and reset the trip odometer to 0. From the airport, we headed down the road to the number five highway. When we hit Wells Gray Road, we made another left. I remembered that it would have been in this general area that Shearing had been involved in that hit and run. Passing Wind Haven Avenue, just before going over the crest of a hill, I knew David had hit David Carter as he lay drunk upon the road.

Heading up the hill and past Spahats, we veered off to the right on the road to Bear Creek Camp.

"David?" Bylo asked over the rumble of the engine in the Ram Charger. "Weren't you a little nervous that someone on this road might see you driving around?"

"Well, yeah, but it was late at night, eh."

"About what time was it?"

"Almost midnight, at least."

"Did you know where you were going before the night you got rid of the truck and camper?"

"Not really. I'd been there before but not exactly that spot."

We came to a Y in the road, and kept to the left following Shearing's instructions. The snow was, as I expected, getting thicker as we gained altitude on Trophy Mountain. We headed straight through to another Y, and once again kept to the left. Finally, our procession ground to a halt. The odometer read 26.9 miles. There was a very pronounced skid trail that led over the edge. Leibel and I got out. I lit a smoke and watched from a distance. Leibel paced around, complaining about my smoking.

Before I could light another cigarette, we were jumping back in the vehicles. Shearing guessed we'd stopped just short of where he'd disposed of the truck, so we proceeded for another two clicks before we arrived.

"Yup, this looks like it," Shearing grunted.

"Dave," Bylo looked at him. "Would you get out here and show me where you drove the truck and camper?"

"Yeah, sure." Dave got out and stumbled over to the edge of the landing. His boots were not all that good on the snow. I climbed out of the car and tried to light another cigarette while Leibel stayed warm inside, chuckling at me and all the other shivering smokers.

I saw Dave point down over the edge of the landing, presumably indicating the logged area where he felt he would have driven the truck and camper. That was the spot, as far as I could remember. They quickly returned to the Ram Charger.

"Dave," Bylo asked once they were seated again. "I noticed several burned logs and stuff on this logged area. The area where you burned the truck and camper, did it have those?"

"Yeah," David answered casually. "There had been a fire nearby."

"What was the reason for burning the truck and camper?"

"To get rid of evidence."

"What did you do after you lit the truck on fire?"

"I walked up north, on the road next to the creek."

"Where did you go from there?"

"I followed the creek down."

"And where did that take you?"

"To my mother's house."

The Ram Charger lurched forward in the snow, and Leibel and I followed. When we got back to Wells Gray Road, we hung a right. Seven klicks later, we hung another.

"What do they call this area, Dave?" Bylo asked as he ordered them to a halt once more.

"The Old Prison Camp."

"Is this where you murdered those people. Four adults and two children?"

"Yes."

The campsite itself was bare, but the area was surrounded by large green pine trees. The grass was untamed and brown. From the road, a cluster of tall, skinny pines reached into the sky. Shearing stepped out of the truck in front of us and proceeded across the campsite to the cluster of trees. That would be where he watched the family from, I thought to myself, as I struck another match. Gerry Dalen was close by, questioning Shearing and recording everything that was said between them.

"Dave, would you show me where the truck and camper was?" He pointed the area out as closely as he could, and Bylo swiftly backed the Ram Charger into that spot. Shearing then directed Ken in to the spot he insisted was the same as that occupied by the Johnson car at the time of the murders. When asked, he pointed to the general location of the tent, which was between the truck and the car a couple of paces towards Wells Gray Road.

"Dave, would you show me where you walked in from the night you shot these people."

He obediently pointed towards the fence line along the road. He then proceeded to walk up behind the Ram Charger, keeping it between himself and the fire pit.

"How long did you stand there and watch them?"

"A few minutes."

"Dave, now show me where the four adults were when you shot them?"

"They were all sitting around here," Dave explained as he walked towards the fire pit. "I think one of 'em was standing."

"Which direction were they sitting?"

"Their backs were kind of turned to me when I was back there."

"David, do you remember where the men were sitting when you shot them?"

"Not really. I couldn't tell you."

Gerry pressed on. "Could you show me from where you shot the four adults?" Dave promptly moved back about ten feet, holding his hands up to his chest as if there were an old Remington pump action .22 within them.

Seeing Shearing standing there with a fake gun in his hands reminded me of a guy we'd arrested a couple years back.

"I've been sitting here beside this guy," the plaintiff began, belching heartily. "I had a couple drinks, and you know, I swear he's been shot! I think you should come and check this out."

Well sure as sunshine, the guy he'd been talking to was dead, shot to death by the owner of the house located deep in the bush. A bootlegger by trade, the shooter was a real rough-looking son of a bitch. He quickly, almost proudly admitted to shooting the guy because he'd run away with a bottle of whiskey without paying for it. As in every investigation, I asked him pertinent questions:

"How were you holding the gun when you shot him?"

"Well," he said dumbly, still drunk. "Give me a gun."

"No, we're not going to give you a gun." Instead, we improvised and in minutes we were watching a drunk stumbling around the place with a section of rubber hose. I shook the thought and returned my attention to Shearing.

"All right," Gerry continued, looking at Dave. "Now where were the girls when you shot them?"

"They were over here in the tent," Shearing clarified, pointing to the area of the tent again.

"Where were you standing when you killed the girls?" David knelt down in the long brown grass, holding his hands as if he were pointing the rifle at them in the tent. He looked up briefly at Gerry, who was still scribbling notes. Boswell took a picture of that. Sitting there, I didn't think it was possible for him to have shot the girls from that position. It didn't sit well with me.

Satisfied, Gerry ordered him back to the Ram Charger, then we all piled back into our respective vehicles and headed off to where he'd left the car.

"David," Gerry asked as we all headed back to Wells Gray Road, "were all the people dead before you loaded them in the car?"

"Yeah," was the quick reply.

The procession came to a halt about 10 miles down the road, then after some discussion headed to the next road and turned right. When the odometer read 60 miles, Gerry and Len followed David to the area where he burned the Johnson car.

"What's the name of that road?" Dalen began on a fresh sheet of paper.

"That's Battle Mountain Trail."

"Does it have any significance to you?"

"Well, just that this is the spot. I've never been back here since."

"Now, why did you burn the car and the bodies?"

"I imagine the same reason as I burned the camper. To get rid of the evidence."

"What time of day was it when you burned the car?"

"It was nighttime, probably about nine or ten o'clock." That would explain why the watch we found was frozen at a couple minutes after ten.

We hadn't been able to decide whether it was ten in the morning, or ten in the evening. During the day, we argued, people could have seen the smoke. At night, we agreed, someone could have seen the flame. There was just no way of telling what time the car had been lit on fire.

"David, when you left here after burning the car, which way did you walk?" Dave proceeded back to Battle Mountain Trail, pointing for emphasis.

"I walked back down this road and down to the main road home."

"Did you catch a ride?"

"No."

At that point, everyone returned to their vehicles and zoomed back down the trail to Wells Gray Road and turned left.

When we stopped again, I got out and headed up to Dalen and Bylo in the Ram Charger. David was sitting in the front seat. I had a slip of paper written by the Crown Counsel that basically said he had the right to appear before the Justice of the Peace within 24 hours. I needed him to sign it, to confirm that he knew of this right.

"David," I began, once he rolled the window down. "I've got a piece of paper here drafted by the Crown Counsel." I explained the paper to him briefly. "Now, we can go back to Clearwater right now and do it, or we can wait a couple of hours and do it then."

David thought about it for a moment. "Nah, so long as I can do it in a couple hours that'll be fine." He initialled the paper as instructed.

I headed back to my vehicle and climbed in next to Leibel. We cruised a bit farther down the road behind the Ram Charger, then cut off to the right. At 70 miles, we stopped.

"David," Gerry said as Len eased the truck forward. "Could you show me where you hid the boat motor and other belongings?"

"Well, that's a bit farther up. This here is where I parked the car and camper that same night." They drove a bit farther. "This here is where I got stuck."

"How did you get out?"

"I used a shovel, and I think I might have used a come along."

"Would you have used the jack?"

"I might have, yup."

"That's from the truck, was it?"

"Nah, I probably would have used my own." A bit farther up, they saw a piece of aluminum sticking out of a tree stump.

"Do you recall hitting any trees or stumps?"

"Only with that boat rack thing that was on the side of the camper. Stop here."

"What's here, Dave?"

"The boat and motor."

"Will you show it to me please?"

"Yeah." The two of them got out of the Ram Charger and moved over to a patch of bush next to the road. Sergeant Boswell followed quickly in their wake to take photographs. When they were at the bush, Shearing leaned forward and pulled a couple of thick branches off the hull. Suddenly, the boat appeared, sitting on its back. The boat had been completely covered. Perfectly camouflaged. Gerry brought Shearing back to the Ram Charger, and Ken, Len and I took a stroll over to examine the boat and whatever was underneath it. The "go all day" gas tank, the motor, and a couple other things were beneath it and all appeared to be in good shape.

When we'd finished poking around, I went back to talk to Dave in the Ram Charger. "All right Dave," I smiled. "Now how do we get back to the road from here? Do we just go straight, or do we have to about-face?"

"We'll just head out this way. Straight, Mike."

"Okay! We'll be right behind you."

We headed back to Wells Gray Road, then headed left. We turned into the driveway marked by a mailbox with the name "F.A.M. Shearing". The house itself sat within a small clearing. Its worn black roof sat upon aged white siding. The grey backdrop of poplar trees was speckled with green from a few conifers that dotted the landscape. Gerry, Len, Sergeant Boswell and Dwight Hoglund, who had caught up with us later, followed Dave into the house.

The interior was plain, but comfortable. Chipboard lined the walls, and most of the furniture appeared homemade. There was a gun rack on the living room wall, visible immediately upon entering.

"Would you now show me the gun that you used to shoot and kill the families? The Johnsons and the Bentleys, that is," Dalen asked as they moved into the house.

"It's this one here," David pointed to the rifle on top. There were two others in the rack, above a gun cleaning kit which sat like an afterthought beneath the three firearms. Boswell snapped a picture, then Hoglund took the rifle off the wall.

"Are there any bullets like those you used to kill the families?"

"There might be some on the rack there," he said, looking. He couldn't find any.

They then proceeded upstairs to Shearing's old bedroom. The bed rested against the far wall. Beside it sat a small bedside table. Shearing leaned down in front of it and opened the top drawer. Within it, they found a Sony Walkman and a leather case containing a Polaroid camera.

Gerry and Len then took Shearing to another bedroom where he picked up some clothes. In minutes, they were back downstairs.

"David, you mentioned some tools. Whereabouts are they?"

"They're over in that shed there."

"Let's go take a look." All of them moved over to the shed. Ken and I hung back for all of this. We tried to keep our noses right out of it, in an effort not to distract Shearing or interfere with Dalen and Bylo.

When they entered the shed, Shearing pointed out a yellow dish pan and a yellow life vest. He also brought their attention to a red plastic tackle box.

"I think these here were from the truck," David said, picking out a small saw and some tin cutters from the yellow dish pan.

"What about sleeping bags. Did you keep any of those?"

"No, I don't think so."

Satisfied, Dalen, Bylo, Hoglund and Boswell exited the shed, locked it up and then returned to the house. Ken and I had been poking around, getting a feel for the place while they were in the shed. There was a really sombre air between us as we realized the significance of our walking around the murderer's house. He'd been two miles away, and we hadn't found him. When we saw them returning, we headed back to the car.

As soon as Shearing was back in the truck, our little convoy turned around and headed back to Wells Gray Road. We then turned back on Highway number five.

"David," Dalen asked over the grinding of the engine. "Since Len and I started talking to you this morning, has any other policeman talked to you, other than Mike Eastham and Ken Leibel?"

"No."

"Has anyone threatened you?"

"No."

"Has anyone promised you anything?"

"No."

"Do you feel you have been treated fairly?"

"Yeah, I guess so."

We all pulled into Clearwater detachment at about quarter to five. Dalen and Bylo rushed Shearing in the back doors, while Kenny and I went in the front. They booked Dave into cells, and we all piled into a car, then headed into town for something to eat.

On Monday morning, November 21, 1983, David Shearing appeared in court and was charged with six counts of second degree murder. Late the night before, I had placed telephone calls to Brian Coxford at BCTV, and our friends at CKNW radio station in Vancouver and gave them a heads up. These were people who had criticized us when necessary, but who had also stood by us and went above and beyond the call of duty in assisting us throughout the previous year and a half. It was no surprise that my phone calls resulted in a media frenzy on Monday.

Although the appearance was short and brief, the courtroom walls strained to hold all of the reporters, courtroom artists, and spectators. Everybody wanted to get a glimpse of the animal who had committed one of the most heinous murders in Canadian history. Security was very tight. There were armed sheriffs and police personnel both inside and outside the courthouse. The last thing I needed was for some fanatic to attempt to kill Shearing. David was quickly remanded until later on that week in order to give him time to find and instruct legal counsel.

It was exceptionally quiet back at the office that afternoon. I think everybody in the building other than the superintendent stopped by to offer us congratulations on a job well done. I ran into Vic Edwards in the hallway, and he was grinning from ear to ear. He shook my hand vigorously and offered his personal congratulations. The superintendent was nowhere to be seen.

I was absolutely fried. I looked like I had just been gassed in the Iran-Iraq War. Gerry, Len, Dwight, Ken and I planned to get together for a couple of drinks later on in the week by way of celebration, but I decided I couldn't wait that long. Instead, I elected to have me a party to sort of warm up for the team's "murder party" later on. After work, I headed off and bought myself a good bottle of champagne.

I knew a bit about fine wines having been introduced and educated on them by Mario Evangelista, a friend who was the sales and marketing manager for Corby Distilleries out of Montreal. I was aware that Dom Perignon was the finest champagne in the world. While at first I was sure I would treat myself to at least a bottle, I soon realized there was another option — Moët & Chandon. They were both beautiful champagnes, but I eventually decided on the Moët. Claude Moët, who founded the House of Moët in the mid 1700s, had established a long line of distinguished Moët & Chandon drinkers. There was Queen Victoria, King Louis-Phillipe of France and the Queen Mother Elizabeth. Most notably to me at that point, however, was undoubtedly Napoleon. Following Napoleon's numerous victories in Austria, Prussia, and Poland, the young general had enjoyed a bottle of Moët all to himself. I reasoned that I had been in a bloody battle for the past two years, and seemed to have emerged somewhat victorious. It just seemed logical that I should celebrate in a similar fashion, so off I went. Me and my bottle of champagne.

I had the house to myself. While the champagne chilled, I lit a huge fire in the fireplace, turned the lights down low, and adjourned to my leather chair. For half an hour, I contentedly watched white flakes of snow tumbling gracefully into the trees from the dark sky above. A simple pleasure perhaps, but one I thoroughly enjoyed.

My own little victory celebration helped distract me, but I knew it wouldn't take long for my mind to drift to the events of the past year or so. The first sight of the car, the charred remains of an entire family that could have easily been my own, the fruitless charge across Canada — it had seemed so unfulfilling until we found the truck and camper, sitting up on a mountain top a couple miles from the murder scene. *Make sure you clean up your own backyard before you start worrying about everyone else's,* I thought to myself.

But we had cleaned up our backyard. We'd spent thousands of man hours combing the million and some acres of Wells Gray Park and come up empty. We'd spent thousands of hours going across Canada at the insistence of 1300 tipsters, to no avail. We'd done everything we could've been expected to do and took full advantage of everything we'd been given. In hindsight, if we hadn't made such a big deal of the truck, those two forestry workers may have written it off as just some burned-out wreck and ignored it. It could have remained unfound while Shearing could have been just as drunk as me right now up in Tumbler Ridge, chuckling at the fact that the police were no farther along now than they had been in September of 1982.

My interview with David lingered in my mind, and I went over and over the events as he told them to me. I couldn't help but think about what it must have been like that evening at Bear Creek. After being so deeply involved in the investigation, it felt like it the bugger had murdered my own two daughters. Pictures of Janet and Karen were so impregnated in my mind that I'd had nightmares throughout that year about how they'd been killed. Instead of being in Wells Gray Park, however, in my dreams they were miles away on the west coast of Vancouver Island. I used to wake out of my sleep because I couldn't move the murders back into the park. I hoped those nightmares would end soon.

Jesus, why the hell did I ever want to be a cop? As I poured myself another glass of champagne, I remembered.

After the bottle of champagne had been uncorked, and I became corked, the more I thought about it, the more I knew in my heart that there was an untold story, and that one day the truth would come out. I was sure of that. I knew then that I had another mission, and hopefully at its conclusion would lie another bottle of that great champagne.

Within weeks of his arrest, David was having his head read by doctors, and we were busily preparing for court. We were tight lipped with the media at this point; we didn't jeopardize any aspect of the investigation.

David had obtained a defense lawyer by the name of Fred Kaatz who worked for the highly respected local firm of Mair Jensen Blair, undoubtedly one of the best in the province. They were a well-established firm with all of the necessary machinery to provide a top-notch defense for David. The fact that members of their firm had received appointments as Supreme Court judges did not escape us. Fred Kaatz was a very well-respected defense lawyer who had spent a number of years as an investigator in the RCMP. If there was anyone around who would be able to get David off, it was Fred Kaatz. That's not to say that our knees were knocking, but with Shearing retaining Kaatz, they sure as hell had us up on our tippy toes. Napoleon had always tried to think positive, so I once again tried to follow in his footsteps.

It's one thing to gather all the evidence, but it's another to prepare it and assemble it for a prosecutor in a court brief. Bob Hunter, the Crown prosecutor, had proceeded via direct indictment, and we knew that the trial would be forthcoming within three or four months. That meant we would have to get our evidence in order well in advance for the prosecution.

Our investigation of David hadn't stopped. Other leads and tips came in that tied David to certain spots at certain times, which were required for corroboration. Frantic phone calls and letters went out to our crime detection laboratory, forensic identification and pathology sections, asking that our reports be given top priority. Whether it was hair and fibre, some type of chemical analysis, or 20 copies of each photograph that had to be assembled in those court briefs, it had to be done pronto.

Every part of the investigation had to be examined and cross referenced where it could be corroborated. Exhibits had to be examined by specialists, returned to us, and accounted for each step of the way.

Bob Hunter was a bloody bear. Nothing was ever good enough for him. It was a definite love-hate relationship between us. The bugger didn't care if was Sunday morning or Thursday night at midnight — when he wanted a meeting, you attended, and you had bloody well better have the answers he was looking for.

When there was a front-page story with pictures in the *Kamloops Daily Newspaper* showing Kaatz with his defense "team," my heart rate bumped up a notch. Not just one bloody defense lawyer, but *three* of them. Christ, I could imagine the hard time Reliable and I were going to have in court. We'd probably be wondering who the accused was — us or David Shearing. I could hear and see Kaatz now: "Uh, Sergeant, exactly what steps did you take when Mr. Shearing suggested that perhaps he needed a lawyer?"

"Well, sir," I'd have to reply, "I went for coffee, sir."

Prosecutor Bob Hunter was unimpressed with the defense team. "But there are three of them!" I whined, standing in his office one day. "So what?" he snarled. He was a really sharp cookie, but I knew the only thing less predictable than one defense lawyer was *three* defense lawyers. He didn't agree. "We've got what we need. Just put it down on paper, assemble it, and bring it to me so I can deal with it." Gee, he made it sound so easy. "Now get out of my office and don't come back until you have those reports I need, Eastham."

Over the next couple of months, things continued to fall into place. It seemed like everybody realized and understood our urgency and consistently got the work done on time. As the reports trickled in, they were assembled and added to Hunter's court brief.

There were no surprises. The results of examinations were positive in every aspect and qualified court experts were prepared to testify accordingly. They were positive for us that is; not so positive for young David. Hunter's court brief was updated every time a new confirmation was received. By now he knew the investigation like he knew the back of his hand and his favourite scotch.

During one of our many meetings with him, I was made aware that Hunter had been passing along a lot of the copies of the documents of the investigational results directly to Kaatz and the defense team. I knew we were responsible for supplying the defense with some particulars, but Jesus! It looked to me like he was giving Fred Kaatz the whole bloody court brief!

"Praise the Lord and pass the enemy our ammunition!" I said to him tongue in cheek.

Hunter (whom I was thinking about calling Igor Gouzenko) glared at me. He politely told me that he was the prosecutor, and that I was the investigator, and to once again get the hell out of his office, and don't let my ass hit the door on the way out otherwise he'd sue me for the damages.

I'd been through many trials with Bob, and knew that his bark was just that. Most of his growling was usually done with a smirk on his face. While I knew he was a teddy bear deep down (and I mean *deep*), in court he was a blood hound. The mere suggestion of inconsistency transformed him into a ravenous beast. When he sank his teeth in during a cross examination, he ravaged his victims. I'd seen it enough times.

The trial date was set for Monday, April 16th, 1984, in Supreme Court in Kamloops. During our many meetings it was evident that Mr. Hunter finally seemed to be pleased with the documentation he had been receiving and the many pre-trial interviews he had been conducting. He had certainly put us through our paces, and he knew it. A couple of days before the trial, Hunter summoned us to his office downtown late one afternoon.

"I wanted to tell you and your team that you have done one hell of a job on this investigation. You have left no stone unturned and are a credit to your Force."

We all stood there and enjoyed the pat on the back. Modestly, we sort of acted like we didn't notice.

"However," he continued, "this case is not going to trial."

Among the four of us detectives, we'd always had something to say. This time, we were speechless. We exchanged confused looks like hockey cards. What the hell was he talking about, "It's not going to trial"? Goddammit! All of the investigators had been studying their notes in preparation for trial to ensure absolutely nothing would be overlooked. We did everything imaginable to present a case so strong it would take an artillery shell to poke a hole in it. So where did we fuck it up? *What the hell is going on here!*

While the four of us contemplated this blasphemy, Hunter got that goddamned smirk on his face.

"Eastham, what is the motto of the Royal Canadian Mounted Police?"

"Well," I said with false enthusiasm, "in English it means 'Maintain the Right,' Bob."

"That's right, Mike," Hunter grinned. "And you and your team have done just that. You did things so right, as a matter of fact, that the defense team you've been so scared of is copping pleas of guilty to six counts of second degree murder on Monday morning, with no concessions whatsoever."

I must have looked shell shocked. *Holy shit!* All of this time on the front lines eating bullets and now it was time to go home. For the first time in almost two years I realized I didn't want to. I had been living this nightmare for so long it was as if it had become me — or I had become it; I wasn't sure. Christ, in the last two months alone I thought I'd dropped 15 pounds from my stomach and added a pound of flesh under each eye. Old "Igor" knew what he was doing all right.

As Hunter explained, there was no use thrashing around in Supreme Court unnecessarily. He told us that Kaatz knew the results of all the forensic investigations, and had copies of the statements in full, along with our notes. He had a list of every exhibit and how they were tied to David. Most important, he knew that he and his team were up against four very experienced detectives who knew their business. Bob further explained that there was no way out for them. While the court might perhaps be persuaded to find fault with one area of evidence, we had it secured in so many different ways we could present each package with a neat little bow around it.

"You guys have done your job; now it's up to me to ensure that justice is served in the eyes of the public. I don't want to see Shearing walk in 15 years. As a matter of fact, I don't want to see him walk for at least 25 years, and that's never been done before on a second degree murder charge. So get out of my office, and let me get to work."

We stood there amazed. We'd basically just been fired.

Bob shook all of our hands and once again politely threw our asses out. "One hell of a job!" he said as he closed the door behind us.

We'd been sent to the rear echelon and he had relieved our tired ranks on the front lines.

Crown prosecutor Bob Hunter was now the man with a mission.

Chapter 21 **COURT DAY**

I had visited Shearing before court the morning of April 16, 1984, in the RCMP lockup across the street. He was tired, but obviously relieved to see a friendly face. I'd kept a close eye on him, visiting him regularly while he had been remanded. He'd always looked forward to my visits.

"How ya feeling, Dave?" I asked kindly.

"Well, not bad I guess, considering." He must have felt like shit. He certainly looked the part.

"I'm going to be straight with you, David," I began, waking him up with my deadly seriousness. "You know, I've been around for a long time. I've been a cop for 22 years, and you know cops hear a lot of stories." He looked at me very passively, but I could tell he was uncomfortable. "Look. I don't have any reason to think that you lied to me, David, but I've got a feeling gnawing in my guts that something else happened that night, and you're not telling me what it is." I could tell just by looking at him that I was right. His eyes quickly lowered to the floor, and he wouldn't make eye contact with me. I knew what that meant. He had done something to those two little girls before he killed them, and I was determined to find out what.

Back in Powell River, I had investigated the alleged suicide of a young woman. Evidence suggested she had either been murdered by having been pushed off a bridge, or committed suicide by jumping of her own accord. While certain evidence suggested one theory, other evidence pointed to the other. In the end, after months of searching, we'd announced that it was indeed a suicide. I promised myself later that I would never close another case being uncertain. Now I had all the evidence I needed sitting in front of me, and I was damned if I was going to let him slip away. "You told me once that you might tell me the whole story one day, and I left it at that. Well, David, the day you're sentenced I'm going to come and collect." I stood, and headed back towards the door. "Think about it, David. I'll be back."

* * *

The historical Kamloops courthouse was already peppered with extra security in preparation for Dave Shearing when I arrived with Ken. The extra presence was there to ensure that nobody shot him. The large, red-brick building loomed above us as we drove up, its landscape littered with reporters and cameras. Relatives of the Johnson and Bentley families were already inside the large, one-room courthouse, mentally preparing themselves for what they were going to hear.

Reporters, cameras, and microphones swarmed around us like bugs over a fresh carcass as we headed in the back of the courthouse. I had the rifle in hand, wrapped in plastic, to submit it as evidence to be used by the court. As I entered the courtroom, I was hardly surprised that it was already almost full. Sitting quietly in the back, the relatives of the victims waited patiently for the proceedings to start.

By the time I returned outside, Len Bylo and Gerry Dalen had arrived with Shearing in an unmarked police car. British Columbia sheriffs held fast around the vehicle as ambitious reporters crowded in trying to get their first glimpse of the Wells Gray Park murderer. Gerry Dalen stepped from the passenger side. He calmly pushed some of them aside as he moved to guide the car back into a parking space near the back door. I hurried past him to keep the door clear as it opened.

I wasn't fazed by the media crews; I'd been dealing with them for years. But I wasn't too excited about having them buzzing around just now. When the case was closed and Shearing was behind bars, then I'd be a little more eager to grab some attention. Until then, it was business as usual.

When the rear driver-side door opened, the atmosphere seemed to pulse with anticipation. Shearing's leg stretched out of the back seat, and he struggled to his feet with his hands cuffed in front of him. As he turned to the left and headed towards the back door to the courthouse, the sheriffs struggled to hold the line of cameras back. Flashes blasted our eyes like a holiday fireworks display, while reporters converged on us. Gerry Dalen led the procession, followed by Bylo, Shearing and myself. I think Ken was inside the courtroom waiting for us at that point.

As we entered the courtroom, there was a sudden hush of voices. Shearing devoured everyone's attention. When he was in the hands of the courtroom personnel, Ken, Len, Gerry and I moved to the back of the courtroom, away from Brian and Linda Bentley. We were silent as everyone waited for the proceedings to start.

Everyone in the courtroom stood as Justice Harry McKay walked authoritatively to his bench and sat down. His salt and pepper hair was trimmed perfectly, but in my opinion his stone-faced coolness was his greatest asset. I looked over at Kenny. He looked pretty calm about the whole affair, as I should have been. We'd done everything possible to cement the conviction, so now all there was to do was hope everything went smoothly.

The clerk stood as we all sat back down again. "In the Supreme Court of British Columbia, holden Kamloops, Monday the 16th of April, 1984," he began, projecting his voice across the courtroom, "Her Majesty the Queen Against David William Shearing." The crown prosecutor stood hastily and moved to the front of the courtroom to introduce himself to Justice McKay.

"My Lord, my name is Hunter, initials R.C., appearing for the Crown. We are ready to proceed."

"Mr. Hunter," the Judge nodded, looking through dark-rimmed spectacles. Shearing's counsel promptly took the floor.

"My Lord, my name is Kaatz, initials I.F, and I am appearing with Mr. Deley, initials D., on behalf of Dave Shearing.

"Will the accused please stand?" Shearing stretched to his full height. He was wearing a brown suit and striped tie, but didn't look like any less of a murderer than he must have carrying that rifle. Off to the left, the clerk stood once more and read out the convictions.

"David William Shearing stands charged count number one, that he, the said David William Shearing, between the 6th day of August A.D. 1982, and the 13th day of August, A.D. 1982, inconclusive, at or near Clearwater, in the Province of British Columbia, did commit second degree murder on the person of Edith Bentley, contrary to Section 212 of the Criminal Code of Canada. David Shearing, having heard count one read, how do you plead? Guilty or not guilty."

"Guilty," Shearing said quietly, staring deadpan at the front of the courtroom.

"The accused David Shearing pleads guilty to count one, My Lord."

The clerk read through five similar convictions for the other members of the family. At the end of each, Shearing answered in a quiet, boyish tone.

"Guilty." *Well, that's one hurdle over with.*

"Now, Mr. Kaatz," Justice McKay began, adjusting himself in his seat to view the defense counsel. "Before accepting those pleas, I have to be satisfied, of course, that the Accused understands what he is pleading guilty to and the consequences of that plea. I assume that you have spent a great deal of time going over this matter with him?"

"That is correct, My Lord," Kaatz answered quickly.

"And you have explained to him in detail just what is meant by second degree murder?"

"That is correct, My Lord."

"And you will have also explained to him the consequences."

"I have, My Lord, and I am convinced that he understands full well the situation that he is facing."

"In particular," the judge reiterated. "You have explained to him that the penalty for second degree murder is life imprisonment?"

"I have."

"With a minimum of 10 years of non-eligibility for parole, and that the trial judge, depending on the circumstances, can increase that period from 10 years to 25 years?"

"I have, My Lord."

"You are satisfied that he understands fully what is going on?"

"I do, My Lord. I am very satisfied that he understands what is happening."

"Mr. Shearing, I am just going to read to you the definition of second degree murder." Justice McKay adjusted his glasses, and continued. "Where the person who causes the death of a human being, means to cause his death, or means to cause him bodily harm that he knows is likely to cause his death and is reckless whether death ensues or not.

"You understand that you are admitting fully and unequivocally to having committed the murders charged against you?"

"Yes," Shearing answered quietly.

"And you understand that, as I have already mentioned to counsel, what the possible penalties are?"

"Yes."

"All right. Well, before I accept—" he paused for a moment, and motioned for Shearing to sit down. He then returned his attention to the Crown prosecutor, "—I would like a brief outline of the circumstances. You can get into more detail later, but I would appreciate a very brief outline."

Mr. Hunter stood and described Shearing's actions as instructed.

"Do you agree with that, Mr. Shearing?"

"Yes."

"Fine. I will accept the pleas of guilty on all six counts."

"Thank you, My Lord," Hunter nodded. "The Crown proceeds now, and I will be lengthy, My Lord, once I start."

McKay thought briefly to himself for a moment, glancing at the clock on the wall to his left. "Would you like me to break for a while before you proceed?"

"Possibly a brief adjournment."

"All right."

We all filed out of the courtroom to stretch our legs and get some smoke into our lungs. All of us knew we were going to be in there all day, going over everything we had learned from Shearing. *Did we miss anything?*

I looked around briefly for the victims' relatives. This had to be a hard time for them. What would be worse, something that I knew and they didn't, was that they weren't going to hear a motive for the murder. We all had a pretty good idea what it was, but we'd never voiced the opinion. I'm not sure if they'd draw the same conclusion when they came away empty-handed at the end of the day. If they had the same suspicions we did, they were very careful about who they told.

Fifteen minutes later, everyone was pushing their way back into the courthouse. Once Justice McKay had returned, Mr. Hunter proceeded with his description of all events leading up to the arrest.

"On the 26th of August, the sergeant in charge of the Clearwater Detachment, Sergeant Baruta, was advised of the circumstances of the two missing families and conducted inquiries in his detachment area and in Wells Gray Park area. Nothing was forthcoming and these people were eventually formally listed as missing and were entered on the police system. The news media was also contacted and the assistance of the general public was requested in an effort to locate the missing families. ...

"On the morning of the 13th of September, information was received by the Clearwater detachment that an individual believed he had seen the missing Johnson vehicle in a burned-out condition on the Battle Mountain Road, which is near the Wells Gray Park ... . As a result of that information, Sergeant Baruta patrolled the Battle Mountain Road and he observed what appeared to be tire tracks of a vehicle which angled off into a heavily brushed area. He followed them down to the vehicle as it had been described. Once he examined it, he observed what appeared to be the remains of totally burned humans inside. The vehicle was approximately a hundred and fifty feet off the road down a slight incline. It had come to rest by being high centred on a log and a big boulder. It was obvious that it had been driven until it became stuck. The vehicle was entirely gutted on the inside with nothing remaining. The only thing remaining on the outside, other than the shell, was approximately 75 percent of the right front tire. The licence plate matched that which was the vehicle owned by the victims. The front driver's door was slightly opened, and the driver's side window appeared to be rolled down. There was a set of five keys in the truck lock which in fact belonged to the vehicle.

"It was apparent that the back seat of the vehicle contained the skeletal remains. Attempts were made to utilize keys to open the trunk, to no avail. A bar was subsequently used to forcibly pry it open. At that time the police discovered what appeared to be two small bodies inside the trunk. These were also burned to the point that they were not visibly identifiable. ...

"Now at this point, My Lord," Hunter continued, "the police received what they could only describe as very reliable information from a citizen who advised that on the 24th of August, he had two occasions to observe what he felt was the Bentley truck and camper in North Battleford, Saskatchewan. He even described the boat on the top and the motor affixed, which was identical to that which the Bentleys would have had. That vehicle was driven by two French-speaking males who did not appear to belong to the unit. It was the same make and model and bore British Columbia plates. The colour scheme was the same. As a result of that information, preliminary inquiries in North Battleford produced another witness who also supported the information from the first witness. A composite drawing of the two French Canadians was produced. That information was circulated across Canada."

And a lot of good that did us, I thought darkly to myself. Sitting there, listening to everything described as it was, I wondered where the hell those two French Canadians ever ended up. The two most wanted men in the country had got through my fingers, yet I'd snatched up a virtual unknown from some small BC town 15 months after the fact. I still hadn't quite figured that one out.

"The police amassed approximately 13,000 tips. Now, My Lord, the Crown points these facts and figures out for two reasons. Firstly, it was undoubtedly the most publicized murder that has ever occurred in Canada with more information given to the public and more information received by the public. This was known to the accused. Secondly, My Lord, it is common knowledge that the truck and camper never left the area, and on the 18th of October, 1983, more than a year after the event, it was found. With that knowledge, My Lord, it is very easy to look in the rearview mirror of life and say that the police should never have conducted the French suspect search or the across-Canada search, but should have concentrated on the Clearwater and Wells Gray Park area. The Crown can only say that the police tracked down all leads, which was their responsibility.

"On the 18th of October, two employees of a Clearwater Forest Department had located the Bentley unit in a burned out condition approximately 24 kilometres north of Clearwater at the 4,700-foot level of Trophy Mountain."

The prosecutor pointed out that pictures of the truck could be found within the first exhibit he submitted. McKay poked his nose through the different pictures, looking at some more closely than others.

"On the 15th of November, 1983, what I can only describe as a little piece of information was received from a resident to the effect that a person by the name of David Shearing had talked about re-registering a 1981 Ford through the British Columbia Motor Vehicles Branch. There was some discussion that it was likely hot and he also mentioned that he wanted to know how to fix a bullet hole in the door.

"Now by this time, My Lord, David Shearing was at Tumbler Ridge, British Columbia. He had been working there. He was presently unemployed and looking for work. On November 19th, 1983, at 1:40 pm. he was approached by Constable German who advised Shearing that the members in Dawson Creek wanted to speak to him about a couple of matters and that German, Constable German that is, would drive him into Dawson Creek for that purpose. Shearing agreed and was not arrested. He was not detained. He was instructed not to be arrested and if necessary would only be for the hit and run.

"At 3:40 p.m., Constable German introduced Shearing to Sergeant Mike Eastham, from the Kamloops subdivision. Sergeant Eastham coordinated the investigation, and had travelled to Dawson Creek to perform the interview. During that time, he was accompanied by Constable Ken Leibel."

Hunter offered the details of the interview as we had supplied them to him. He included all those fussy details like reading his rights under the Charter and so on. Several quotes were mentioned from the interview pertinent to Shearing's involvement in the hit and run, and eventually Hunter ended up reading out the entire statement as written by Shearing.

"That statement was then signed, My Lord, by Shearing."

Hunter then proceeded to explain how Shearing's body language had steadily shifted from slightly uncomfortable to depressed. It was odd hearing Hunter read out my words aloud before the whole courtroom. I could feel some people glancing in my direction, including Kenny, but I just stared straight ahead. I kept telling myself I'd done it the right way, and hoped that everyone who was looking at me was thinking the same thing.

Hunter read out the statement I'd recorded for Shearing. "Because of the number of people killed, and the distances travelled, he was asked if anyone was with him. He said 'I was alone.' He was asked 'Why? Can you think of any reason for killing them?'"

Everyone in the courtroom was absolutely silent as we all listened for the response. I couldn't even hear anyone breathe. "'No.'"

The atmosphere changed completely at that point. I'm not sure what everyone was expecting. Something as simple as impulse, or as complicated as a psychological disorder.

"Now, My Lord, I am prepared to speak to sentence now, and I would only ask the Crown be afforded the privilege of replying to anything that my friend might say and that might arise during his submissions."

"All right," McKay quickly agreed.

"Mr. Shearing, My Lord, has a criminal record that in 1981 at Clearwater he was charged and convicted of possession of marijuana — I'm sorry, of a narcotic that was in fact marijuana. He was given a $50 fine and in 1983, at Dawson Creek, he was charged and convicted of care and control of an automobile with a blood alcohol reading of point zero eight and was fined $500. My friend admits that record, My Lord, on behalf of his client."

"That's correct, My Lord," Kaatz spoke for the first time. There had to be a lot of thinking going on behind those eyes.

"All right, thank you," McKay said.

"I file that as an Exhibit," Hunter mentioned.

"Exhibit eleven."

"Yes, My Lord," the clerk answered obediently.

"My Lord," Hunter continued, "that concludes the facts that, as the Crown is aware of them, implicate Mr. Shearing in the six murders which he committed. The Criminal Code requires that Mr. Shearing be sentenced to life imprisonment. The issue here, with respect, is the Court's discretion as to when Mr. Shearing is eligible for parole — a period of somewhere between 10 and 25 years.

"In the case of first degree murder," he pointed out, "there is no discretion in the Court; 25 years is mandatory. In order for there to be first degree murder, it is necessary that the crime falls squarely within one of the definitions of the Criminal Code. Six, or for that matter one hundred and six second degree murders, do not constitute first degree murder, but the senseless murder of six totally defenceless people is deserving of the maximum as reflected in no eligibility for parole for 25 years.

"There is never an excuse for murder, My Lord, but there is usually a reason. Here the Crown submits that there is not even that. There was no alcohol and no drugs involved. There is not the slightest suggestion that these six people annoyed the accused or even insulted him. There is nothing. It was a senseless killing of six innocent and totally defenceless strangers.

"The Crown must ask Your Lordship to consider the stark horror the Johnson and Bentley families encountered that evening, sitting around a campfire, the two young girls in the tent. Within seconds, I suggest, four adults are dead and then the accused goes over to the tent and kneels down and kills the young, defenceless children. The real horror, it is suggested My Lord, is the killing of the two children. The shots would be ringing in this gentleman's ears after he quickly kills the adults, and I, with respect, suggest that that would stop anyone from going further. He goes to the tent, kneels down, opens the tent and kills two more young children. Then he cleans up the campground, puts the four adults in the car, empties the trunk and puts the two children in the trunk. He takes down the tent, puts everything in the camper, drives the car and hides it. He comes back. He drives the truck and hides it. He goes home, then goes to work the next day. He returns home, then goes through their belongings. He takes the car with the six dead bodies, drives it into a secluded area and burns everything so that none of the bodies are identifiable. A couple of nights later he does the same with the truck and camper. When he's asked why, he says, 'To burn the evidence.'

"The question I am sure will be asked by everyone, including the Court, is, why does he kill these six people? The Crown has no evidence to offer you as to the motive. None," Hunter reiterated. "My Lord, the maximum sentence of which I submit the mandatory eligibility for parole provisions fall into, can only be reserved for the worst type of an offender. I am sure that when Your Lordship deliberates as to the sentence to be imposed in this case, that you will consider that aspect and we submit that you will undoubtedly be able to think of crimes that will be as bad and possibly worse than this. It is with respect that I caution Your Lordship that they too should receive the maximum.

"In this case, My Lord, the Crown is asking that Your Lordship impose the maximum life imprisonment without eligibility for parole for 25 years." He didn't mention that this would be the first recorded case in Canadian history that it would apply to.

"Thank you, Mr. Hunter," McKay turned his attention over to Mr. Kaatz. "Would you prefer that I adjourn now for the luncheon adjournment, or would you prefer to get started?"

Mr. Kaatz stood slowly, conferring shortly with Mr. Dley. "Perhaps, My Lord, I expect to be an hour, perhaps an hour and a half and I think that it might be in order to adjourn now, and then I could commence without interruption."

"You will have no trouble finishing? You say an hour, perhaps an hour and a half?"

"I would say approximately an hour and a half."

"We will adjourn, then, until 1:30 this afternoon."

And it was about time too. My stomach was growling like a Harley. Everyone had fallen into an exit routine, so as we all filed out we headed out for a bite to eat.

Chapter 22 **WHO IS DAVID SHEARING?**

It felt so much better to be sitting down with a full stomach. We'd eaten so fast, we'd hardly even had an opportunity to discuss the proceedings. The four of us had sounded like a tractor-pull competition in the back row. We wanted Shearing to put in the 25 years he deserved, and Fred Kaatz was going to do everything in his power to try and stop that. That meant taking our case and turning it upside down. I didn't think he could do it, but I'd been surprised before.

"Are you ready to proceed, Mr. Kaatz?" McKay began, donning his glasses.

"Yes, My Lord. Mr. Hunter did not address Section 671 and what the exercise is about that we are going through here, and I think we should perhaps review that and address the criteria that should have been addressed in speaking to your Lordship about eligibility for parole for Mr. Shearing. Section 671 is fairly clear and precise." Kaatz picked up his notes, and began reading from them. "It says that 'At the time of the sentencing of an accused under Section 669 who is convicted of second degree murder, the judge presiding at the trial of the accused or, if that judge is unable to do so, any judge of the same court may, having regard to the character of the accused, the nature of the offence and the circumstances surrounding it's commission, and to any recommendation made pursuant to Section 670, by order, substitute for 10 years a number of years or imprisonment, being more than 10 but not more than 25, without eligibility for parole, as he deems fit in the circumstances.' ...

"The Accused by statute, and I think it should be made very clear, will be sentenced to life imprisonment and life imprisonment means precisely that. The rest of his natural life. What we have to deal with is simply when he will be eligible for parole ..."

Kaatz told the court about Shearing's "remorse" and his cooperation during the investigation.

"I am saying these things because when I get into Mr. Shearing's character, you will see that these things also fit into his character. There were things that he said during the statement that I think go to establish as well the fact that he was crying and he mentioned God."

He did? I don't remember that. Ah well.

"He mentioned a number of things. He also mentioned shooting himself at one stage, so I think from the circumstances—"

"I have none of that before me," McKay interrupted quaintly.

"My Lord," Hunter quickly explained. "I believe he was asked on the second occasion on the next morning whether he had written a suicide note."

"Yes."

"That is what that alludes to."

"I remember the mention about suicide."

Kaatz promptly took the floor back. "I believe there is also the statement made— maybe Mr. Hunter did not read it in. It is one of the statements where he says, 'I should shoot myself.' This is the kind of comment I think that simply shows the remorse for the situation he was in."

No, that's a sign that you bet all your money and lost.

"Now I think the next question Your Lordship must consider is David Shearing's character. Who is David Shearing, and how does David Shearing, as a person, as an individual, come to court? He is 25 years of age. His date of birth is April 10th, 1959. His place of birth is New Westminster, BC. He lived there until he was five years of age. He then moved to the Clearwater area with his parents, his brother, and his sister. He was educated in Clearwater, BC, and graduated Clearwater Senior Secondary School with an approximate 70 percent average.

Kaatz read out a letter from Shearing's high school principal, who recalled him as "a good average student." Another letter from a counsellor at the same school said pretty much the same thing and described him as "a very quiet person who responded politely and respectfully." The impression given was of an unremarkable, rather forgettable kid.

Kaatz continued by displaying David Shearing's marks throughout his high school years. He then explained that David had attended Cariboo College where he studied mechanics for six months. Shearing had done quite well in that course, receiving an award for standing second in the class.

We sat still, listening to Kaatz trying to build Shearing up into a victim of everything but his own ruthless desires. In my mind, I didn't care if he was the proprietor of the Nobel Peace Prize. And make no mistake: Although they'd chosen second degree murder over first degree, his actions were completely premeditated. He'd stalked them the first night, then he came back and killed them. You don't get much more premeditated than that. We just couldn't prove that he'd been there before he committed the murders.

Yet another letter was read out, this time from the employer Shearing had been working for at the time of the murders. Once again, he was described as "always polite and helpful."

"That is the last letter," Kaatz continued. "In regard to his family background, David's parents were both born in Canada and raised on farms in the Prairies. His mother, who he describes as a little old-fashioned-type woman, presently resides in Clearwater in an apartment for senior citizens. ...

"David's father died of lung cancer in March 1982, at the age of 67 years. He had been ill for approximately one year."

"How old did you say he was?"

"He was 67, My Lord. That was March of 1982. I will address that a little more fully later on. Now, I received this information from both David and his brother Greg, who is present in the courtroom, I believe. He was here this morning, in any event. Information from David and his brother Greg allows me to say that David had a good childhood. His mother and father seldom argued and his father was not a drinker. David speaks very highly of his father and describes him as a well-read and intelligent man. He said his home was always full of old books and his father had an interest in photography, stamp collecting, ancient civilization, astrology, Greek mythology, et cetera.

"He was that kind of individual. David admired that, admired the fact that his father was a conservationist and never hunted even though they lived in one of the prime hunting areas of the province. David advised me ... that he did a lot for his father and took his father's death very, very hard. He said when his father died he felt that he'd lost a friend as well as a father. This was some four months prior to the murders. Three or four months.

"David described himself as an avid reader, reading mostly mechanic's magazines, handyman books, science fiction, and mainly attracted to mechanics, science, and chemistry. Those were the areas that he liked to pursue. He said he could have had better marks in school if he'd worked harder. He chummed with a number of people at the school that smoked at noon hour in the washrooms, with the kids, he said, that had the honours marks, even though his marks were not as high.

"He admits to experimenting with marijuana and there was a charge before the court in that regard. In his school years and on a couple of occasions he said he had experimented with acid but he was not really involved in that to any great deal, and he says to me it wasn't any more than most of the kids that he chummed with. He has always used alcohol and on occasion to extreme. Near or around the time of his father's death — there is a letter that I will be reading from his brother — he used it moreso. He tells me he liked the country life, and enjoyed the large garden that he had at home, approximately an acre. He enjoyed the dogs, the cats, the pigs, and the rabbits they had that went with the country living.

"David was not a hunter but he did enjoy fishing and hiking in the Wells Gray Park area. He went on numerous backpacking trips with his brother and friends or neighbours, some of them lasting a week at a time. He said that he was very attracted to that area, and the beauty of the mountains was a main reason that he went hiking so much.

"In regard to music, My Lord, he said he is self taught on the electric guitar and enjoys playing and singing western music. He also described himself as a very emotional person.

"Now, when dealing specifically with the offences before the court, David has advised me that after the offences he on many occasions contemplated suicide, and went so far as to choose a mountaintop upon which he would take his own life. He said that, I believe, he even wrote a note. I think that is before Your Lordship in the evidence from the statements. He said that he could not go through with this plan. He tells me that, and I have discussed in full with him, that he is fully aware of the consequences of his guilty pleas today and he is fully aware of the mandatory life sentence. He understands what that is about and he understands what he is facing.

"When I discussed with him procedures on the trial on this matter, he told me that he did not want the family and friends of the deceased or his own family to go through with the traumatic experience of the trial, and he says that is because he is guilty. He also advises me, and I think this information should be before Your Lordship, that it is in his intention to cooperate fully and totally with the prison authorities and with the psychiatrists and whatever else or anyone else that he is required to cooperate with while he is in custody."

Kaatz continued by pointing out that he had several other letters. He proceeded to read before the court, all of them with the same message: *David was a charming young man, who was always busy trying to help other people. He was a bit shy, but had a nice sense of humour when he got comfortable. The acts of violence for which he stands accused are completely out of character.*

The last letter was from his brother, Greg. Although it was very touching, the four of us were struggling to feel any compassion for Shearing.

"'Dear Sir,'" Kaatz began. Although Justice McKay had already read the letter, he'd suggested it be read for the record. "'Please accept this letter from my hand and use it should you find merit in its contents to address the Supreme Court, His Lordship and my fellow countrymen. Please use it to acquaint the learned court with the following matters which I feel must be disclosed about this man, my brother, David Shearing, and his character as well as our, the family's, shocked state upon hearing of his arrest.'"

Everyone's eyes were on David as the letter was read before the court. He was visibly affected by the words of his brother, a man he loved and respected, a man he had so drastically dishonoured.

"'Firstly, I would just like to say that I have intense sympathy for the members of the Bentley and Johnson families and their relatives and friends. My heart goes out to them. When I first heard mention of this crime I was overcome with a feeling of sadness as I am today. When I was informed by the police that my brother was suspected of this crime last November, I was completely shocked and unbelieving that he who was a kind, considerate brother could even contemplate thinking of such a thing. It was a totally devastating blow which is unexplainable to most people except to those who have received similar crushing messages under similar circumstances. Both myself and the whole family were completely taken aback and still find it hard to believe... .'"

Greg's letter explained his credentials by insisting that he'd had enough experience with the court system as a deputy sheriff to make an unbiased critique of his brother's character. "'Please note that I respect our justice system and what it stands for, and would not intentionally try and corrupt that respect at any time.'"

The courtroom was dead silent as Kaatz read on, describing everything we'd been told from a perspective only a brother could offer. It was clear that the two of them were very close.

"What happened to this young man of good character? He was kind, sympathetic and a sensitive person. I know him to be a hard-working, compassionate, sensitive man, with above-average intelligence, and although at times he drank to excess, his drinking was not an obvious problem to the family.

"Since his arrest, I have visited David regularly in the prison system and I still see a lot of good in him. He shows extreme remorse as to what he has done. He is in pain with himself, as he is a very sensitive man, for the terrible deed he has committed.

"I can only ask the courts that when they punish him, and indeed he must be punished, that they consider his character as I have set out as his brother. Respectfully yours, G. A. Shearing."

Kaatz put the letter down before him, then continued. "My Lord, although this crime is a horrendous crime, and keeping in mind what the test is for Your Lordship and Your Lordship's function in regard to Section 671, when he is eligible for parole, I think that I would ask Your Lordship to bear in mind the letters that I have read of his background, his character, his acquaintances, and bear in mind that although the crime is somewhat frightening and horrendous as Mr. Hunter said, that David Shearing is still a human being. Please bear that in mind when you consider what he might be eligible for and when." Kaatz's summary was customarily wordy, saying the same thing over and over again, just a little differently every time.

"Thank you." Justice McKay turned towards Hunter. "Mr. Hunter?"

"No, I have no reply, My Lord."

Judge McKay cleared his throat. "I am going to reserve overnight. I want to read this material again. I suppose I also have to, in setting sentence on the mandatory requirements of Section— what is it? 98?"

"Yes, My Lord," Hunter acknowledged. He then discussed with the judge what was to be done with the gun. Once that issue had been dealt with, the session was done for the day.

"The accused will be remanded until 10:00 am tomorrow morning," Judge McKay announced.

And that was it. As far as I was concerned then, it could have gone either way. His lawyers certainly had made Shearing look pretty spectacular, but it wouldn't be until the next day that we would find out if it had been spectacular enough.

Chapter 23

TEN OR TWENTY-FIVE?

The following morning, the four of us proceeded to the courtroom once Shearing was in the proper hands. We all moved to our respective places, and waited to witness the culmination of 18 months of work. Everyone in the courtroom stood quickly to their feet as Justice McKay entered the room. Once he was settled, the clerk opened up the proceedings. The Bentley relatives sat as if alone in a completely different realm, so patiently were they waiting for the sentence to be announced.

"In the Supreme Court of British Columbia, holden at Kamloops, Tuesday, the day of the 17th day of April, 1984, Her Majesty the Queen versus David William Shearing."

Justice McKay cleared his throat before he began. "Mr. Shearing, would you stand please?" Shearing did so. "The Prisoner has pleaded guilty to six counts of second degree murder. The facts as they emerge from his statement show the senseless, ruthless, cold-blooded slaughter of six innocent and defenseless victims, a slaughter that devastated three generations of a single family.

"Two of the victims — the grandparents, Mr. and Mrs. Bentley — were enjoying their retirement years. Mr. and Mrs. Johnson were raising a family and in the prime of life. The other two young girls, one 11 and the other 13, had their whole lives ahead of them. The victims were enjoying a family reunion and a camping trip in one of our wilderness areas when this senseless slaughter occurred. The adults were sitting around a campfire at the end of a no doubt enjoyable day, and the young girls had retired to their tent for the night.

"What a tragedy. What a waste, and for what? As best as I am able to judge, the only motive for this mass killing was that the prisoner coveted their possessions. The sentence for second degree murder is life imprisonment. The only issue before me is as to the period the prisoner must serve before becoming eligible for parole."

Justice McKay reviewed all the points Mr. Kaatz had made regarding David Shearing's character and how all who knew the man were shocked that he could have committed such a horrific act.

"But obviously, there is another side to him of which even his family and closest friends are unaware," Justice McKay continued. "A side that makes him, in my view, a very dangerous man. There is the David Shearing who, without any apparent motive, walked into the campfire light and deliberately shot and killed four adults and who then knelt at the tent flap and shot and killed the two girls. There was the David Shearing who carried out the elaborate and time-consuming cover up, the details of which I need not repeat. There is the David Shearing who inquired about the registering of a hot pickup, and as to how one could repair a bullet hole in the door of that pickup. Yes, I agree that I must consider the character of the Accused described by his friends and acquaintances and by his family, but I must also keep firmly in mind the other David Shearing. The one who committed the dreadful crimes."

Now the judge got to the crux of the matter. We waited impatiently to hear what 18 months of work would get us.

"Dealing with the nature of the offences and the circumstances surrounding their commission, I must, of course, be careful to ensure that I do not treat these murders as though they were first degree murders, thus requiring a period of ineligibility for 25 years. The Crown elected to charge second degree murder in each case and I assume that was because of the perceived frailty in the evidence relating to the planning and deliberation as those words have been defined in the jurisprudence on the subject.

"However, I must emphasize that there are degrees of second degree murder, just as there are differences between murders. It was for those reasons that Parliament gave to sentencing judges a discretion ranging from a minimum of 10 years of ineligibility to a maximum of 25. At the lower end of the range of culpability is the second degree murder with which we are all too familiar involving one of more such things as lack of actual intent to kill, a family dispute, real or imagined grievances, sudden anger, provocation falling short of the provocation which justifies reduction of murder to manslaughter, defense of the person falling short of justifiable killing in self defense, diminished capacity by reason of alcohol, drugs or mental impairment and so on.

"That is not the case before me. This case is in the upper range of culpability. The victims were unknown to the prisoner. They did not in any way provoke him. He knew they were camped at the site and carefully scouted the situation. He went home and then returned either that night or the next with a loaded .22 rifle. Why? We don't really know, but it seems it was either to rob or to kill. He, and these are his words, 'walked down through the bush to the old campsite, snuck up to the camper, walked around the camper and started to shoot the people.' And then these, too, are his words. 'Went to the tent and shot the other two.' There are absolutely no ameliorating or mitigating factors. The killings were clearly intentional. Most of the victims were, as he said, shot in the head and some may have been shot more than once. There is no suggestion that his mind was in any way affected by alcohol or drugs. There is no suggestion of diminished capacity or evidence of mental illness. There is no suggestion of real or imagined grievances against the victims.

"What we have, put very simply, is a cold-blooded and senseless execution of six defenceless and innocent victims for no apparent reason other than he possibly coveted some of their possessions."

Everyone in the courtroom was completely still. A bomb could have gone off outside and nobody would have noticed. Justice McKay was building a very strong foundation for a 25-year sentence, but none of us knew for sure at that point what the end result would be.

"The sentence I impose must in conjunction with such matters as protection of the public in general and specific deterrence have proper regard to public opinion and must express in clear terms the revulsion felt by the great majority of our citizens for this senseless and vicious mass killing such as we are here dealing with. Parliament has decreed that sentencing judges may, on conviction for a second degree murder having regard to the criteria set out in Section 671, increase the period of ineligibility for parole from 10 years up to the maximum of 25 years. Obviously an increase to the maximum of 25 years would be a rare event. I am unaware of it being done in any other case to date. In my view, however, this is an appropriate case for such drastic action. The enormity of the crimes demands the maximum sentence."

Twenty-five fucking years, David, I thought to myself, but I still wasn't satisfied. I was still determined to find out what really happened, even if it would never be revealed in court.

"Mr. Shearing," Judge McKay continued over the rush of whispers spreading across the courtroom. "With respect to each of the six counts of murder to which you have pleaded guilty, I sentence you to concurrent terms of imprisonment for life without eligibility for parole until you have served 25 years of your sentence."

Justice seemed to have been served — finally!

When we left, the reporters were accosting everyone. Nobody was spared, except us, and only because we left by the back door. We left Vic Edwards there to satisfy the press and media.

Bylo, Dalen, Leibel, Hoglund and I walked proudly out the back to where our vehicles were parked. Standing victoriously upon the podium of justice, the five of us greeted the silence none of us had enjoyed for over a year and a half. You could only enjoy so much silence, and once Shearing was safely back in cells there was only one thing to do.

Murder party!

It was a ritual for us. For long cases, and even some of the short ones, you're overwhelmed with pressure from every direction. You live a miserable existence, working ridiculous hours in excruciating conditions. When it was all over and the bad guy was behind bars, it was time to head out and do what came naturally. I can't remember the official RCMP terminology for it, but I think it was something to the effect of "getting absolutely shit faced."

Dalen was already planning it as we walked out. "C'mon Mike!" he said eagerly. The others looked at me apprehensively.

"You guys go on and start without me, I'll be there a bit later." I turned, heading towards the RCMP lockup where Shearing was waiting. "It's time to collect."

At that point, I was satisfied that Shearing had been given as much time as he deserved under the circumstances. They didn't have the gallows anymore, and capital punishment had itself been executed almost a decade earlier. David had been given the stiffest sentence at the disposal of the justice system.

It was clear a lot of people wanted him dead — an eye for an eye and a tooth for a tooth. Of course, that opens up the whole debate about capital punishment. Some argue that if the system takes the life of a killer, the system itself is no better than that killer. Others say taking away a killer's life also takes him away from suffering the burden of his punishment. Few debates on capital punishment ever end without some sort of verbal knife fight, but in this case, where it was so cut and dried, it was hard to field an argument against it. Dave Shearing was usually an obliging, polite, considerate man who, without warning, could shift into a raging, methodical killer — two distinct personalities he showed no ability to control.

A family of six is dead: George and Edith Bentley, Bob and Jackie, Janet and Karen Johnson. Shearing said he did it. He said he shot them in the back of the head. He said he lit the cars on fire. He watched them burn. Television and radio interviews across Canada were sending us a very distinct message:

Hang the son of a bitch.

I knew that, regardless of what kind of morbid details I could suck out of him during our last visit, it wouldn't affect Justice McKay's sentence. David received the equivalent to a first-degree murder sentence and couldn't receive more than 25 years without eligibility for parole, so he really had nothing to lose by telling me what I wanted to know. I was going to make very sure I pounded that fact into his head right from the beginning.

He didn't smile at me this time when I walked in. The son of a bitch had just been sentenced to 25 years he wasn't expecting, and he could tell from my stern glare that I wasn't there to fuck around. I knew he had had a meeting with his defense team after his sentencing and had the facts of life explained to him. *Twenty five big ones, David.* He'd be an old man when he got out, and I kind of wondered what he'd look like. If he looked this bad after only six months in gaol, in 25 years he'd look like a beady-eyed sewer rat. His hollow green eyes sat motionless, while his neatly trimmed mustache bordered tightly sealed lips.

"What's up, David?" I said, sitting down across from him in the interview room.

"Not much, Mike," he replied, his eyes focused on the table between us.

"You know why I'm here, David." He nodded dumbly. "There's a couple things that don't sit well with me and you know what they are. What's gnawing at me right now is, I think you sexually abused those girls before you killed them." I laid it right out on the table. I wasn't here to dance with him.

I could hear the hum of fluorescent lights as he sat motionless before me, looking at the floor. "You told me some time ago that you would consider telling me the rest of the story after you were sentenced. Well, I'm here to collect, David, and I'm not taking no for an answer. You're in for 25 big ones, and what I tell the parole board about you may affect you for the rest of your life. I've got you by the sac, David. I'm right about the girls, and you know it."

The beads of sweat came instantly, on both him and me. His forehead glistened in the light of the room. His skin was chalky and pale. *Come on you son of a bitch!* my mind screamed so loud I'm surprised he didn't hear me.

"I'm going to have to call my lawyer."

"Good, let's go call your lawyer." At that point, I really didn't give a shit if he called in all three of his lawyers. I was driving that fucking bus and he wasn't getting off it until I decided to stop. He must have been under the impression he was big time now. Before he talked to the cops, he'd have to confer with his lawyers.

His lawyer's office was right across the street. I just sat there, staring at David while we waited for Fred Kaatz to show up. He was obviously uncomfortable as my eyes sat like bowling balls on his shoulders. While I glared menacingly at David, my mind sifted through all the misery and frustration that had accumulated throughout the investigation. Daughters, dead daughters. Even my own daughter, whom I had neglected for the past two years because of this goddamned case, had suffered immeasurably from my absence. I made up my mind right then and there that when I was done I was going to go home and give her a big hug.

Jesus, it's time for a new job.

Fred Kaatz arrived after what must have seemed an eternity to David. I gave him my usual "don't fuck with this idea" look as I walked out, and stood outside the door. By law, Shearing didn't have to tell me anything. But I also knew, and he should have known, that he wasn't going to benefit by not telling me. I had the poison pen and Fred knew I would be writing the parole report. Fred also was trying everything he could to get Shearing in General Population so he could "do his time comfortably" and not like a caged animal as Clifford Olson was. That was probably what they were talking about as I waited outside, charging myself up, getting pumped. It was like I was preparing for the first interview all over again.

Fred finally came out and told me he had instructed David that whatever he was going to tell me was his decision, although not telling me anything at that point would have been like slamming the gate after the horses ran out.

When I opened the door, David was sitting there with his hands hanging down at his sides. His face was expressionless. Deadpan. I wasn't too sure what he was thinking, but he meant business. He wasn't a stupid guy. He had an above-average education and experience in several different fields. He was a hard worker and was relatively well liked among his peers. He was going to give me a good run at it.

What was it that motivated a guy like that? Reluctantly, I admitted to myself that Shearing had been fairly cooperative throughout the investigation (well, except for being so damned hard to find) and at times showed some signs of being a good-mannered sort of guy. His friends, family, and employers had said the same thing. Where did the train switch directions? How did he feel, really feel about what he did? What the hell was he thinking about when he planned these murders? How could he justify in his own mind slaughtering six people to satisfy his sick pleasures? Sure, he'd also run over a guy in the park and killed him while he was drinking, but that was of little consequence in my mind. That was one thing, but two little innocent girls and their parents and grandparents? Jesus, how on bloody earth could he plan that?

And who knows if he's going to tell me the truth this time?

"All right, Mike. You got it."

I almost fell out of my chair. "You understand, if you tell me I do have to notify my superiors in Vancouver, and the family of the victims. Whether you want your family to find out or not is a burden that has to remain with you."

He nodded slowly. After a few minutes of collecting his thoughts, Shearing started talking.

"I guess I saw them there at the Bear Creek site one of those nights on my way home from work." No emotion.

"You remember which night?"

"I think it was Thursday or Friday I saw the family there. A couple of older folks and these two young girls. I guess I got it in my mind that I wanted them."

Just like that! He really wanted those little girls. Reflecting back on what we had unearthed during our investigation, Shearing did have an interest in young girls. An older woman in his universe was about 16. Whether it was some sort of sick social behaviour, or perhaps a lack of self confidence, we weren't sure. Young girls were in his life, and he related to them.

"I went back, and I'm not sure if it was that night, or the following night I knew I was going to have to kill those other four to get the girls." He described his point of entry, having actually gone across Fage Creek from his house, and then moved through the bush to the back of the campsite.

"I watched them for about 45 minutes, sitting up on this sort of hill where I'd watched them the nights before. I showed it to you back when we went to the park."

I remembered the spot. There was a collection of shrubs that would have concealed him perfectly as he peered down at the vacationing family. The sick bastard was probably sitting up there playing with himself as he watched the family enjoy their last night together.

Once he was satisfied the girls were in the tent, he proceeded back towards Fage Creek and walked along its edge until he reached Wells Gray Park Road. He then headed south until he reached the campground and crept behind the camper with the rifle in hand.

"When I was there, one of the women saw me—"

"Which one?"

"I don't know. It was pretty dark."

"What happened then?"

"Well, she started standing up, and I said 'Don't move! I gotta gun.' Then the younger guy stood up and I shot him."

"Where did you shoot him, David?"

"I think I hit him in the throat, because he was gurgling and making a lot of noise. Then the older guy started running back over to the truck, and I shot him next to the passenger-side door.

"The mother of the girls was running for the tent, and I shot her in the head about halfway between it and the fire. Then I headed around to get the older woman, who was trying to get into the camper. I just came up behind her and shot her in the head too." No remorse. No feelings. It was like he was telling me about a Girl Guide field trip he was on. "Once they were all dead I went over to the tent. The girls were in there, kind of sitting up on their elbows. They asked me what all the noise was, and I said there were some bad people out there and that their parents had told me to stay back so they could go and get help. They asked if it was motorbike people, and I said, 'Yeah, don't come out. Whatever you do don't come out.'"

As he told me the story, everything I'd seen in my mind for the past two years was played back for me again. I felt like I was there, watching over the campground when the first shot was fired. I could see Bob Johnson falling to the ground. I could hear his dying breaths as Jackie screamed for him. Then to see her father shot down only feet from her, the trees would have echoed her screams for miles. The girls would have been panicking if they'd heard even a whimper from their mother, and now she was screaming in terror. Those girls wouldn't have been sitting there, wondering what the hell happened. They'd have bolted out of that tent and run to their father for protection. They'd have seen their parents and grandparents murdered. He'd have had to chase them down in the forest, and I could only imagine what sort of fear he'd had to plant in their minds to get them to stop ...

My imagination was gradually overwhelmed by David's voice as he continued.

"Then I went back out and had to shoot the younger guy—"

"Bob Johnson," I said, firmly. "He's got a name, David."

"Yeah, Bob Johnson. I'm not good with names. Anyway, I shot him again because he was making all this noise. Then I had to put the bodies in the car."

"That must have been pretty tough," I suggested. Lugging four adult bodies from the ground to the backseat of the car would have been no easy task. He would have been absolutely smeared with blood. Technically, once a body is dead, it doesn't actively bleed. The heart isn't beating, so blood is not being forced out of the body. However, gravity bleeds blood, and it would have been pouring out of the wounds.

"It wasn't easy," Dave agreed. There's a prize understatement. Manhandling four bodies into the back seat of a car, and stacking them up— Christ, with all the blood — the mere thought of it choked me up. I tried to visualize how the hell he would've piled four people on top of each other in the backseat. I recalled my first dead drunk that I'd had to load into the backseat of a PC, and that was no easy feat. We're talking about four bodies covered in blood. He would have been smeared with it, no matter what he'd said before. "I had a little blood on my hands." *My ass!*

"I covered 'em up with a blanket when I was done, and went back and cleaned up some of the other stuff. There wasn't too much sitting around, so it didn't take too long. I went over to the tent when I was done and crawled in."

I knew what he was going to tell me as soon as he was in that tent with those girls, but there was no experience in the RCMP that could have prepared me for my reaction. It had all been just supposition before that. It had been just an ugly theory in my head. Now, all of my thoughts had been confirmed. As he explained what happened, I sat absolutely breathless. Anyone who had any questions about capital punishment should have sat down beside me and listened for themselves. Shearing was lucky I wasn't armed. On second thought, I think *I* was lucky I was unarmed.

"After I got dressed," he continued without missing a beat, "I got them to help me take down the tent. They asked where their parents were a couple times, and I told them they got away to get help. We cleaned up the rest of the site and put most of the stuff in the camper. I guess they believed me, because they were doing everything I said. They didn't see me shoot the parents, so I guess they didn't have any reason not to believe me."

I knew that was bullshit. Both the women must have been screaming at the top of their lungs when Bob Johnson was shot, and the report of a .22, while not very loud, is a real awakening snap. I firmly believed that they had seen it all: Their dad being shot down in mid sentence. Their grandfather being killed near the truck. Mummy struck down by a bullet as she ran to save them. Grandma stalked and shot in the back of the head at point blank range. I was sure they'd seen it, and no amount of telling was going to convince me otherwise. Those girls would have been so scared, I'm sure they would have done anything he asked them out of blind fear.

"We got in the car, and I told them to sit in the front beside me."

With their dead parents and grandparents piled in the back seat. The blood would have been trickling under their feet. The girls would have been crying ... I could see it all so clearly.

"I drove back around to Wells Gray Road and headed up to the ranch. When I got to where I wanted to be, I got the girls to set up the tent. I told them those biker people were still around looking for them, so they weren't to leave. They were so scared, they did everything I told 'em to." He explained that he then had to walk back to the Bear Creek campsite and pick up the camper, with the intention of hiding it somewhere within the wooded confines of his family's 160-acre ranch.

I instantly recalled the show and tell that David had taken us on right after his initial confession. He'd left the girls near the same place he'd hidden the boat and motor. The forest's canopy was so dense and so dark that the children must have been absolutely terrified, even during the day, let alone at night! I could imagine the animals prowling around them, and the trees crackling, and the wind howling, and the rain pouring ...

When he returned with the truck, David said he told them how he had saved their parents and helped them to get away. "They really thought I was their hero," Shearing repeated, trying to convince me. *You're so full of shit.* Once they were set up in the tent, Shearing warned them not to go anywhere because the bears and the wolves and the bikers would find them. If the bears showed up, he told them they could hide in the camper.

"They were scared shitless, and did everything I wanted them to do. When they were settled I went back home, and went back to work the next morning as usual."

Just like that. He leaves two little children alone in the forest with their dead family in the car — "I've gotta get some sleep because I've got a busy day tomorrow. Had a busy day today, had to kill four people and load up their bodies. Had to walk way back to the campsite to get my new truck and camper." *You fucking sick bastard.*

He didn't remember seeing them that morning, but he did see them that night. "I brought them milk and bread and stuff on Wednesday, I think it was. Might have been Thursday."

"And you murdered the parents on—"

"I'm pretty sure it was Monday."

"All right." It wasn't all right. I was about to lose it.

"That next day, Tuesday I mean, I came back that night to see them and I was still their hero. I told them that I had talked to their parents, and that they told me it was safest for them to just stay there with me. They were pretty happy with that story, and they trusted me. We talked a lot at night before they went to sleep, and I had some beer out there with me to drink in the camper. Both the girls slept in the tent because the younger one had a fear of the camper and was kind of claustrophobic."

That Friday night, Shearing returned and told them that their parents were going to meet them at a remote fishing cabin. They left from the ranch and began working their way through the dense brush in the dark. "It was raining like hell. I tried to light a fire for them, because they were really cold and wet, but I couldn't." Shearing explained that they camped out underneath a sheet of plastic he'd brought with him and suspended with some string between a couple trees. He claimed the girls slept in one bag, and he in another. I was suspicious of that too. After 20 years in the force, you know when your guts are telling you something. He had them completely isolated, and he knew he wasn't going to let them live to tell the tale. Talk about planned and deliberate — holy shit!

The next day, he explained casually, they continued on down the trail from the ranch. Upon reaching the river, they turned downstream and scampered about a mile to the cabin. He hung their clothes out to dry with the sleeping bags, and generally just sat around and tried to talk to them about anything. That night, they slept in the cabin with the same sleeping arrangements as the night before. The two girls were allegedly in one sleeping bag, and he in another.

"That's Sunday morning now," David explained. "And when we got up, we saw some prisoners fishing in the river. My dad was a prison guard once, and I'd been around them before so I wasn't too worried about it. Apparently, they didn't see the girls were there with me. One of them [who later turned out to be Don Gordon, a prison guard at Clearwater Correctional Centre] came up to the door and told me that there were some real mild prisoners fishing in the river and that we shouldn't be alarmed."

"Where were the girls?"

"I hid them behind the door and told them to be quiet. They did everything I said."

As an operations commander for hostages and barricaded persons, I recalled from one of the courses I took how victims in captivity are so easily swayed to believe in their captors. The Patty Hearst kidnapping case was one such incident that gained international attention. These two innocent children would have been so naïve, it probably hadn't taken long before they believed in David and what he was doing to them at his leisure. Even if they had seen their family murdered in cold blood, I was certain they would have chosen to make it a lie. I knew those girls truly believed their mother and father would eventually come and get them. It was all just a bad dream.

"The guy asked me if I was camping, and I said yeah. I think he told me to have a good time and then turned back around and went back to the group." For God's sake, if only Don Gordon had poked his nose in the cabin, or if one of the girls had coughed, or sneezed, or screamed, or ran! They would have been alive today.

When the coast was clear, David and the two girls headed back to the ranch. "The girls were real slow on the way back. I guess they were really tired from all the walking we'd been doing. When we got back to the ranch, everything was still set up the way we left it." Not long after they returned, Shearing asked Karen to go for a walk with him to talk about a personal matter. Karen followed him obediently. Once they were out of hearing range from the camp, they stopped.

"I told her that I had to take a piss, so she turned around. I had the .22 stashed there, so when she wasn't looking I shot her in the back of the head."

The words cut through my chest like a bayonet, leaving me with the dirtiest, bloodiest taste in my mouth. Sitting there deadpan, Shearing explained it so matter of factly I thought I was going to be sick. My eyes widened, but I couldn't do or say anything at that point. I was so disgusted. So angry. My body felt like it had been thrown in the oven, and I had difficulty breathing. The feeling inside me was so intense and so overwhelming— *"When she wasn't looking I shot her in the back of the head."* The words echoed through my mind as he proceeded, tunnelling deeper into my memory. What is a person supposed to feel when they're being told something like that? How was I supposed to feel? How did Dave think I felt about what he was telling me?

Even to this day, I sit back and I know something else happened on that trail. He knew what he wanted, and what he was going to do. Murder, kidnapping, sex, torture — what other acts of depravity were left for this guy to commit? Cannibalism?

"When I went back to the camp, I had a beer and sat around. When Janet asked where Karen was, I told her that I had tied Karen to a tree."

"Tied her to a tree?" I thought to myself. *Where in hell does that fit in? What was going through her mind? Little sister is in the woods tied to a tree somewhere ...*

"And that night, Janet and I were in the camper."

I listened, my guts aching, as he told me the rest.

"Janet was a virgin, and didn't know a lot about sex at all." I just wanted to stand up right then and there and punch the dirty prick right in the face. My hands were shaking, and I was sweating. I was furious. Burning up.

"She didn't know how to do anything, so we just stayed up most of that night and talked about everything."

She was only 13, David! I was livid. He had no conception of exactly how disgusting and horrible his actions were.

"That morning, Tuesday I think, I asked Janet to come for a walk with me down that trail. She came, and when I got to the spot where I'd hid the rifle I asked her to turn around so I could take a piss. When she did, I shot her in the back of the head and killed her also."

The words ended with such abrupt finality, I was left hanging there with nowhere to go. I didn't have any other questions. I didn't want to know anymore. I was literally numb. It occurred to me that I had been expecting him to tell me exactly what he had told me, but for some reason, I hadn't expected it to come at me the way it did.

"I loaded the bodies in the trunk, and went home to bed." *Good Christ!*

The next night, Shearing came back to the car, and drove it up to Battle Mountain. By that time, it'd been almost 10 days and nights that the bodies had been decaying in the back seat. Four adults, dead, in the backseat of that car, decomposing for that period of time. Then he's got to climb in there and drive them up the mountain. What kind of trip is that? Driving down the road with cars going past, wondering if anyone you drive by knows you've got six bodies in the back.

Shearing eventually drove the vehicle into the trees and swerved until he got stuck. He told me he tried to get it in there farther, but the car was really and truly stuck. He used five gallons of fuel in the front and back and set the car on fire. After watching it burn for a while, he proceeded home. What was going through his mind as the vehicle ignited and exterminated the existence of the three generations of that family? I couldn't even hazard a guess.

Right about the time the tourist alert came out, around the 23rd of August, Shearing took the truck and camper up to Trophy Mountain to torch it.

"I knew that area pretty well," he explained. "There's a big gully there, and I wanted to drive the truck off that cliff. That way nobody would have found it." Unfortunately for him, he got stuck again. It had been raining again very steadily that night, and the ground had turned to mush. He saturated the truck in gasoline and lit it up. It smoldered a bit at first, then was quickly engulfed in flames. Satisfied, Shearing walked the two miles back home along a heavily wooded path that led him right to his own backyard.

I sat there, stunned, not even realizing that I had committed to paper almost everything David had told me. I felt as if *I* had been murdered six times and cremated. I was totally exhausted and saturated with perspiration from the 30 minutes it had taken David to tell me the story.

I knew he had left out a lot of the details, but I knew enough. I suppose I could have interrogated him for more of the story, but I was sick enough by the thought of what I had to tell my associates and eventually the victims' family. Christ, just hours before I had been talking to someone about how great police work was. *So you want to be a cop, eh? I don't think they put this stuff in the manual.*

"Come on, David," I said, hours of silence condensed into only a few seconds. "I'll put you away and I'll probably see you tomorrow."

When I finally got outside, I went and sat alone in my car. In that brief period of uninterrupted solitude I had a real chance to take a look at my life and some of those I had seen destroyed in my 22 years as a cop. David's motivation can never be explained. These cold-blooded murders defy description even now, but as long as someone out there is willing take another person's life, there's going to be a cop who has to sit back in his car when it's all over and wonder what the hell went wrong.

If ever anything in my life had hurt, sitting there alone in my car for an hour was probably the most painful experience in my life. Immersed in my own desolate thoughts, the lives of a thousand strangers passed by me and I didn't even notice. There were no feelings of jubilation or bravado for getting Shearing to talk the second time. Only heartbreak.

The following day when I could sit back and analyze the second confession with a bit more objectivity, the grim reality of it all was that I had already known the answers to most of the questions I had asked Shearing. All I had been lacking were the sordid details I eventually had to hear from Dave himself. I wasn't overly proud of myself for what I had succeeded in unearthing from David's sick past, but what was done was done.

I soon set about transcribing my notes in memo form to the officer commanding. While writing this memo, I wondered if I was going to be in shit for getting the information now, as opposed to earlier. There was a chance that if I'd been able to present this evidence sooner we could have charged David with first degree murder. Of course, in his case a first degree murder sentence was really no different from the second degree conviction he actually received, other than by title. First degree was 25 years and in this case so was second degree.

To my surprise, I wasn't scolded at all for my inability to provide that evidence. Instead, the brass questioned the authenticity of the information.

"Don't believe it," the superintendent told me. "It's self serving, and he's not credible. Besides, why would he tell you that now?"

For a minute there, I felt like I was the bloody accused, not Shearing. I really didn't give a shit whether they believed Shearing's new statement or not, but when it came down to questioning my judgement, I had to act. We soon got in touch with Don Gordon, the prison guard who had met Shearing that fateful day. He recalled the incident vividly. Yes, he'd had a team of prisoners out for a Sunday morning fishing trip, and he remembered seeing the smoke billowing from the small, one-room cabin by the river. The fellow whom he described having seen there was almost certainly David Shearing. The guy stood fast at the door and didn't go outside. Basically, Don recalled their encounter exactly as David had described it.

With that information, I decided to send Reliable Liebel to corroborate everything David said. "Kenny, the brass is looking at us sideways insofar as the recent information from Shearing is concerned. I need you to get to the cabin and see what you can establish in the way of any supporting evidence. Go and talk to Shearing, but only about what you may find at the cabin. Oh, and don't get into any details about what he has already told me."

"All right Boss, I'm gone."

The following day, Reliable came to me with a smile on his face. As usual, he had come through for me.

"As a result of speaking with Dave, I headed out to the cabin and found what I was looking for. The writing's on the wall, Boss. David said he carved his initials in the wooden logs of the cabin. I found them, along with another set."

"What exactly was on the wall, Ken?"

Reliable took a deep breath before saying: "DS+JJ."

There was a long silence between us. "The photos will be ready in an hour or so. Do you need anything else?"

"No, Ken, you done good."

By May 1984, Gerry Dalen, Kenny Leibel, Len Bylo, Dwight Hoglund, and I looked as if we'd made sleep deprivation a career. I still had bags under my eyes that I could trip over, and I think I'd now lost about 20 pounds since the investigation began. I was smoking like a chimney, bankrupt, exhausted, and drinking enough for all five of us. To top it off, the superintendent wasn't about to lay off his offensive against my bar, the Brass Rail. He was still insisting that I had violated the RCMP Act by contracting debts I was unwilling or unable to pay, and that I was involved in some type of conflict of interest. He may have been right about being unable to discharge the debt, but there was no conflict, other than between him and me. To add to this delightful workplace setting, my personal life and my financial situation seemed to be quite the conversation piece around the water cooler. I think everyone in Kamloops knew that I was in the shit.

Although we had successfully concluded the investigation, there were still a couple of loose ends we had to tie up before we could wrap it up completely. The giant machine we'd fired up almost two years earlier was still generating public attention, and we were still getting phone calls from those who hadn't read a newspaper in four months, offering us more clues. We politely informed them that the case had been concluded, and thanked them for being good Canadian citizens. Some of Shearing's friends from school were still calling in, insisting that we'd coached Shearing into pleading guilty and that we were no better than the Gestapo. We thanked them for their concern. After hanging up, we bitched among ourselves about how this case was never going to really end. *Christ, someone throw out the fucking anchor!*

While we were cleaning up the aftermath of the Wells Gray Park murders, the superintendent busied himself squashing any and all attempts to congratulate us for our work on the case. There was such devotion to duty by my guys, the first thing I did was suggest it was time for some kind of official recognition. I knew what everyone had gone through and what an incredible weight had been put upon them. Not just the members, but their families as well. Frank Baruta had also been put through a wood chipper in Clearwater and had gone way beyond the call of duty.

The senior Crown prosecutor, Bob Hunter, took it upon himself to call up the deputy commissioner at our headquarters in Vancouver and suggest we all receive Commissioner's Commendations, the most prestigious award in the RCMP, for the incredible amount of work we'd put into the investigation. We had wrapped the case so tightly there had been no defense. He knew we had covered every possible loophole from here to the moon, and in doing so had saved the taxpayers hundreds of thousands of dollars by not having to go through a two- or three-month trial.

The deputy commissioner himself agreed that our performance may have warranted Commissioner's Commendations. Unfortunately, as if it would have been some tremendous embuggerance for the Codfather to allow any of us that sort of recognition, the superintendent shot the idea out of season and strapped it to the hood of his car. We had the satisfaction of knowing we did our jobs, but to this day, it burns my ass big time that nobody got any official acknowledgement of the years of effort. *Fuck'em,* I thought to myself. We couldn't take a Commissioner's Commendation to the bank anyway.

As I look back, probably the most difficult part of the investigation was battling against my own office. Right in the middle of it all the superintendent had me audited to make certain I wasn't wasting the force's resources. As the audit showed, the operation was as efficient as could have been expected under any circumstance. Unsatisfied, he had the process repeated. As if I didn't have anything else to worry about, I was continually stepping through huge mounds of bureaucratic bullshit.

Now that it was over, he had to destroy what little sense of appreciation we might have been able to pry out of the upper echelons. Naturally, you don't do your job just so that you can trip over everyone bowing at your feet, but as the story goes, every old dog likes a pat on the back every now and then. The team was burned out and any indication that our work had been appreciated would have been a good first step to rejuvenating our morale. I guess I had asked for too much. After almost two years of walking through the desert without a drop, it was obvious our first drink of water was going to be just a handful of sand.

I knew the superintendent wanted me to quit. He had hinted at it a few times as the file was winding down. He'd pushed, and eventually made my life miserable enough that I decided to let him win. It was time to move on and I knew it. I'd wash the damned police cars, so long as it wasn't in Kamloops. It wouldn't be long before I was history in his subdivision anyway. I'd either be transferred to the midnight shift, or whisked away to some God-forsaken detachment somewhere horrible. He'd pushed my performance review down 16 percent from the year before, which was pretty drastic. At that rate, the Vancouver Canucks would be winning the Stanley Cup before I got another promotion.

I began to actively review my options. The first call I made was to the staffing officer in Vancouver, Inspector Dave Dore. He'd interviewed me several times in the past, and we'd talked about me driving a desk for a couple years. He had also tried to motivate me into moving up to the commissioned ranks. While being a pencil pilot had been the second-last thing on my mind (the last being a commissioned rank), it had certainly become an attractive alternative. I was simply too damned tired to do anything else.

"David, I'm fried. I've got 23 years in, 19 of which have been on the front lines with the detective office. I've had nothing but blood and guts and bullshit since I got here. I've paid my dues, and it's time to move on. You guys talked to me about it before, getting out of here and into another line of work. I didn't want it then, but Dave, I'm ready now. Find me a nice, safe, quiet job where I can relax for a bit. My marriage is falling apart, my financial situation seems to be the talk of the detachment, and my boss doesn't have any use for me whatsoever. I just spent the last two years involved in the most disgusting case of my life, and I'm burned out. My guts are aching constantly, Dave. Do what you can to get me the hell out of here."

"All right Mike, slow down," he said comfortingly. "Let me see what we can do." The next day, Friday, I got a call from him. *Holy shit! He was listening!*

"Mike, I've got a position for you. Now I know it's not exactly what you were looking for but hear me out." He paused for a second, probably wondering how to put forth his proposal.

I paused too, tightening up my sphincter muscles. If I'd known then what he was up to, I'd have hung up the phone and headed to the bar. (Not my own, because I still wasn't allowed to be seen there.)

"We've got a member who is being commissioned in Burnaby."

Oh God! Burnaby? I hoped he was joking. I'd never wanted to work in the Lower Mainland of British Columbia, primarily because I had little experience in big city policing. Burnaby, population 175,000, was a big city to me, and the detective office wasn't exactly what I'd call a "nice, safe, quiet job."

Dave proceeded with the punch line. "In order to make this work out, I need a sergeant to make a sideways move to Burnaby GIS."

Not very funny. On average, somewhere between five and fifteen people would be murdered in Burnaby every year, not to mention all of the other bullshit that went with it. I visualized myself meeting with the next of kin, having to tell them their loved one was dead. The way I looked, they'd probably think I was the Grim Reaper himself. "I kind of had something a little quieter in mind, David." Murders and rapes and robberies, oh my.

And then to make matters worse, he said: "Trust me."

Yeah, trust you. Just like I trusted the bank. Just sign here — my ass!

"You only need to go to Burnaby on paper, until I can find you a soft spot down here. "

I knew I was getting railroaded, but what choice did I have? "All right Dave, if you say so." *Dammit! Penetrated again!*

Bob Byam, who was second in charge at the Burnaby detachment, had been a really close friend at one point in my career. We'd sort of drifted apart, but I'd made sure to keep in touch with him over the years. I'd been the best man at his wedding when we were young detectives and we used to play a lot of ball together. We'd shared a lot of good times, and some bad. One of the main reasons I decided to accept the proposal was that I knew Bob would have my best interest in mind, even if Dave Dore didn't. Later it turned out that the two buggers were in cahoots! Once Dave got off the phone with me, I knew there must have been a couple of phone calls between the two of them before they figured out how to lure me down to Burnaby. They both wanted me to work down there, and I wasn't going to any soft spot — unless robbery, homicide and sex crimes was what they called a soft spot.

As soon as the transfer was on paper, the superintendent was charging around, honking about how I had engineered my own transfer. He was right, of course, but I wasn't going to give him the satisfaction of owning up to it. I vehemently denied the charge as I packed my bags for the big city. If I hadn't left, there was no doubt in my mind that he'd have had other ways of "nursing" me into early retirement.

I was out of Kamloops within a month and they had me give a farewell speech at the social. Everyone at subdivision HQ came, thinking I was going to go ballistic on the superintendent after a couple of beers. I didn't owe him anything, that was for sure, and he certainly didn't have any of my respect. If I'd have lashed out against him, however, I knew he would have won the war. There's quite a skill in telling someone you dislike exactly how you feel about them, without actually spelling it all out. It was a skill with which I'd become quite proficient in the last few years.

"There are a lot of things that I could say right now, and you probably know what they are. You know what we've all been through." My stomach churned as I thought out my next few words. *We are a part of best police force in the world, so why the fuck do we have to work against our own superintendent?* "You all know that you can't make chicken soup out of chicken shit." I paused, thinking very, very carefully about what I was doing. "At least, not very easily. Thanks to all of you guys, we eventually did it." *I wonder if he'll ever figure that one out.* I heard a deep-throated grunt beside me. He got it all right.

"Come on, Mike!" some members in the crowd shouted. "Tell us about it! Are you going to miss Kamloops?" The superintendent just stood there, waiting for me to do myself in.

"Well, I'm going to be saying goodbye to a lot of close friends. Of course, you all know who you are, and you know who to call if you need a spare room in the city." It wasn't long before I was on my way to Burnaby.

When I walked in on my first day, with the ink on my transfer papers still wet, the guys in Burnaby had a surprise for me. We'd had five members working in subdivision GIS in Kamloops. Here, there were about fifty. There were emergency response teams, bomb squads, dog squads, criminal intelligence squads, drug squads, and all the support, stenos, and computers a guy could wish for. I wasn't sure why half of the detectives were wearing bullet proof vests. Back in Kamloops, I didn't even wear my sidearm half the time.

I'm sure a couple of sets of city dick eyeballs followed me to my office, probably wondering if this old worn-out fart from the north country knew what the hell city life was about. One thing that was clear to me was that I'd been ripped off. If I'd had access to all of this manpower at the beginning of the J/B investigation, Shearing would have been cooling his heels in the bucket a lot sooner.

I'd been in the building long enough to find my office, the can, and the coffee pot when a bloody alarm started wailing in the background. *Great,* I thought to myself, *let's play follow the constable out the door.* I looked around and everyone was grabbing every piece of equipment that went bang, and stuffing shotgun shells into the breeches of sawed-off shotguns as they raced out the door. A young detective came to my office, smiling at me.

"Hey Boss, I'm BJ from robbery." Standing about six foot three, and weighing about 240 pounds, BJ stood like an oak in my doorway. His jet-black hair and full mustache matched the barrel of the shotgun he carried, and the silly grin he had stretched across his face suggested that this man wasn't happy unless he were within range of absolute mayhem. "We've got a bank to visit ASAP. We don't want to miss the bus!"

Christ, I wasn't even on the bus, and I already wanted to get off. Only minutes earlier, three armed men had stormed a bank downtown. Using big iron bars and large concrete blocks, they had smashed through the windows and apparently started firing automatic weapons into the ceiling and walls. They quickly liberated the counting room and vault of thousands and thousands of dollars (it was being counted before the bank opened), and then proceeded back out to their getaway vehicle.

I followed BJ and another detective out to a new unmarked Crown Victoria. They got in the front and I jumped in the back. Sirens and lights, we knifed through the city streets behind a fleet of police vehicles. BJ was driving like a fucking maniac, and I knew that we'd be filling in PC MVA (motor vehicle accident) forms if the day ever ended. Getting to the scene in any more than one piece didn't seem to be one of BJ's top 10 priorities. I don't know if I was suffering from indigestion or excitement. Maybe I was scared. My heart was banging against the knot in my stomach, and judging by the God-awful racket, either my teeth were chattering or BJ had ripped the transmission to shreds.

"Shots fired!" someone warned over the radio.

I instinctively reached for my sidearm ... nothing! Shit! It was sitting in my briefcase with my transfer papers back at the office, probably the only firearm left in the whole goddamned detachment. *Great. I'm in the back seat of a hurricane, heading towards angry men firing guns, and my detectives look like they drink diesel fuel for breakfast. What the hell have*

I gotten myself into this time? My only consolation was that I was probably going to die in a car accident before I got shot at. The young guys seemed to eat it up. Judging by their bravado if they weren't shot full of holes and bleeding all over the place, including me, it would have been a wasted trip.

"How do you want to handle this, Sarge?" the detective in the passenger side asked. I must have looked like he just told me I was going to get a root canal without an anesthetic. "You want an ERT alert? Where do you want the perimeter set up? If they're still in there, we'll have to set up a quick command post, unless we get an all clear from the bank. The dog teams are almost on scene, waiting for instructions. Do you want 'em to back off?"

I just looked at him. Was he talking to me? *Am I in charge?* I wanted to stick my head in the sand, but judging by my luck up to that point I'd have had my ass shot off. To add to the orchestra of chaos, the police radio was blurting out RCMP codes and instructions pertinent to the bank robbery. Most of the calls were disguised, in case the robbers were monitoring the channels.

"Don't worry, Boss," BJ said nonchalantly, sensing my discomfort. "We'll just play it by ear when we get there."

We were almost on top of the bank, and my armpits were rivers of sweat. I was silently willing myself to wake up when BJ shouted: "Ah fuck! They're gone!"

Thank Christ they were gone! In seconds we were on the scene with the ambulances, fire trucks, and the media. A lot of the reporters were asking who was in charge, and with poorly hidden smiles they were pointed in my direction.

"Hey Mike!" said one man from within a gaggle of gawking reporters. I recognized several of them from Clearwater. "What the hell are you doing here?" I explained my transfer to a dozen microphones. "So you got a promotion?"

"Yeah," I answered acerbically. "I got a promotion all right."

ERT showed up at the scene only because they had been en route to a training session, but I thought they were carrying out orders I didn't remember giving. The dog squads were moving around a perimeter I didn't remember setting up. I didn't know it then, but my new corporal, Franky, whom I hadn't even met yet, and BJ were standing behind me choreographing the scene. With a sly grin, Franky'd nod or shake his head as different members came to me with questions. I learned quickly that he was a really great guy to lean on, and was probably one of the smartest cops I'd ever worked with.

Later that day, when I got back to the detachment without even a bullet hole in my chest to brag about, I staggered into the inspector's office. My first day on the job had consisted of two bank robberies and a body reported in a ditch that turned out to be a skinned bear. It was as if I'd been caught in the middle of a bad John Wayne movie. But Bob Byam was smiling at me as if I were wearing hosiery and a tutu.

"What the hell did you get me into, Byam?" I asked, crumpling in my chair.

"Hey Mike, don't worry about it. That's just everyday big city policing. You'll get used to it."

Yeah, getting shot at quickly becomes second nature when you're over 40. At times like that, I'd have traded everything I owned to be 20 again, when eating bullets was just a halfway point to being a man.

Just when I thought it couldn't get any worse, he said, "Trust me."

Where had I heard those two words before?

"I know you're probably feeling a bit overwhelmed, but with time you'll adapt. It's no different than Kamloops. Things just happen a little faster, and a bit more often."

There goes my sphincter muscle again.

"You're taking over the robbery, homicide, and sex crimes details. You have the experience we need, and I intend on taking advantage of it. These guys know their jobs, so it should be easy for you."

Great. I get to deal with a bunch of rapists and bank robbers and murderers — and lots of them. Big city police work was so much more complicated than the smaller town stuff I was used to. There were so many more factors in the equation. More variables. More bloody headaches, and I was already one headache over the legal limit. While I was sitting there, trying to digest all of the rah rah crap, Bob dropped some more good news on me.

"Mike, let me ask you something," he said, leaning slightly over his desk towards me. "What do you know about the Paper Bag Rapist?"

"Very little," I answered honestly. I had seen articles about him in the paper several times in the past few months. How could I forget the headlines: "Terror Strikes Hearts of Lower Mainland Citizens — Paperbag Rapist Claims Another Victim."

"This son of a bitch has been terrorizing the Lower Mainland for the last 13 years, indiscriminately raping women and children at will in local parks. When the sun shines, this prick is out there looking for potential victims. He's a predator among predators. Summer is just around the corner, and so is he. Somebody is going to wind up dead here pretty soon if we don't put the arrest on him, and I don't want that happening in Burnaby, Eastham. Do you understand?" There was a very clear message in his tone: You're not here to fuck around, Mike.

"Yeah."

"There's three filing cabinets in the back office that you had better go to bed with," he said, motioning over his shoulder.

I didn't know what to say. One part of me loathed the task, while another was anxious to face it. I was no stranger to trouble, and trouble was certainly no stranger to the big city.

Byam leaned back in his chair to grab a three-inch-thick folder he had sitting behind him. It slammed on the desk in front of me like the world's biggest slap in the face. "This file is an overview of what we suspect of him. You'd better catch up on your reading, Mike. It's your responsibility now."

Responsibility had a hell of a price tag, and I had been so depleted from the Johnson and Bentley murders, I'd have to pick pockets to pay for it. Even with all the support I apparently had, the Paper Bag Rapist was not going to be an easy score. Several task forces had already been formed to identify this bastard, but he was still at large, and had been for 13 years. He made David Shearing look like a virgin quail in comparison, having wrecked the lives of hundreds of women and children. He left his victims soiled with the horrendous memories of his crimes, perhaps the worst punishment of all.

The Paper Bag Rapist was unquestionably one of the most dangerous criminals in Canadian history, but there was an awfully long road to walk before I began living the horror of apprehending that predator. Little did I know then how close we would come to losing him, and some of his victims.

I collected the file in my arms and headed back to my own office. It was close to quitting time, but adrenaline was still pumping through my system. Before I'd put the papers down on my desk, the alarm sounded again.

As if on cue, BJ and Franky were standing at my door carrying enough weapons and equipment for all of us. Franky passed me a bullet-proof vest, and BJ was carrying an extra shotgun.

"For me?" I asked him, taking it and checking to see if it was loaded. It was, of course.

"We've got to keep you healthy, Boss. You're the only one who can sign our overtime." BJ gave me that shit-eating grin I would come to know so well, then turned and went downstairs.

By the time I got down to the underground lot, BJ was already in the driver's seat of our PC, revving the engine and testing the siren. He then tossed the portable red light over the roof of our car, which hadn't had a scratch on it except for the one he had just made with that damned light! Shit, I knew we were going to get it this time.

"Are these pool cars?" I asked as we piled in.

"Nah," Franky said gingerly. "It's your car."

BJ was still smiling when I demanded that he hand over the keys and get in the back seat. One thing I did know was how to drive.

"Burnaby D4," I said on the police radio as we headed into harm's way. "Eastham, BJ Brown, and Frank Mogridge are 10-8 and en route to the scene. Update please ... "

Here I go again ...